MARVEL GRAPHIC NOVEL

UNCANNY X-MEN #6

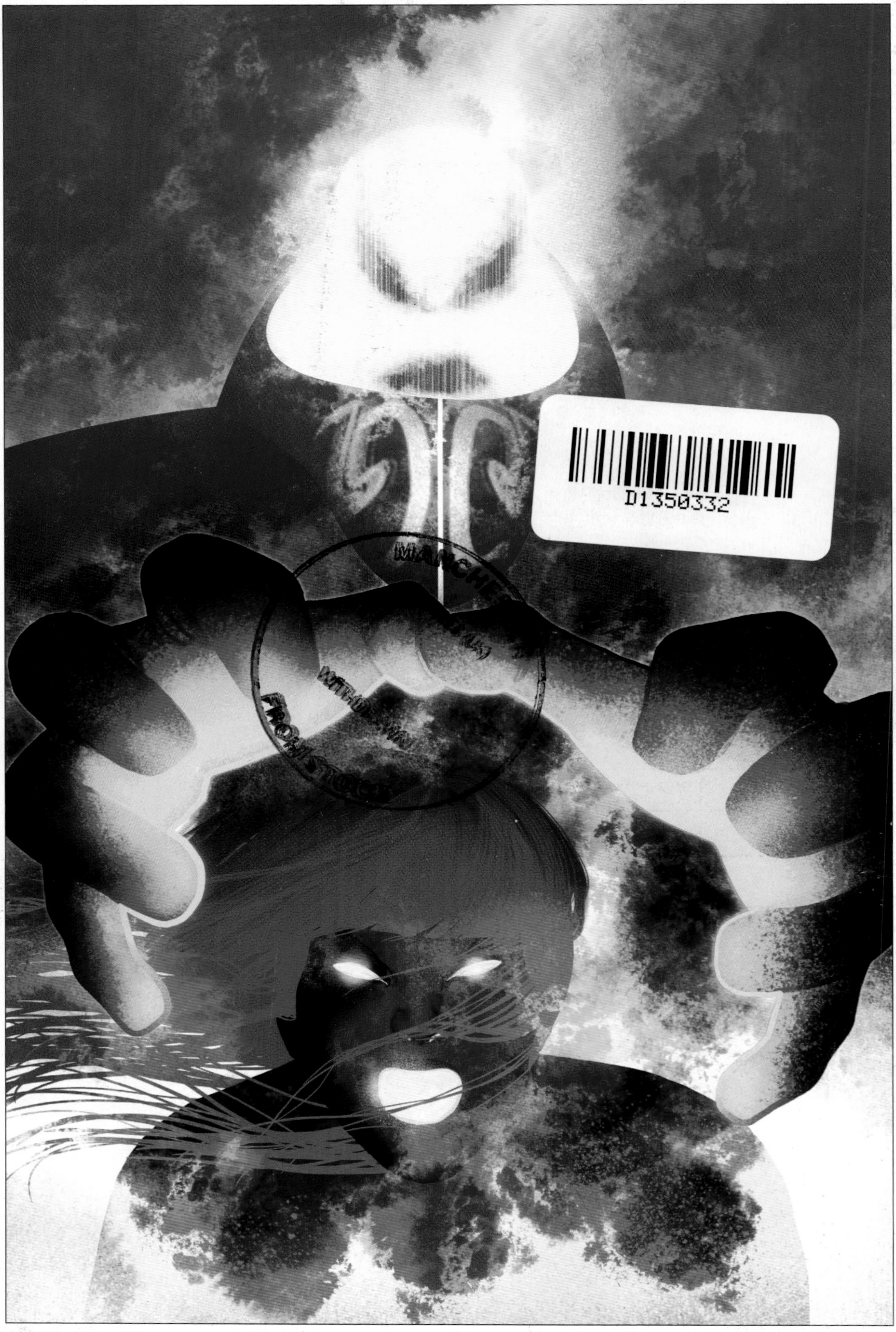

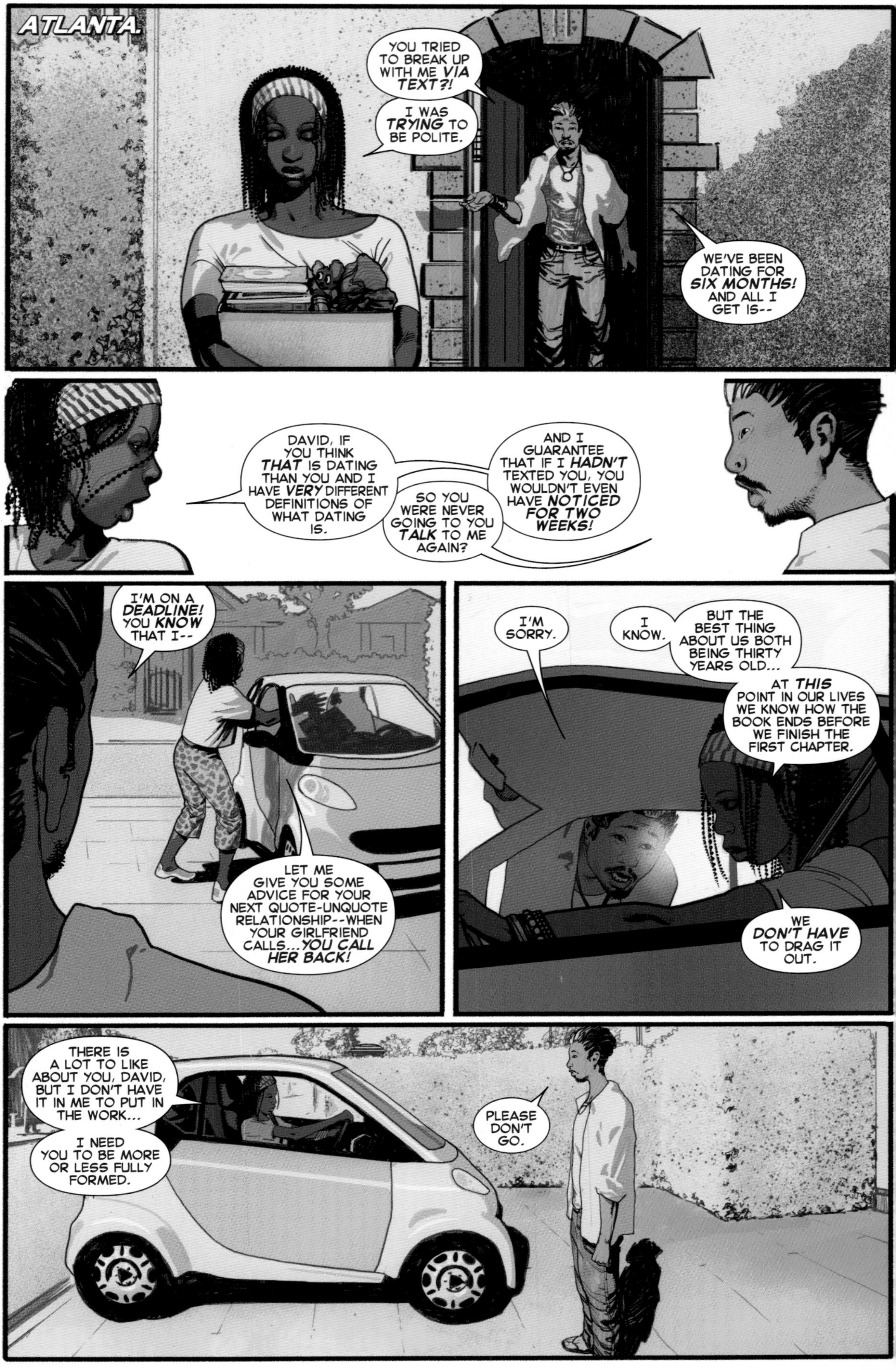
ATLANTA.
YOU TRIED TO BREAK UP WITH ME *VIA TEXT?!*
I WAS *TRYING* TO BE POLITE.
WE'VE BEEN DATING FOR *SIX MONTHS!* AND ALL I GET IS--
DAVID, IF YOU THINK *THAT* IS DATING THAN YOU AND I HAVE *VERY* DIFFERENT DEFINITIONS OF WHAT DATING IS.
AND I GUARANTEE THAT IF I *HADN'T* TEXTED YOU, YOU WOULDN'T EVEN HAVE *NOTICED FOR TWO WEEKS!*
SO YOU WERE NEVER GOING TO YOU *TALK* TO ME AGAIN?
I'M ON A *DEADLINE!* YOU *KNOW* THAT I--
LET ME GIVE YOU SOME ADVICE FOR YOUR NEXT QUOTE-UNQUOTE RELATIONSHIP--WHEN YOUR GIRLFRIEND CALLS... *YOU CALL HER BACK!*
I'M SORRY.
I KNOW.
BUT THE BEST THING ABOUT US BOTH BEING THIRTY YEARS OLD...
AT *THIS* POINT IN OUR LIVES WE KNOW HOW THE BOOK ENDS BEFORE WE FINISH THE FIRST CHAPTER.
WE *DON'T HAVE* TO DRAG IT OUT.
THERE IS A LOT TO LIKE ABOUT YOU, DAVID, BUT I DON'T HAVE IT IN ME TO PUT IN THE WORK...
I NEED YOU TO BE MORE OR LESS FULLY FORMED.
PLEASE DON'T GO.

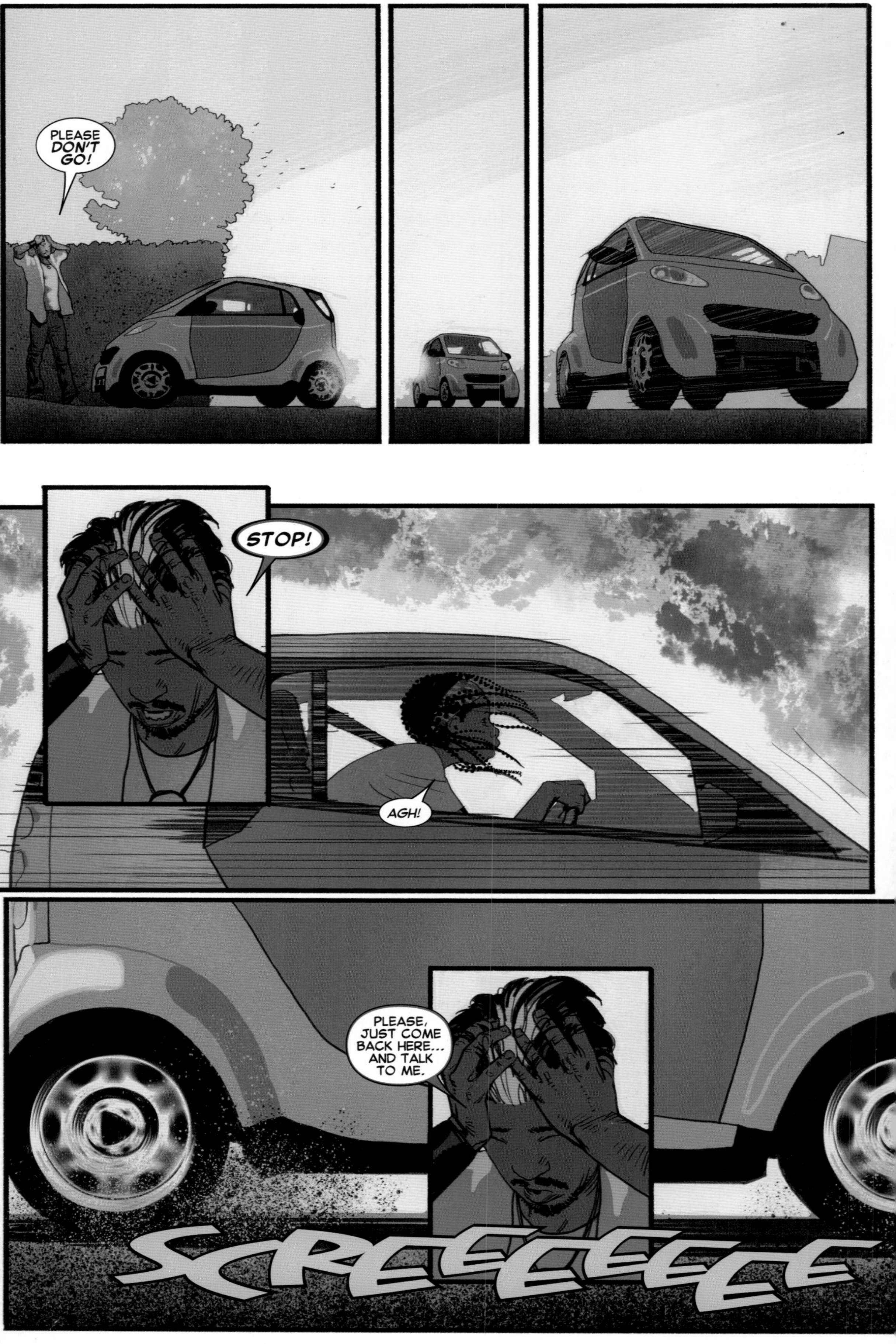
PLEASE DON'T GO!
STOP!
AGH!
PLEASE, JUST COME BACK HERE... AND TALK TO ME.
SCREEEEEEEE

ERT
THANK YOU.
SEE? WE CAN TALK ABOUT THIS. YOU KNOW I--
WHAT THE #$%&?
WHAT?
WHAT?! COME ON!
COME BACK!
SCREEEE
AGH!
ROOOMM
WHOA!

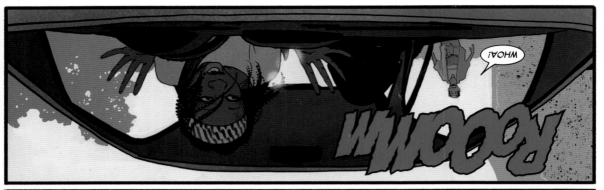

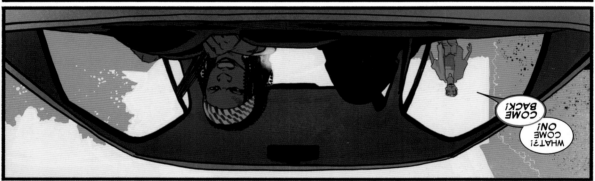

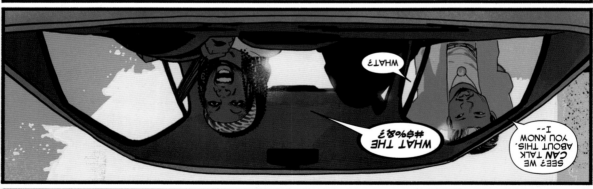

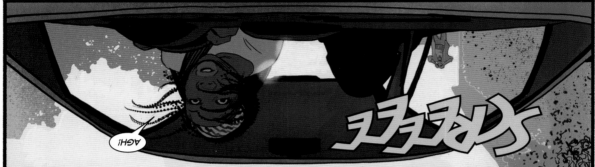

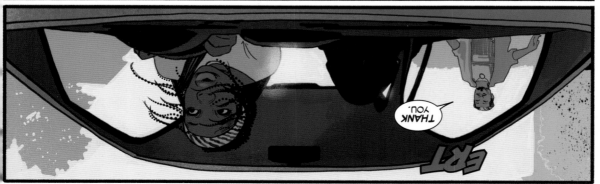

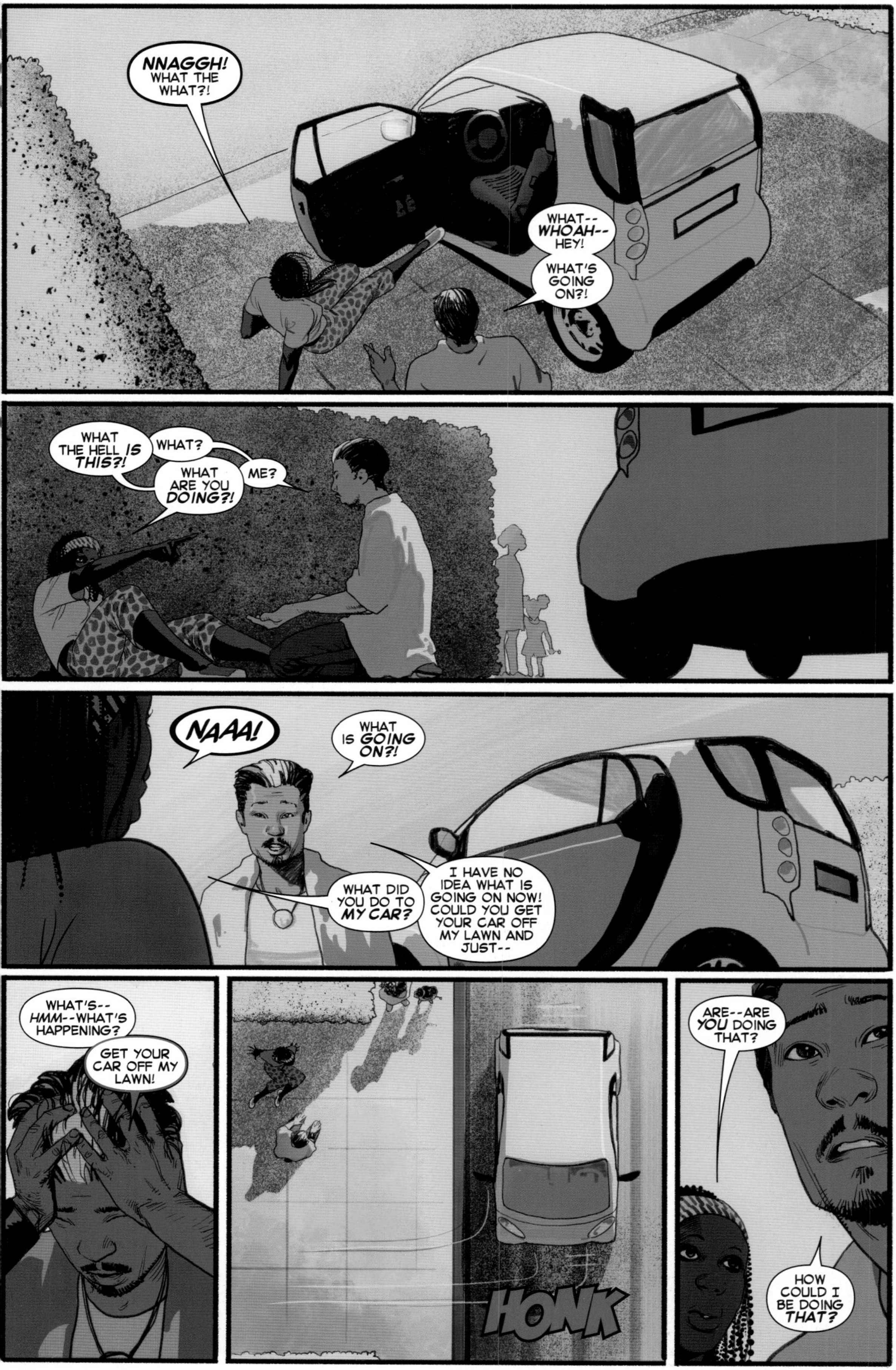
NNAGGH! WHAT THE WHAT?!
WHAT-- WHOAH-- HEY!
WHAT'S GOING ON?!
WHAT THE HELL IS THIS?!
WHAT?
WHAT ARE YOU DOING?!
ME?
NAAA!
WHAT IS GOING ON?!
WHAT DID YOU DO TO MY CAR?
I HAVE NO IDEA WHAT IS GOING ON NOW! COULD YOU GET YOUR CAR OFF MY LAWN AND JUST--
WHAT'S-- HMM--WHAT'S HAPPENING?
GET YOUR CAR OFF MY LAWN!
HONK
ARE--ARE YOU DOING THAT?
HOW COULD I BE DOING THAT?

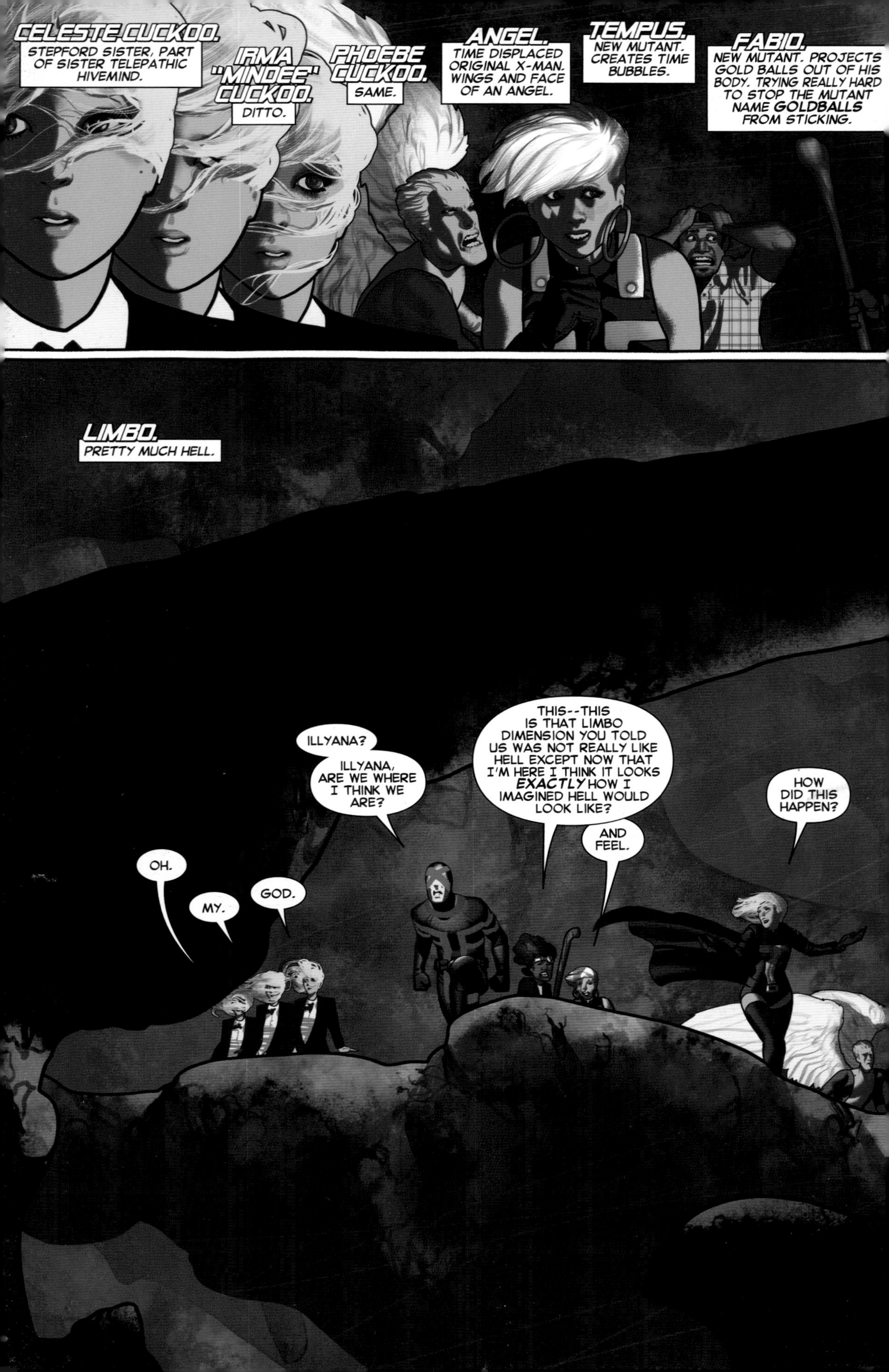
CELESTE CUCKOO. STEPFORD SISTER, PART OF SISTER TELEPATHIC HIVEMIND.
IRMA "MINDEE" CUCKOO. DITTO.
PHOEBE CUCKOO. SAME.
ANGEL. TIME DISPLACED ORIGINAL X-MAN. WINGS AND FACE OF AN ANGEL.
TEMPUS. NEW MUTANT. CREATES TIME BUBBLES.
FABIO. NEW MUTANT. PROJECTS GOLD BALLS OUT OF HIS BODY. TRYING REALLY HARD TO STOP THE MUTANT NAME GOLDBALLS FROM STICKING.
LIMBO. PRETTY MUCH HELL.
ILLYANA?
ILLYANA, ARE WE WHERE I THINK WE ARE?
THIS--THIS IS THAT LIMBO DIMENSION YOU TOLD US WAS NOT REALLY LIKE HELL EXCEPT NOW THAT I'M HERE I THINK IT LOOKS EXACTLY HOW I IMAGINED HELL WOULD LOOK LIKE?
AND FEEL.
HOW DID THIS HAPPEN?
OH.
MY.
GOD.

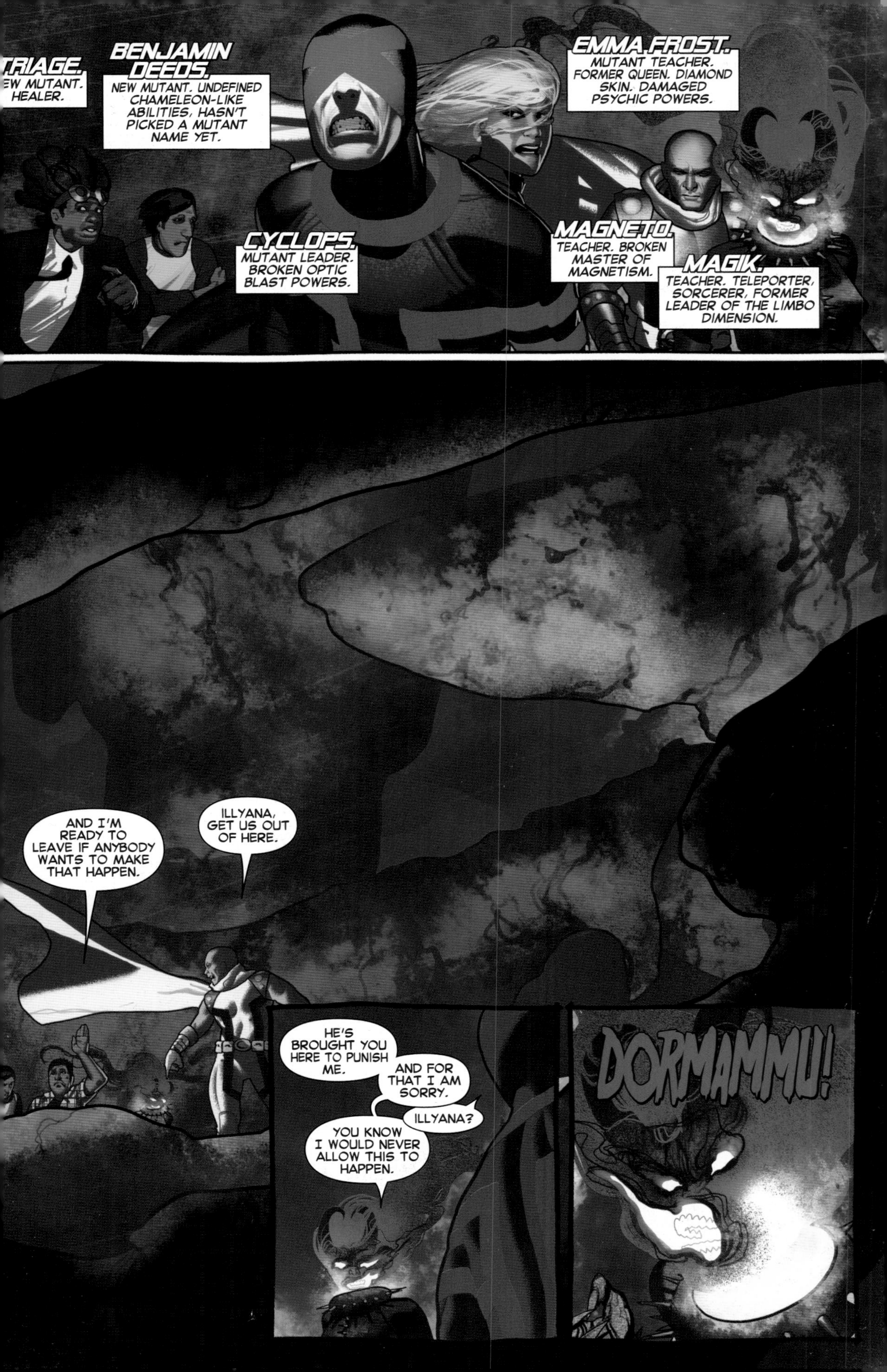
TRIAGE.
EW MUTANT. HEALER.
BENJAMIN DEEDS.
NEW MUTANT. UNDEFINED CHAMELEON-LIKE ABILITIES, HASN'T PICKED A MUTANT NAME YET.
EMMA FROST.
MUTANT TEACHER. FORMER QUEEN. DIAMOND SKIN. DAMAGED PSYCHIC POWERS.
CYCLOPS.
MUTANT LEADER. BROKEN OPTIC BLAST POWERS.
MAGNETO.
TEACHER. BROKEN MASTER OF MAGNETISM.
MAGIK.
TEACHER. TELEPORTER, SORCERER, FORMER LEADER OF THE LIMBO DIMENSION.
AND I'M READY TO LEAVE IF ANYBODY WANTS TO MAKE THAT HAPPEN.
ILLYANA, GET US OUT OF HERE.
HE'S BROUGHT YOU HERE TO PUNISH ME.
AND FOR THAT I AM SORRY.
ILLYANA?
YOU KNOW I WOULD NEVER ALLOW THIS TO HAPPEN.
DORMAMMU!

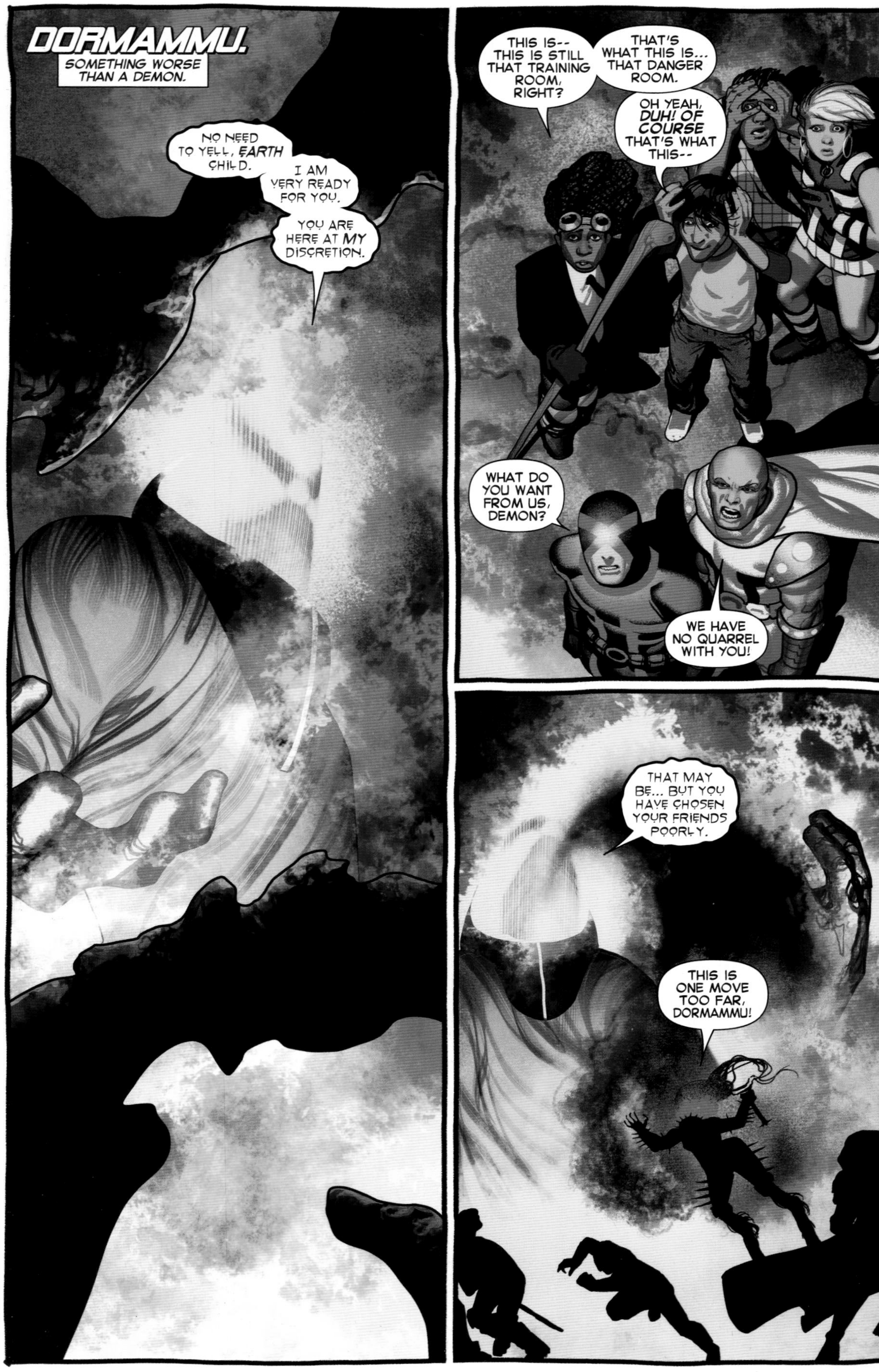
DORMAMMU.
SOMETHING WORSE THAN A DEMON.
NO NEED TO YELL, EARTH CHILD.
I AM VERY READY FOR YOU.
YOU ARE HERE AT MY DISCRETION.
THIS IS-- THIS IS STILL THAT TRAINING ROOM, RIGHT?
THAT'S WHAT THIS IS... THAT DANGER ROOM.
OH YEAH, DUH! OF COURSE THAT'S WHAT THIS--
WHAT DO YOU WANT FROM US, DEMON?
WE HAVE NO QUARREL WITH YOU!
THAT MAY BE... BUT YOU HAVE CHOSEN YOUR FRIENDS POORLY.
THIS IS ONE MOVE TOO FAR, DORMAMMU!

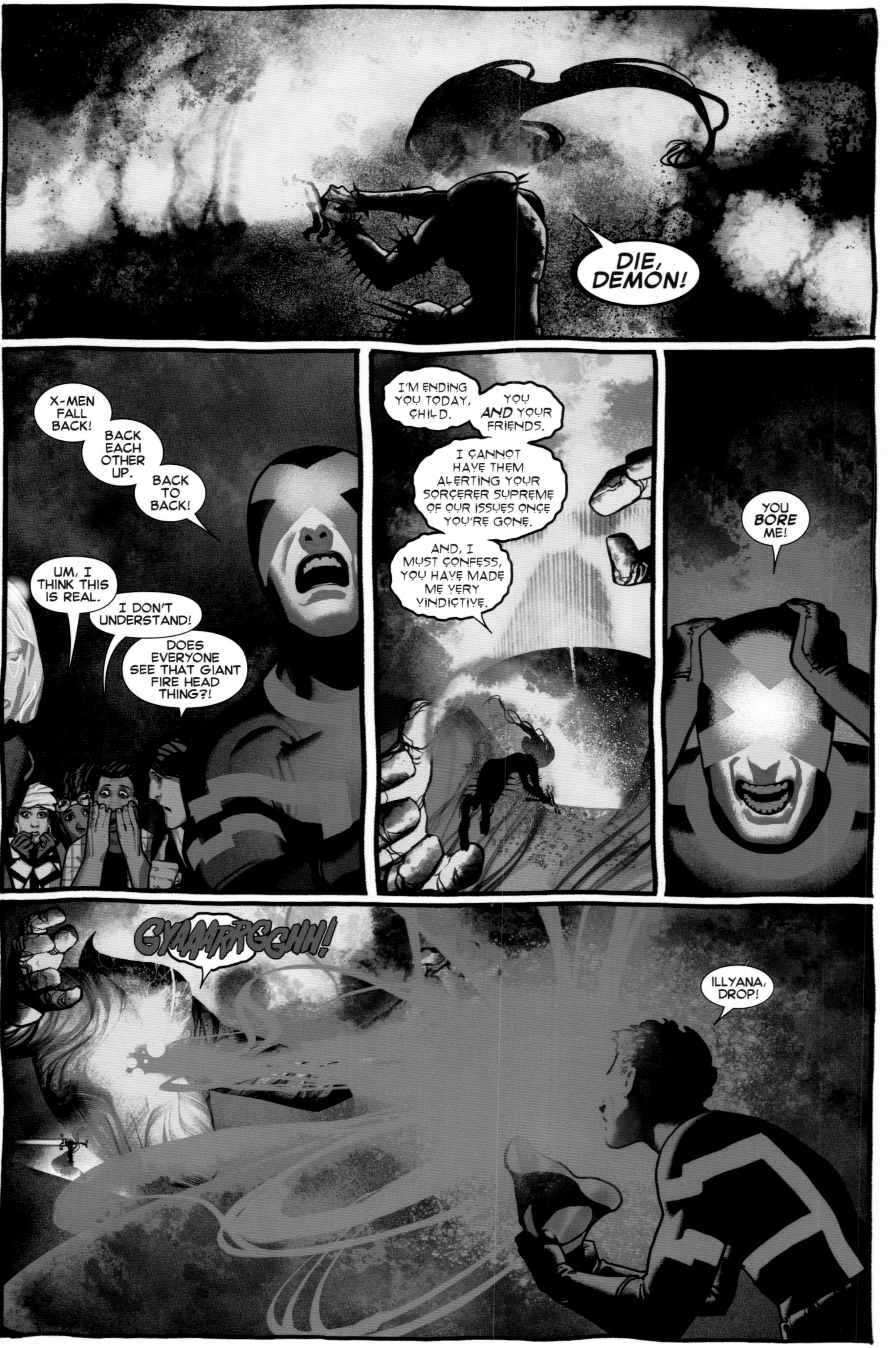
DIE, DEMON!
X-MEN FALL BACK!
BACK EACH OTHER UP.
BACK TO BACK!
UM, I THINK THIS IS REAL.
I DON'T UNDERSTAND!
DOES EVERYONE SEE THAT GIANT FIRE HEAD THING?!
I'M ENDING YOU TODAY, CHILD.
YOU AND YOUR FRIENDS.
I CANNOT HAVE THEM ALERTING YOUR SORCERER SUPREME OF OUR ISSUES ONCE YOU'RE GONE.
AND, I MUST CONFESS, YOU HAVE MADE ME VERY VINDICTIVE.
YOU BORE ME!
GYAAARRGGHH!
ILLYANA, DROP!

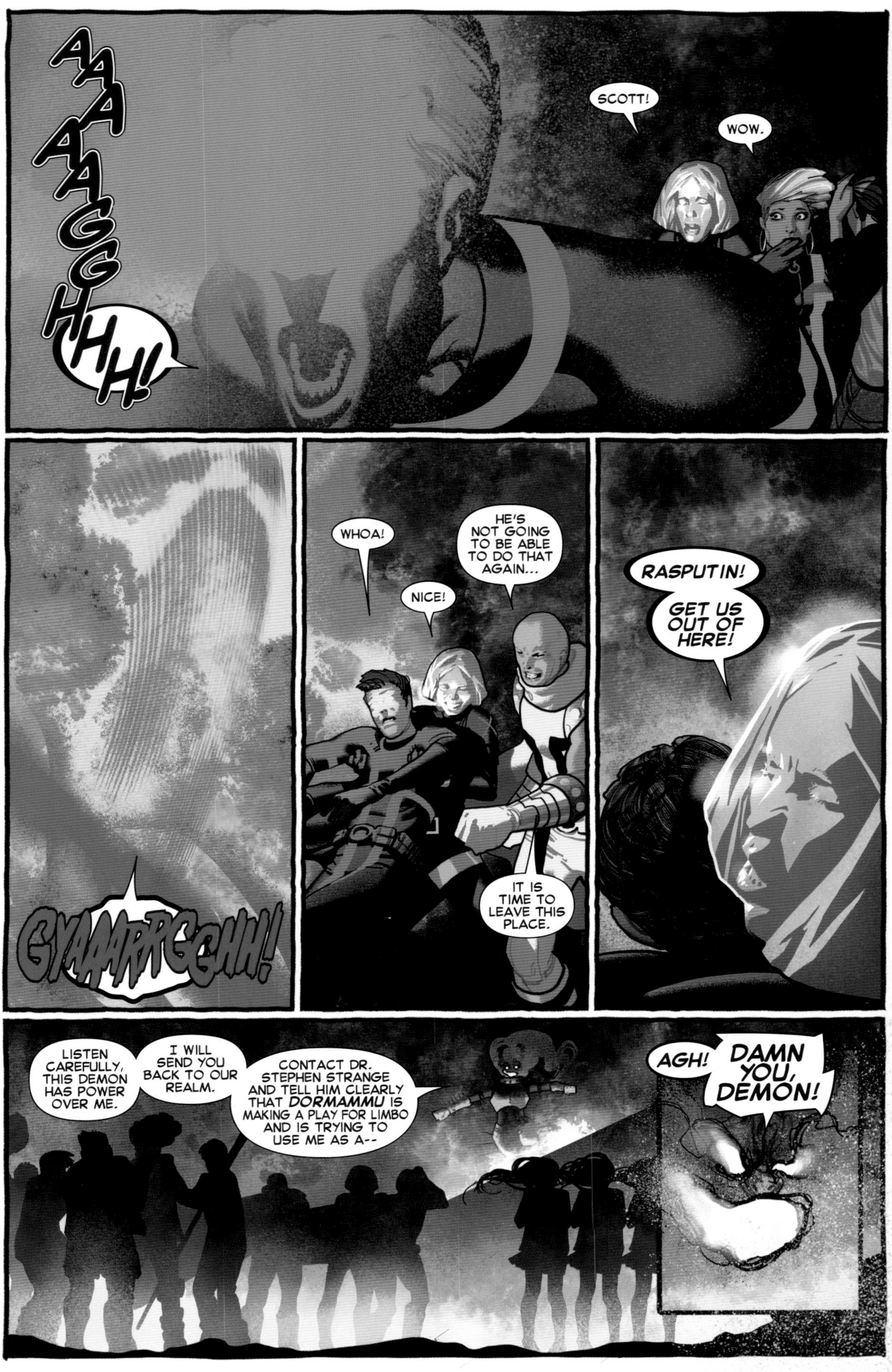
AAAAAGGHHH!
SCOTT!
WOW.
GYAAARRGGHH!
WHOA!
NICE!
HE'S NOT GOING TO BE ABLE TO DO THAT AGAIN...
IT IS TIME TO LEAVE THIS PLACE.
RASPUTIN!
GET US OUT OF HERE!
LISTEN CAREFULLY, THIS DEMON HAS POWER OVER ME.
I WILL SEND YOU BACK TO OUR REALM.
CONTACT DR. STEPHEN STRANGE AND TELL HIM CLEARLY THAT DORMAMMU IS MAKING A PLAY FOR LIMBO AND IS TRYING TO USE ME AS A--
AGH!
DAMN YOU, DEMON!

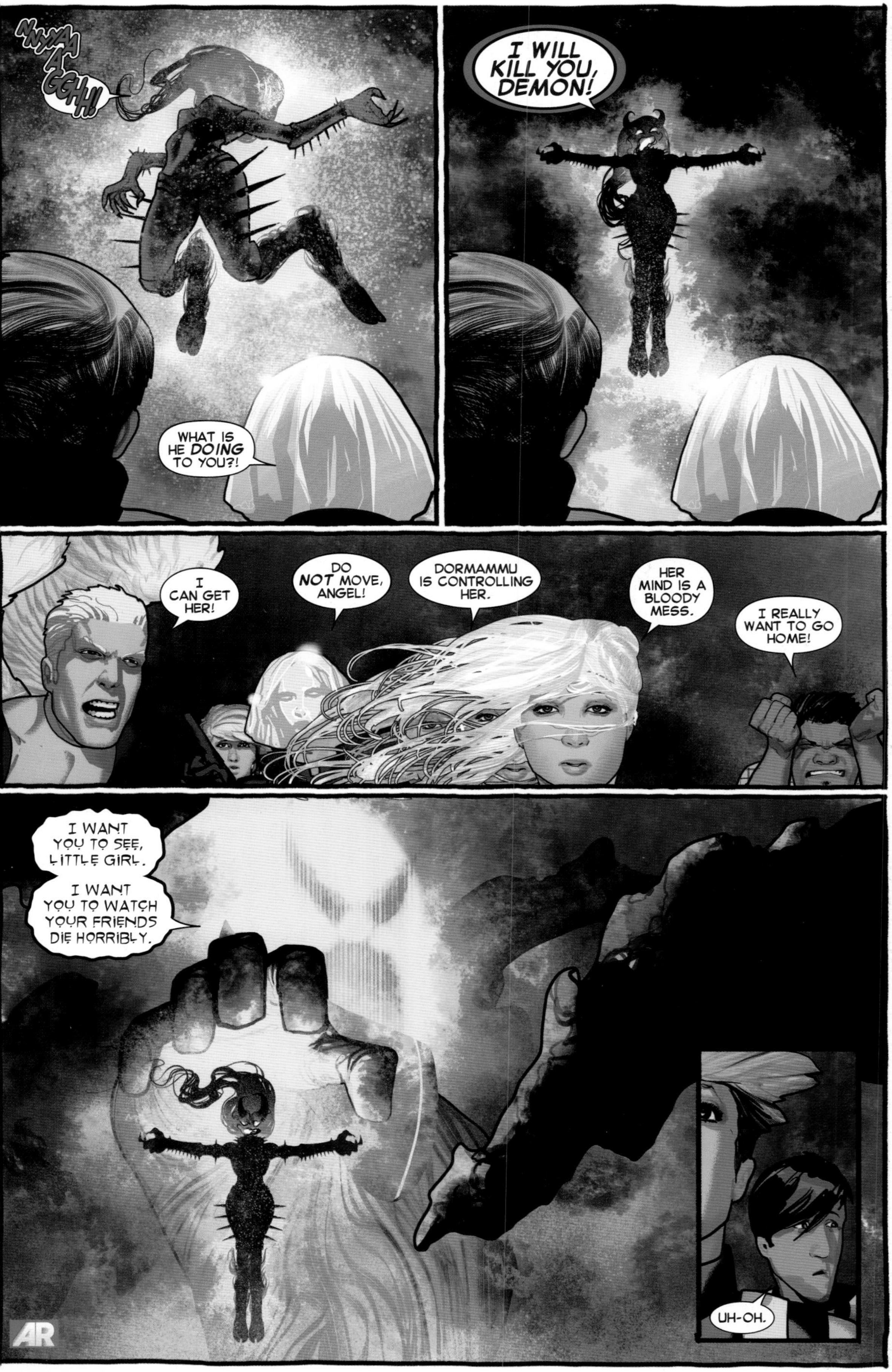
NNYYAAAGGHH!
WHAT IS HE DOING TO YOU?!
I WILL KILL YOU, DEMON!
I CAN GET HER!
DO NOT MOVE, ANGEL!
DORMAMMU IS CONTROLLING HER.
HER MIND IS A BLOODY MESS.
I REALLY WANT TO GO HOME!
I WANT YOU TO SEE, LITTLE GIRL.
I WANT YOU TO WATCH YOUR FRIENDS DIE HORRIBLY.
UH-OH.

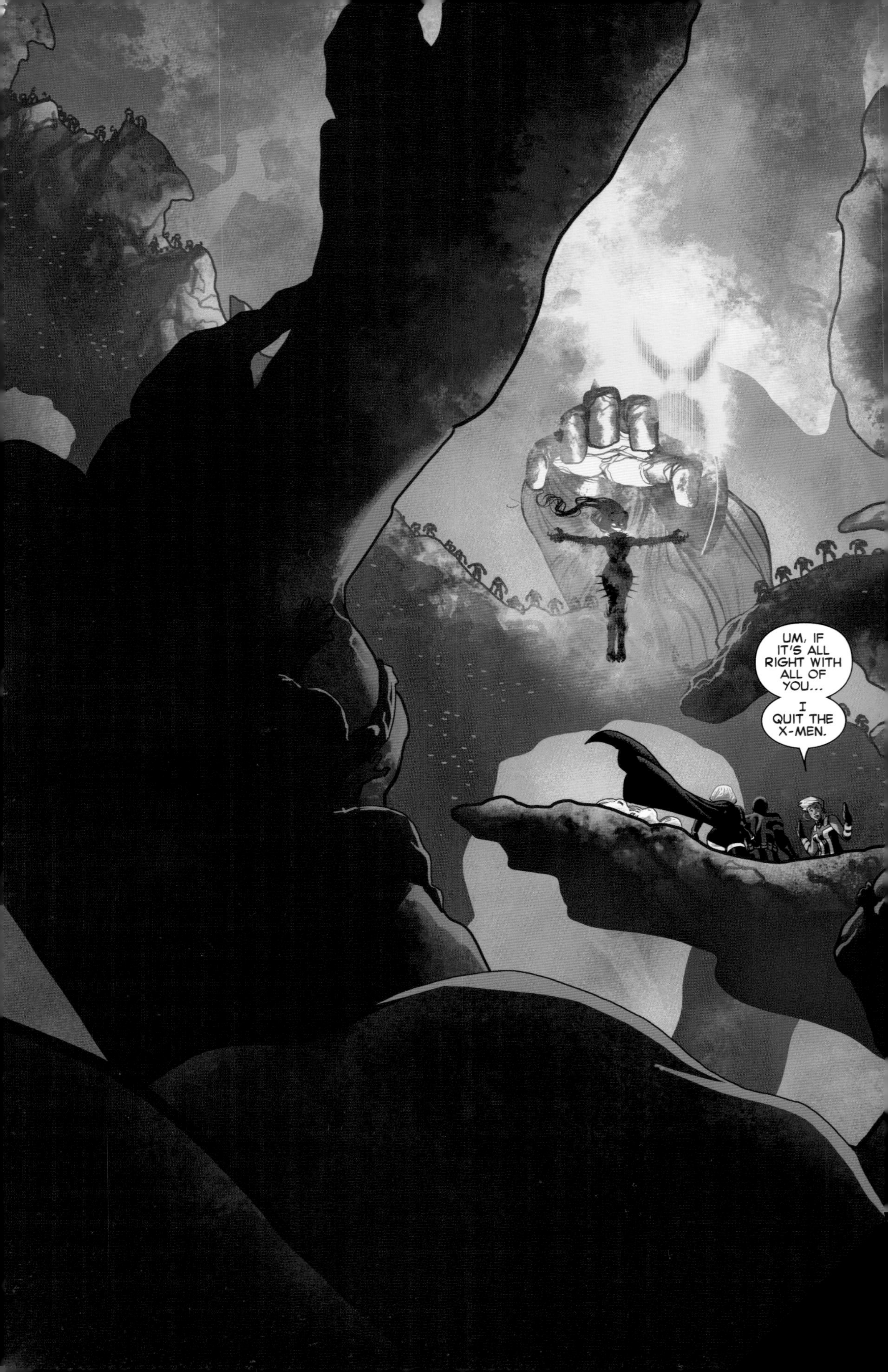
UM, IF IT'S ALL RIGHT WITH ALL OF YOU...
I QUIT THE X-MEN.

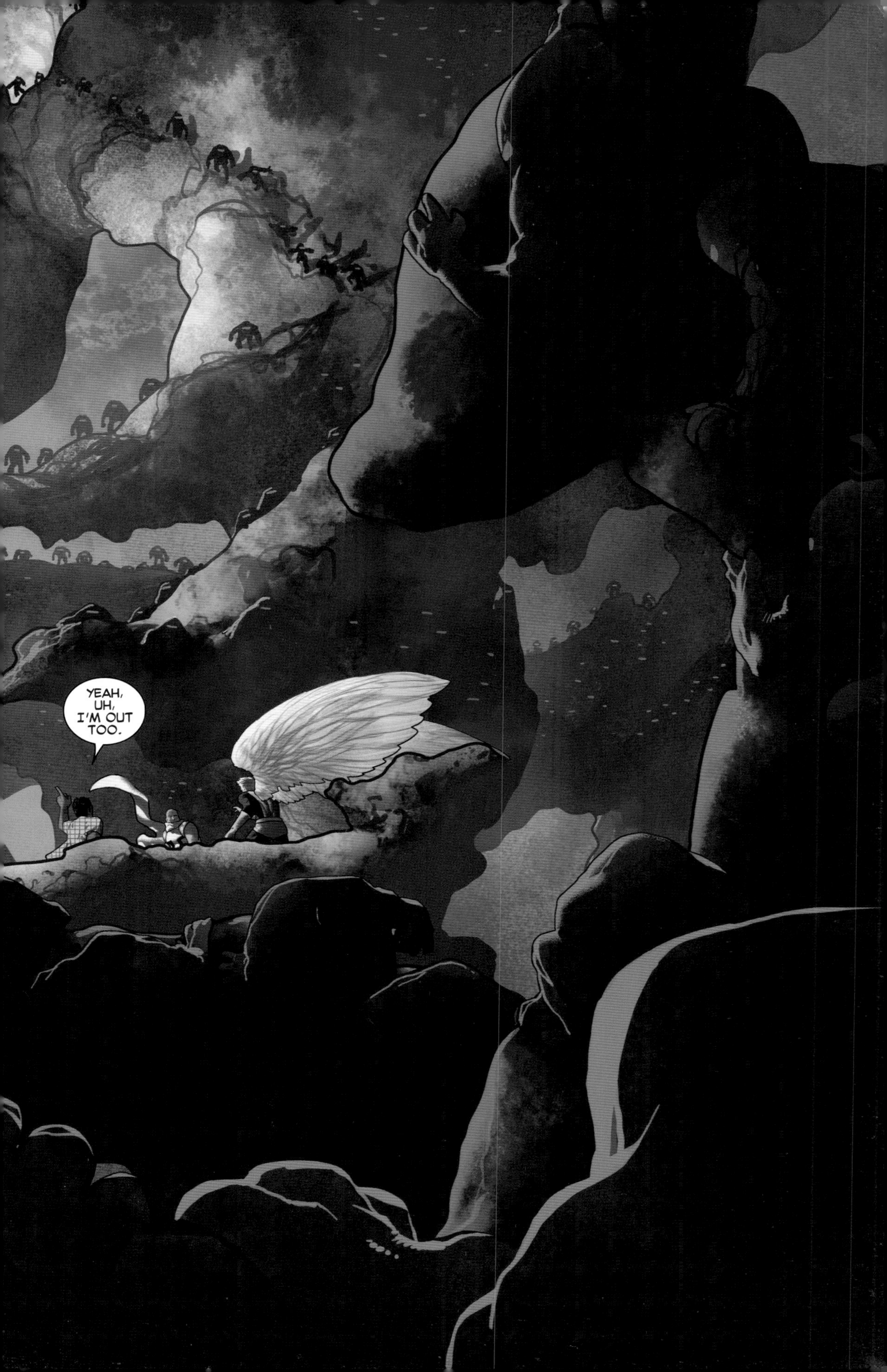
YEAH, UH, I'M OUT TOO.

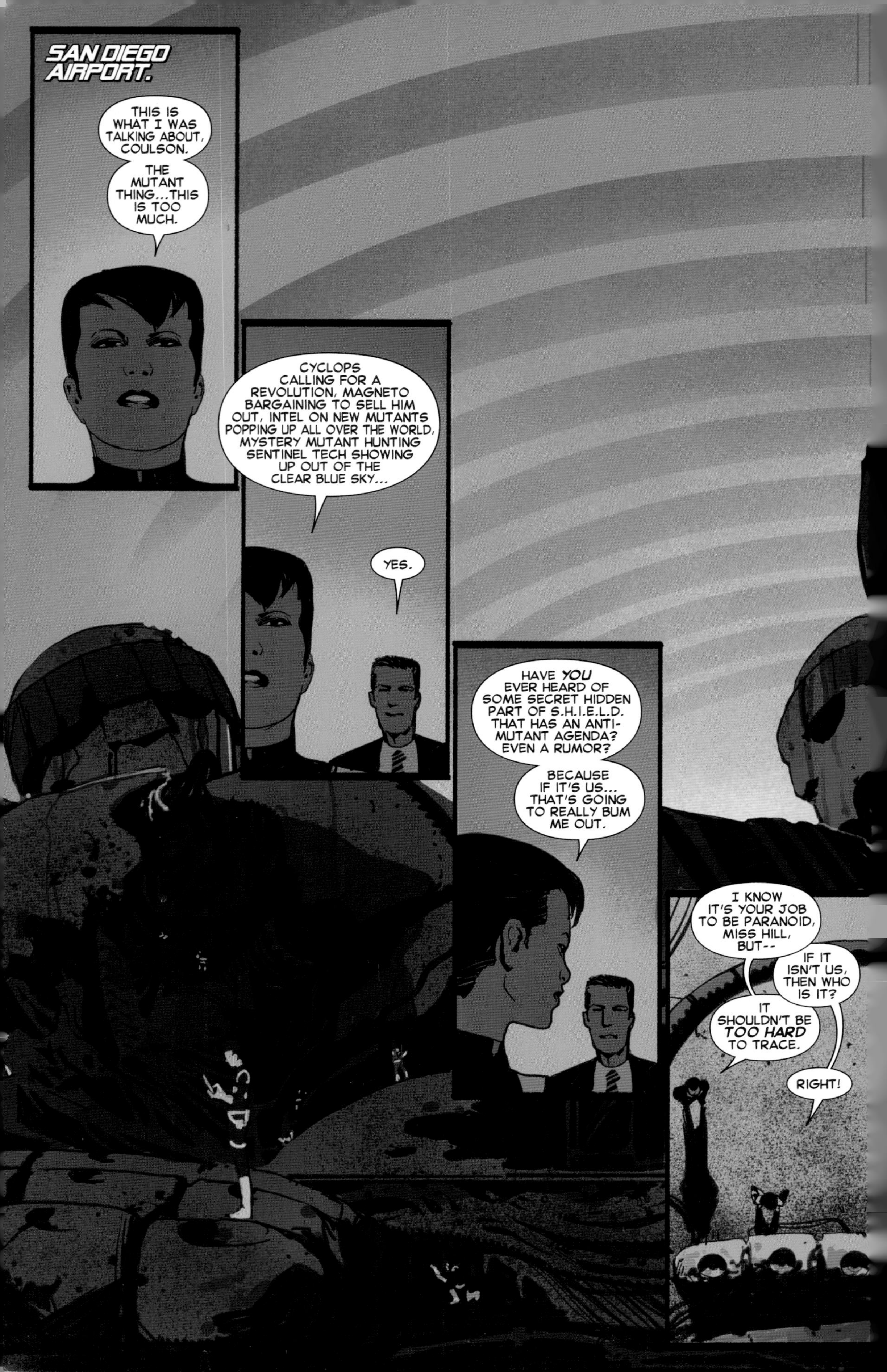
SAN DIEGO AIRPORT.
THIS IS WHAT I WAS TALKING ABOUT, COULSON.
THE MUTANT THING...THIS IS TOO MUCH.
CYCLOPS CALLING FOR A REVOLUTION, MAGNETO BARGAINING TO SELL HIM OUT, INTEL ON NEW MUTANTS POPPING UP ALL OVER THE WORLD, MYSTERY MUTANT HUNTING SENTINEL TECH SHOWING UP OUT OF THE CLEAR BLUE SKY...
YES.
HAVE *YOU* EVER HEARD OF SOME SECRET HIDDEN PART OF S.H.I.E.L.D. THAT HAS AN ANTI-MUTANT AGENDA? EVEN A RUMOR?
BECAUSE IF IT'S US... THAT'S GOING TO REALLY BUM ME OUT.
I KNOW IT'S YOUR JOB TO BE PARANOID, MISS HILL, BUT--
IF IT ISN'T US, THEN WHO IS IT?
IT SHOULDN'T BE *TOO HARD* TO TRACE.
RIGHT!

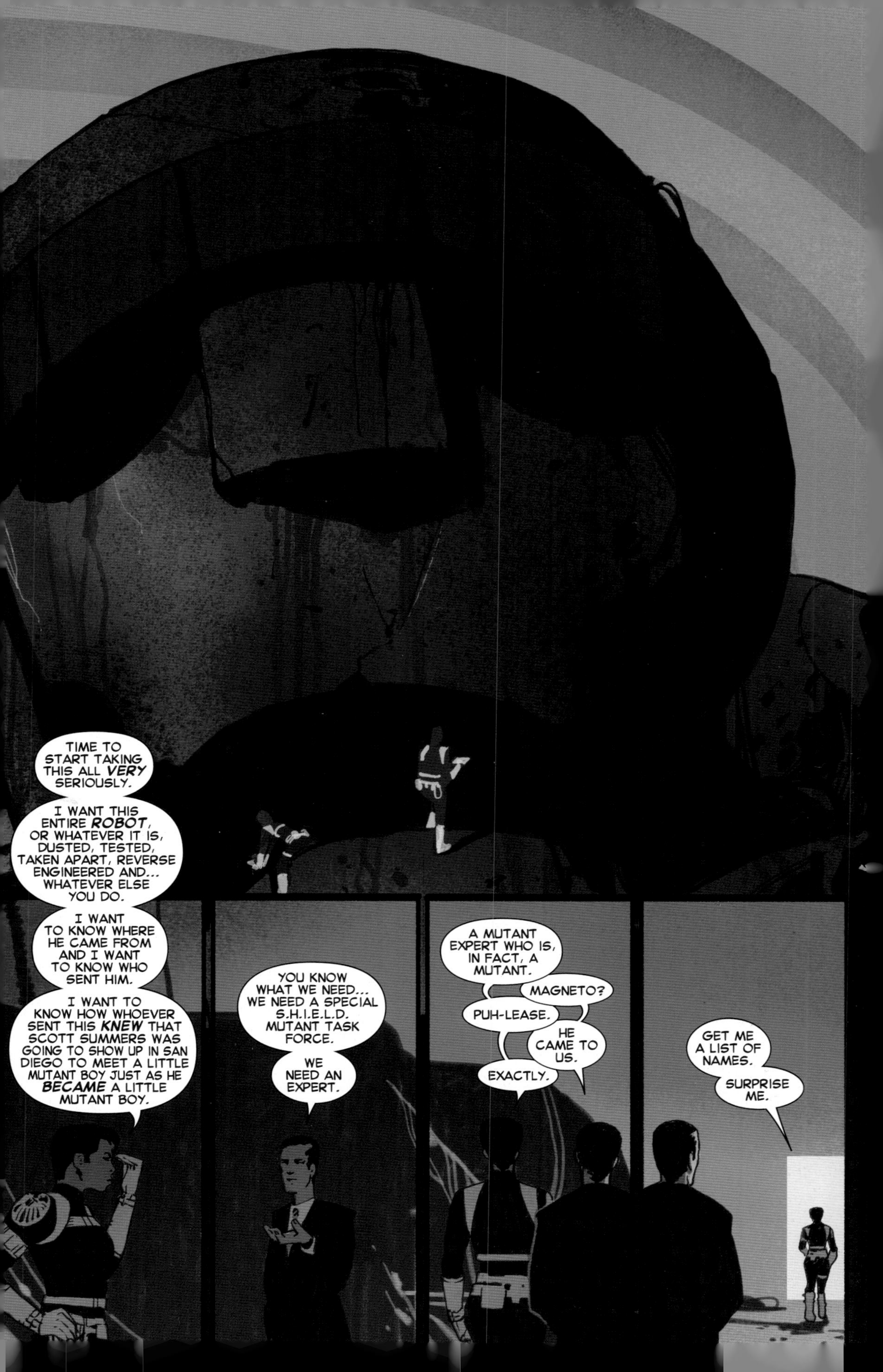
TIME TO START TAKING THIS ALL *VERY* SERIOUSLY.
I WANT THIS ENTIRE *ROBOT*, OR WHATEVER IT IS, DUSTED, TESTED, TAKEN APART, REVERSE ENGINEERED AND... WHATEVER ELSE YOU DO.
I WANT TO KNOW WHERE HE CAME FROM AND I WANT TO KNOW WHO SENT HIM.
I WANT TO KNOW HOW WHOEVER SENT THIS *KNEW* THAT SCOTT SUMMERS WAS GOING TO SHOW UP IN SAN DIEGO TO MEET A LITTLE MUTANT BOY JUST AS HE *BECAME* A LITTLE MUTANT BOY.
YOU KNOW WHAT WE NEED... WE NEED A SPECIAL S.H.I.E.L.D. MUTANT TASK FORCE.
WE NEED AN EXPERT.
A MUTANT EXPERT WHO IS, IN FACT, A MUTANT.
MAGNETO?
PUH-LEASE.
HE CAME TO US.
EXACTLY.
GET ME A LIST OF NAMES.
SURPRISE ME.

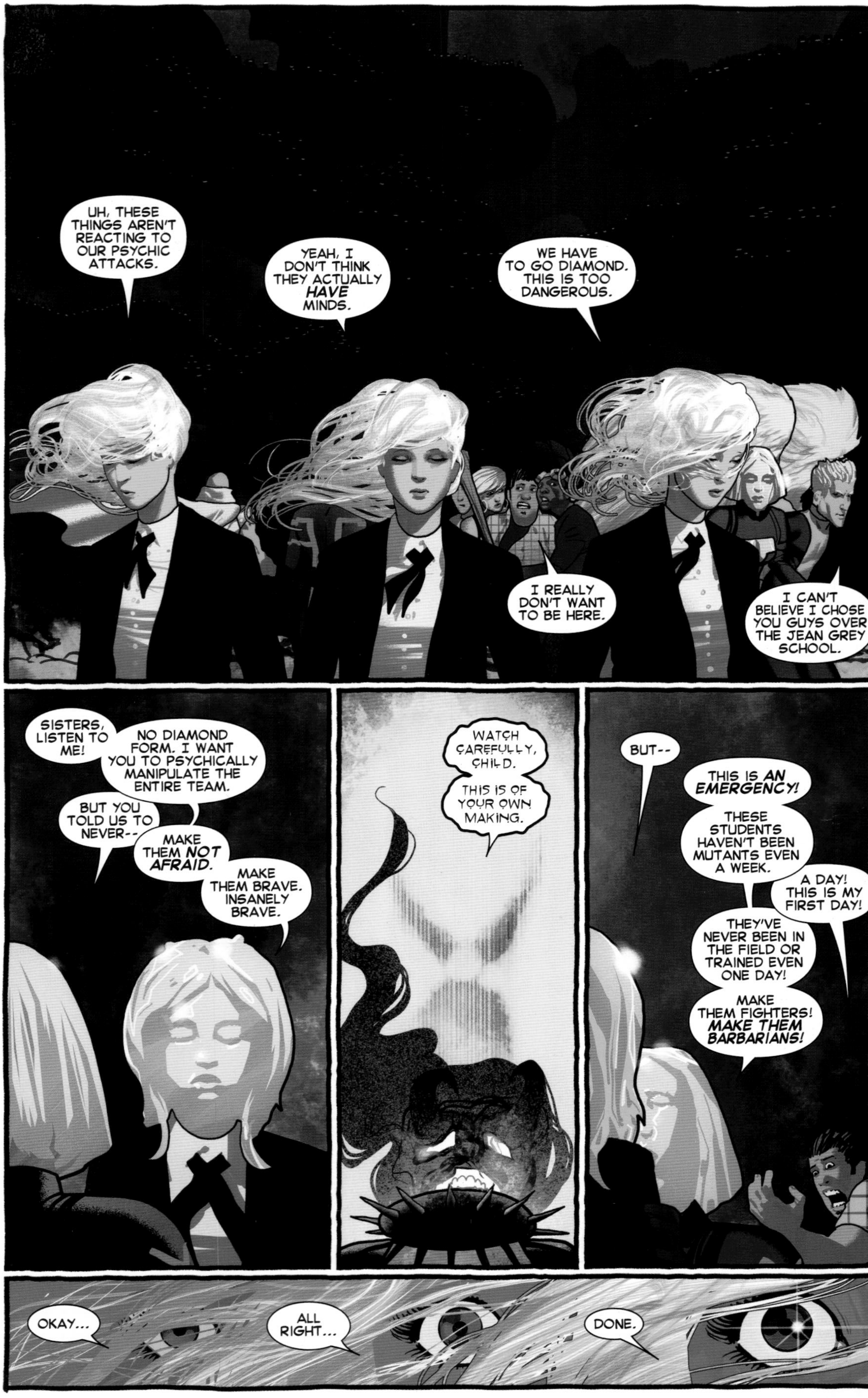

UH, THESE THINGS AREN'T REACTING TO OUR PSYCHIC ATTACKS.
YEAH, I DON'T THINK THEY ACTUALLY *HAVE* MINDS.
WE HAVE TO GO DIAMOND. THIS IS TOO DANGEROUS.
I REALLY DON'T WANT TO BE HERE.
I CAN'T BELIEVE I CHOSE YOU GUYS OVER THE JEAN GREY SCHOOL.
SISTERS, LISTEN TO ME!
NO DIAMOND FORM. I WANT YOU TO PSYCHICALLY MANIPULATE THE ENTIRE TEAM.
BUT YOU TOLD US TO NEVER--
MAKE THEM ***NOT AFRAID.***
MAKE THEM BRAVE. INSANELY BRAVE.
WATCH CAREFULLY, CHILD.
THIS IS OF YOUR OWN MAKING.
BUT--
THIS IS ***AN EMERGENCY!***
THESE STUDENTS HAVEN'T BEEN MUTANTS EVEN A WEEK.
A DAY! THIS IS MY FIRST DAY!
THEY'VE NEVER BEEN IN THE FIELD OR TRAINED EVEN ONE DAY!
MAKE THEM FIGHTERS! ***MAKE THEM BARBARIANS!***
OKAY...
ALL RIGHT...
DONE.

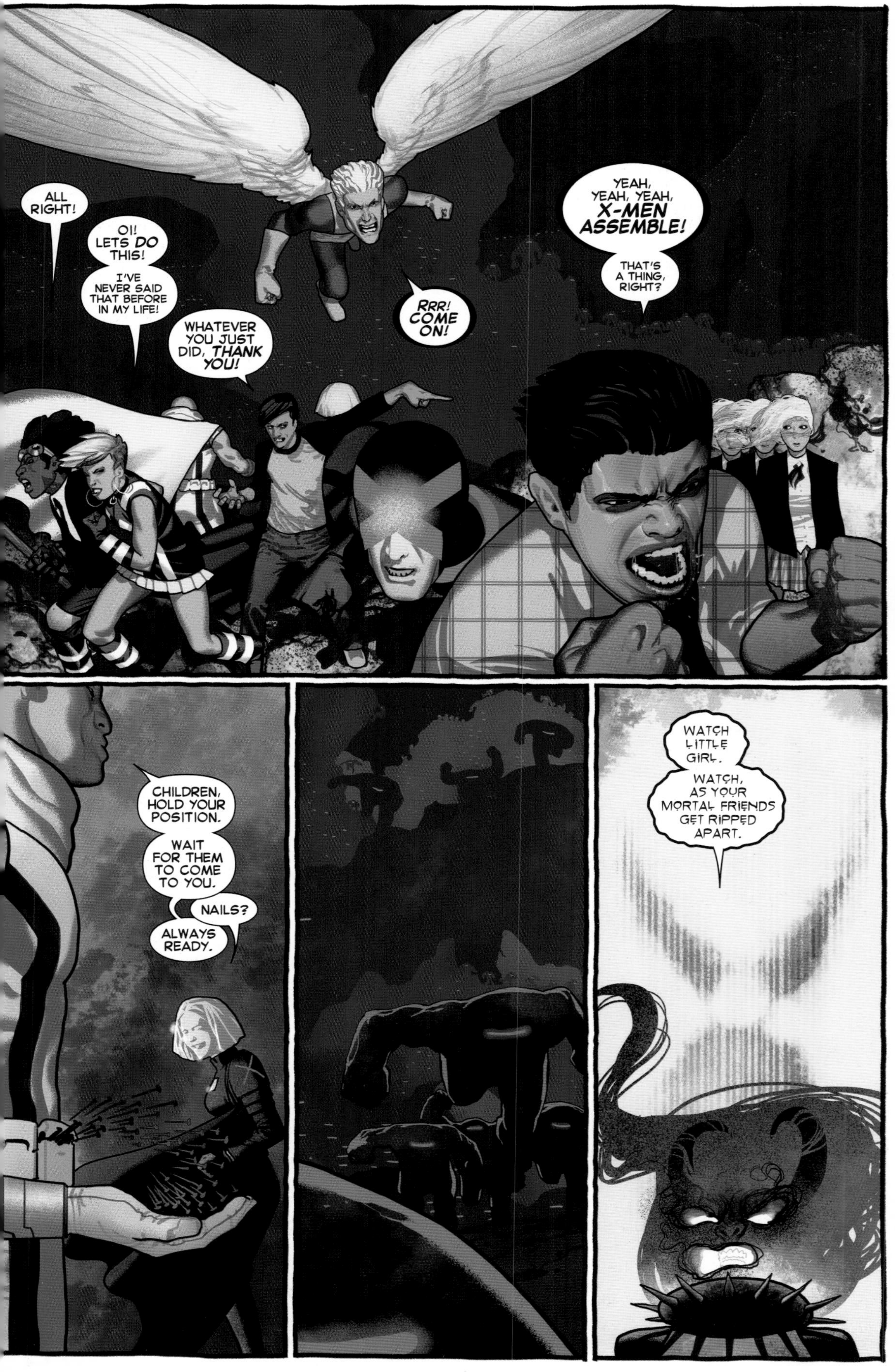
ALL RIGHT!
OI! LETS DO THIS!
I'VE NEVER SAID THAT BEFORE IN MY LIFE!
WHATEVER YOU JUST DID, THANK YOU!
RRR! COME ON!
YEAH, YEAH, YEAH, X-MEN ASSEMBLE!
THAT'S A THING, RIGHT?
CHILDREN, HOLD YOUR POSITION.
WAIT FOR THEM TO COME TO YOU.
NAILS?
ALWAYS READY.
WATCH LITTLE GIRL.
WATCH, AS YOUR MORTAL FRIENDS GET RIPPED APART.

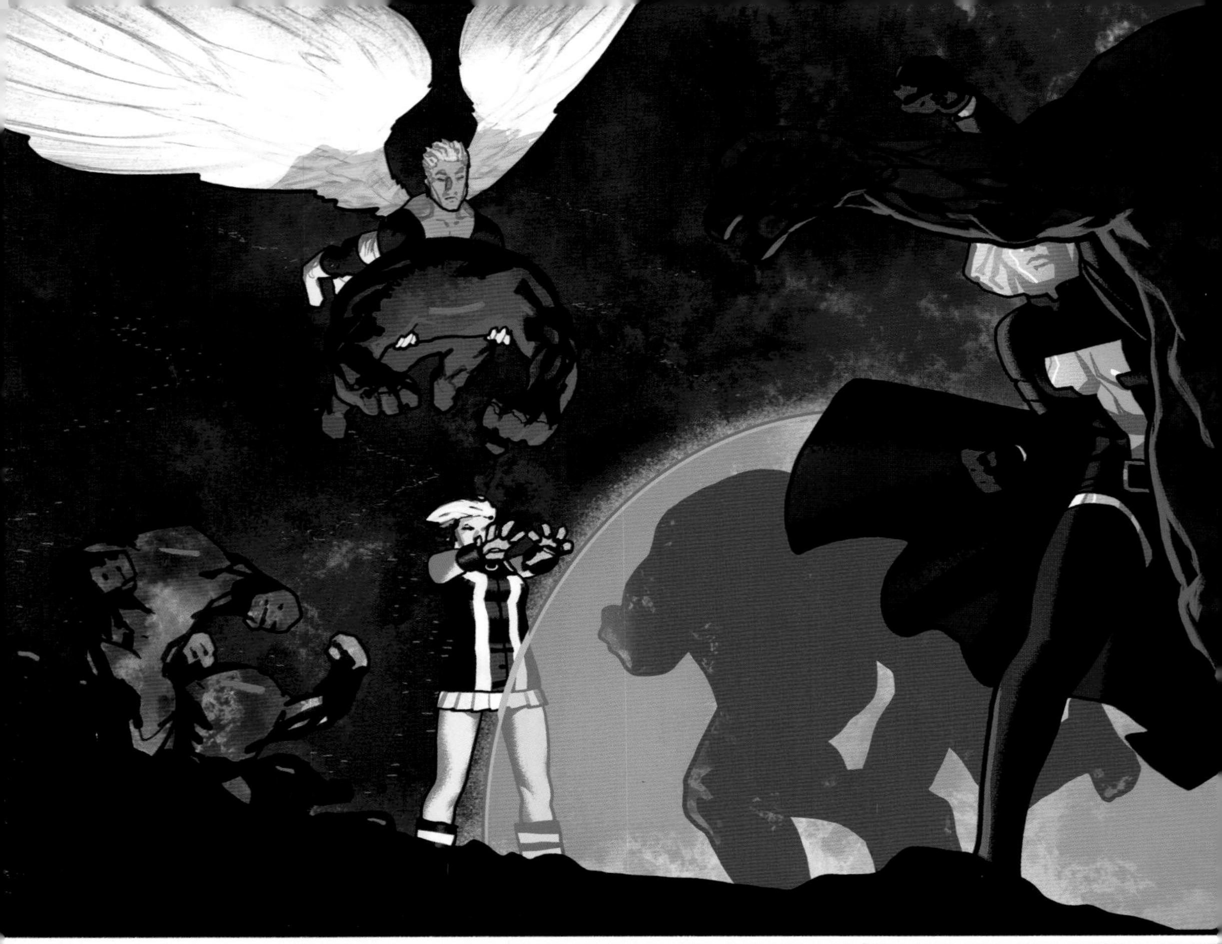

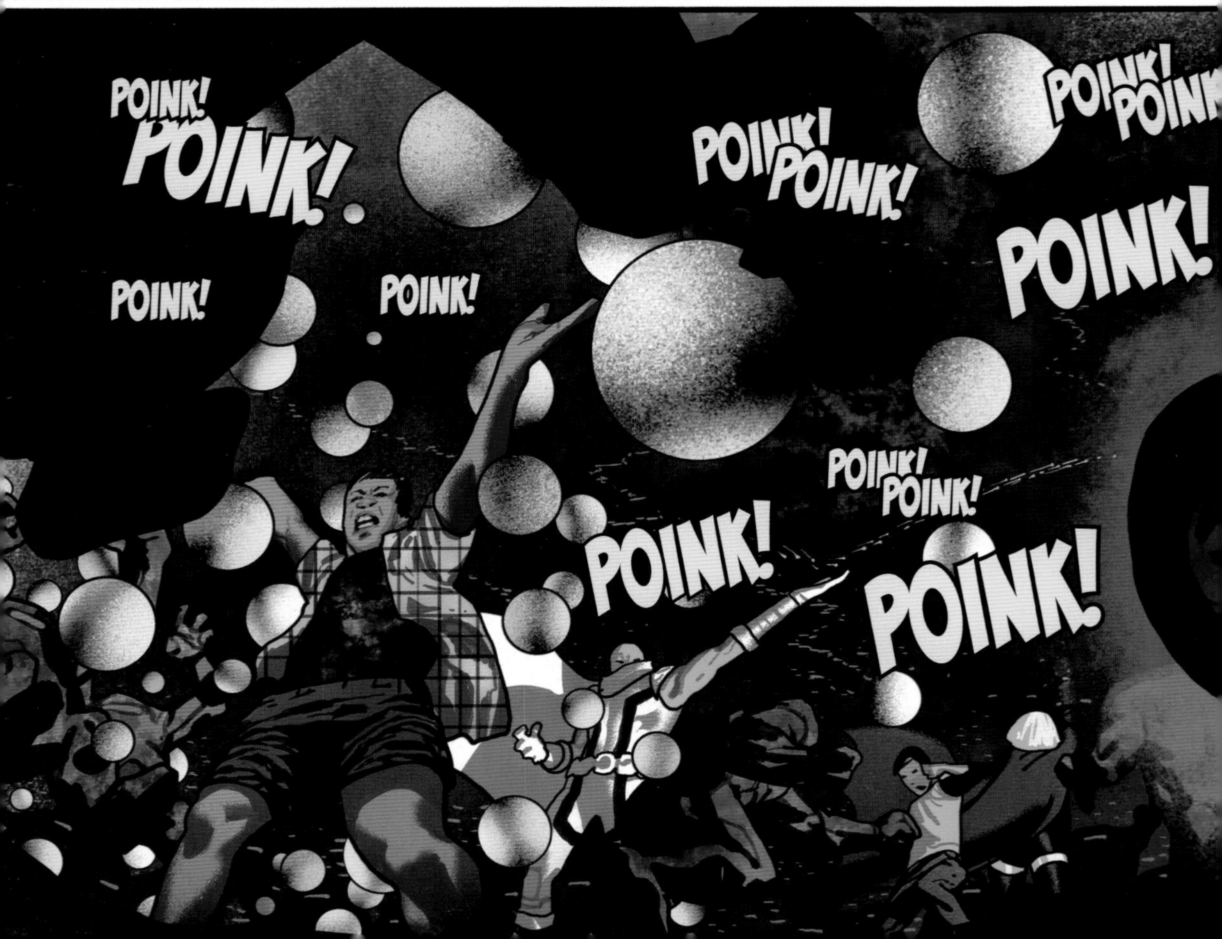
POINK!
POINK!
POINK!
POINK!
POINK!
POINK!
POINK!
POINK!
POINK!
POINK!
POINK!
POINK!

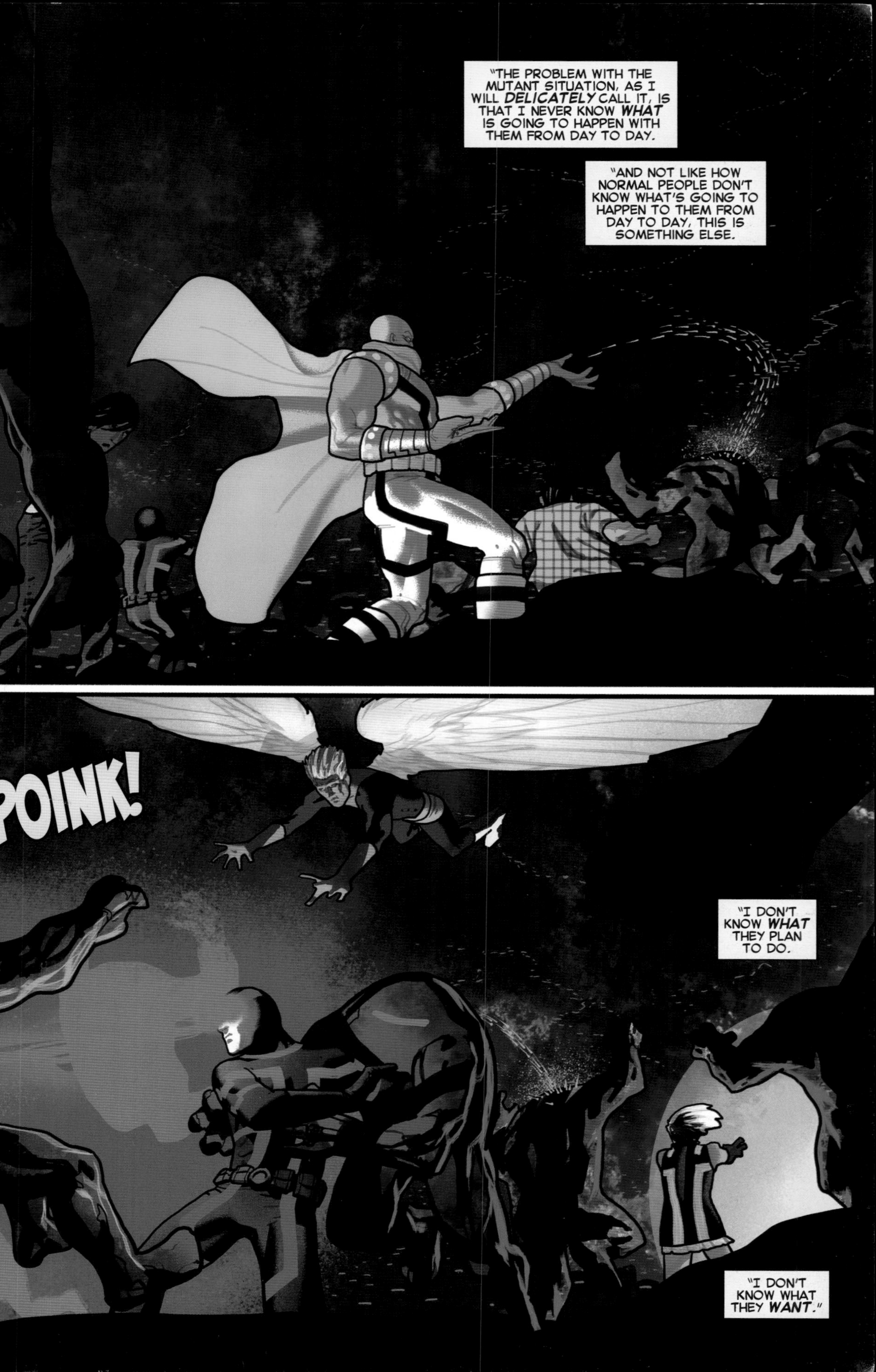
"THE PROBLEM WITH THE MUTANT SITUATION, AS I WILL *DELICATELY* CALL IT, IS THAT I NEVER KNOW *WHAT* IS GOING TO HAPPEN WITH THEM FROM DAY TO DAY.
"AND NOT LIKE HOW NORMAL PEOPLE DON'T KNOW WHAT'S GOING TO HAPPEN TO THEM FROM DAY TO DAY, THIS IS SOMETHING ELSE.
POINK!
"I DON'T KNOW *WHAT* THEY PLAN TO DO.
"I DON'T KNOW WHAT THEY *WANT*."

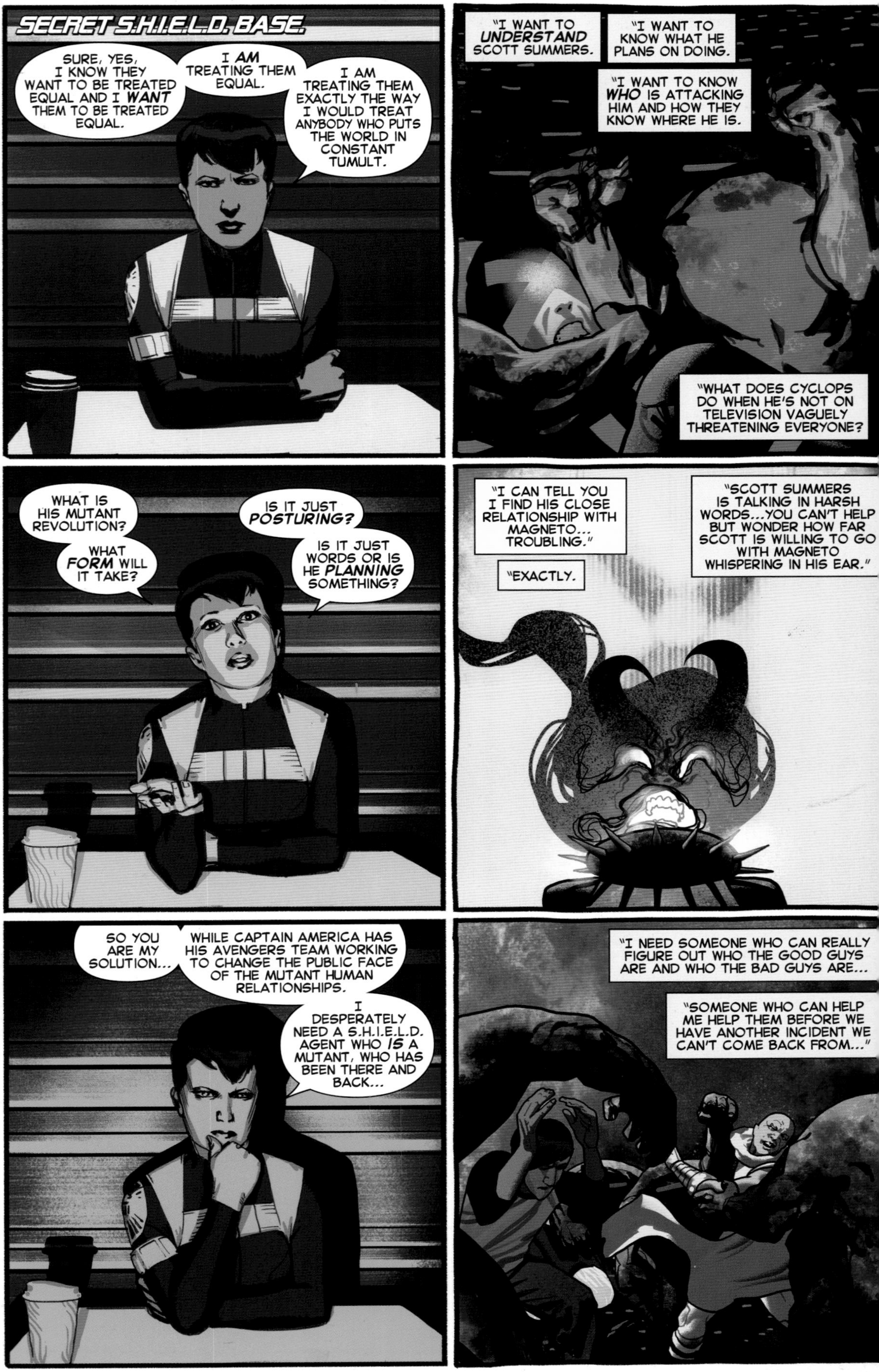
SECRET S.H.I.E.L.D. BASE.
SURE, YES, I KNOW THEY WANT TO BE TREATED EQUAL AND I WANT THEM TO BE TREATED EQUAL.
I AM TREATING THEM EQUAL.
I AM TREATING THEM EXACTLY THE WAY I WOULD TREAT ANYBODY WHO PUTS THE WORLD IN CONSTANT TUMULT.
"I WANT TO UNDERSTAND SCOTT SUMMERS.
"I WANT TO KNOW WHAT HE PLANS ON DOING.
"I WANT TO KNOW WHO IS ATTACKING HIM AND HOW THEY KNOW WHERE HE IS.
"WHAT DOES CYCLOPS DO WHEN HE'S NOT ON TELEVISION VAGUELY THREATENING EVERYONE?
WHAT IS HIS MUTANT REVOLUTION?
WHAT FORM WILL IT TAKE?
IS IT JUST POSTURING?
IS IT JUST WORDS OR IS HE PLANNING SOMETHING?
"I CAN TELL YOU I FIND HIS CLOSE RELATIONSHIP WITH MAGNETO... TROUBLING."
"EXACTLY.
"SCOTT SUMMERS IS TALKING IN HARSH WORDS...YOU CAN'T HELP BUT WONDER HOW FAR SCOTT IS WILLING TO GO WITH MAGNETO WHISPERING IN HIS EAR."
SO YOU ARE MY SOLUTION...
WHILE CAPTAIN AMERICA HAS HIS AVENGERS TEAM WORKING TO CHANGE THE PUBLIC FACE OF THE MUTANT HUMAN RELATIONSHIPS.
I DESPERATELY NEED A S.H.I.E.L.D. AGENT WHO IS A MUTANT, WHO HAS BEEN THERE AND BACK...
"I NEED SOMEONE WHO CAN REALLY FIGURE OUT WHO THE GOOD GUYS ARE AND WHO THE BAD GUYS ARE...
"SOMEONE WHO CAN HELP ME HELP THEM BEFORE WE HAVE ANOTHER INCIDENT WE CAN'T COME BACK FROM..."

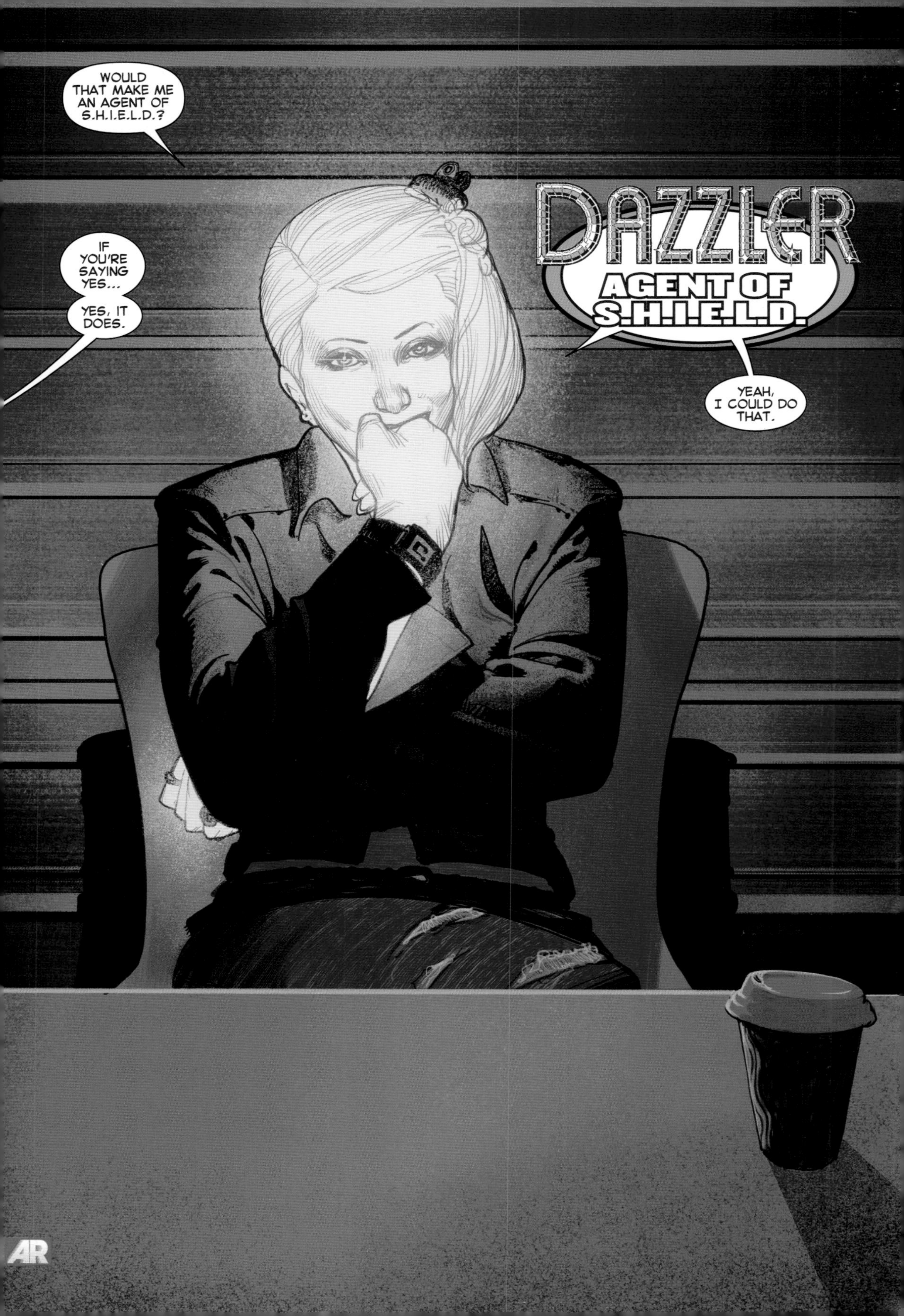
WOULD THAT MAKE ME AN AGENT OF S.H.I.E.L.D.?
IF YOU'RE SAYING YES...
YES, IT DOES.
DAZZLER
AGENT OF S.H.I.E.L.D.
YEAH, I COULD DO THAT.
AR

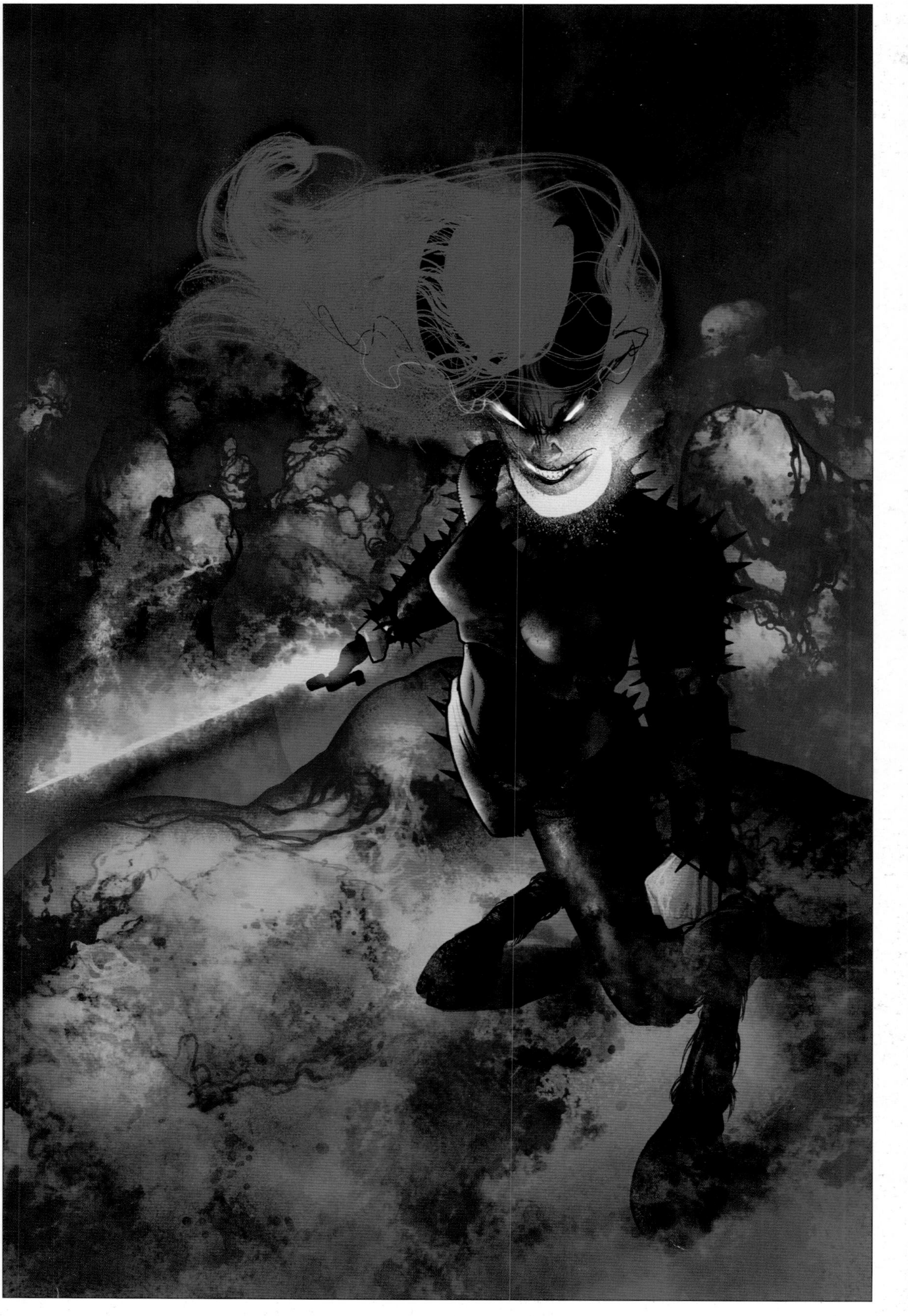

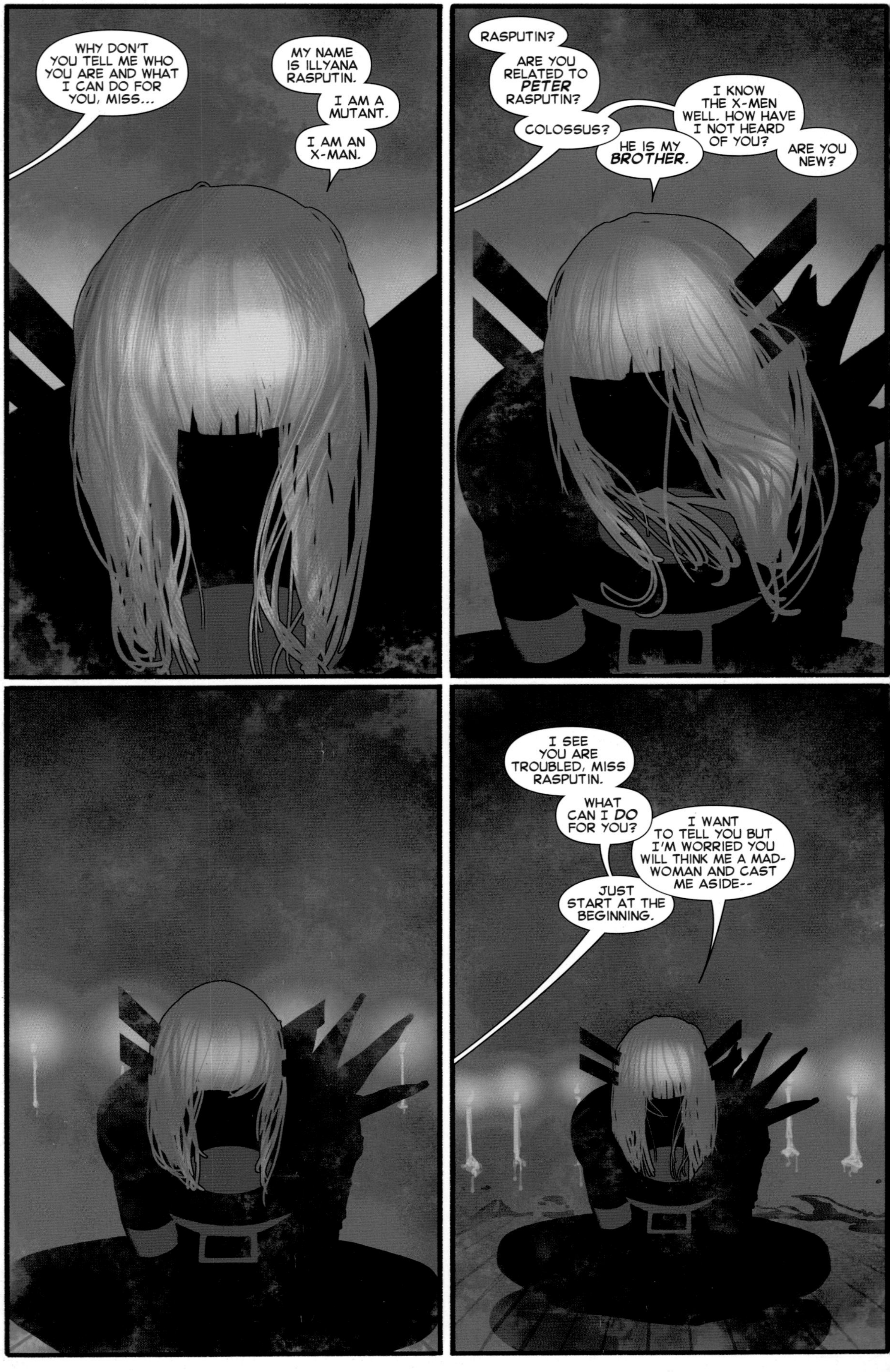
WHY DON'T YOU TELL ME WHO YOU ARE AND WHAT I CAN DO FOR YOU, MISS...
MY NAME IS ILLYANA RASPUTIN.
I AM A MUTANT.
I AM AN X-MAN.
RASPUTIN?
ARE YOU RELATED TO ***PETER*** RASPUTIN?
COLOSSUS?
HE IS MY ***BROTHER***.
I KNOW THE X-MEN WELL. HOW HAVE I NOT HEARD OF YOU?
ARE YOU NEW?
I SEE YOU ARE TROUBLED, MISS RASPUTIN.
WHAT CAN I ***DO*** FOR YOU?
I WANT TO TELL YOU BUT I'M WORRIED YOU WILL THINK ME A MAD-WOMAN AND CAST ME ASIDE--
JUST START AT THE BEGINNING.

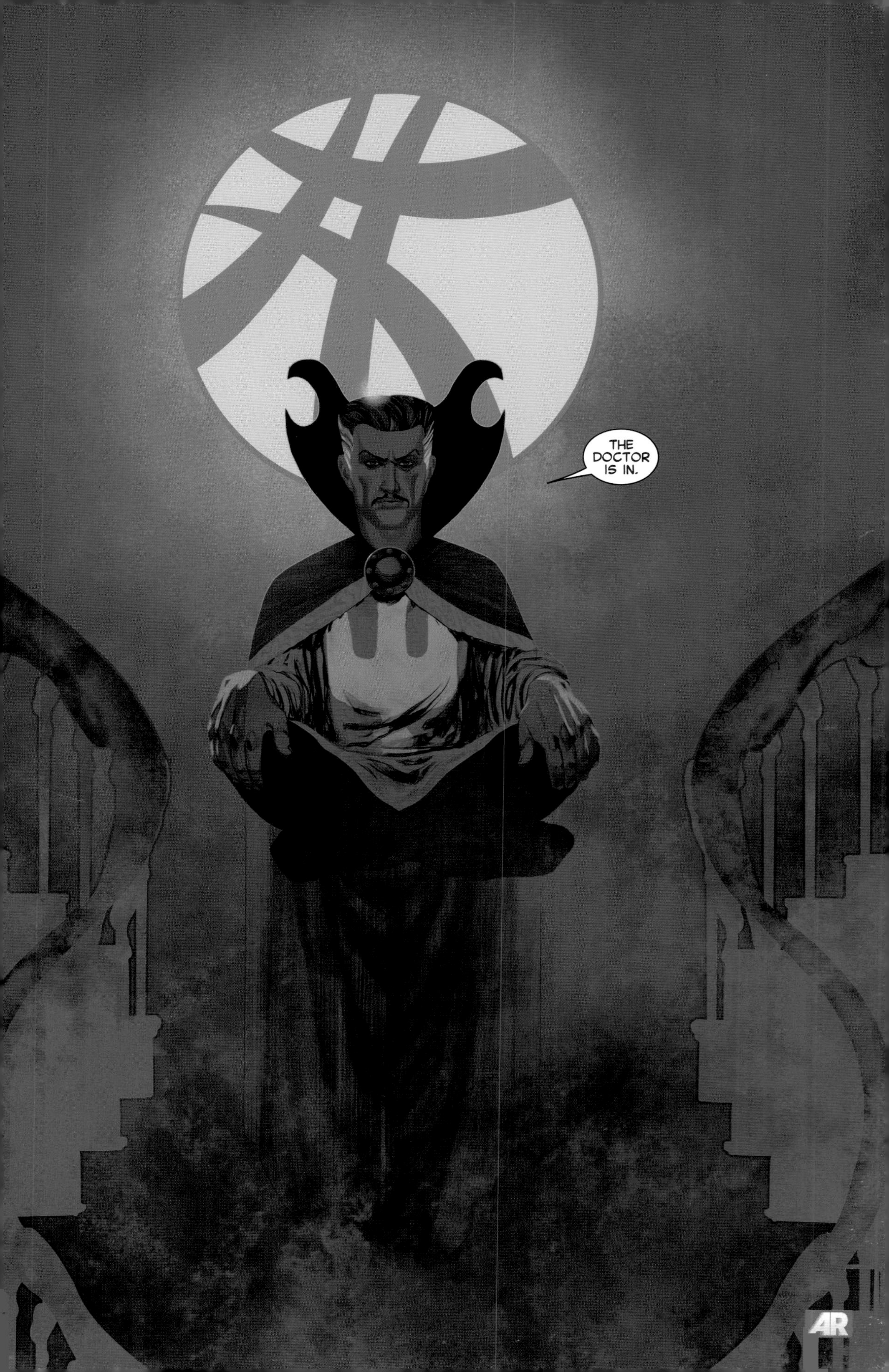
THE DOCTOR IS IN.

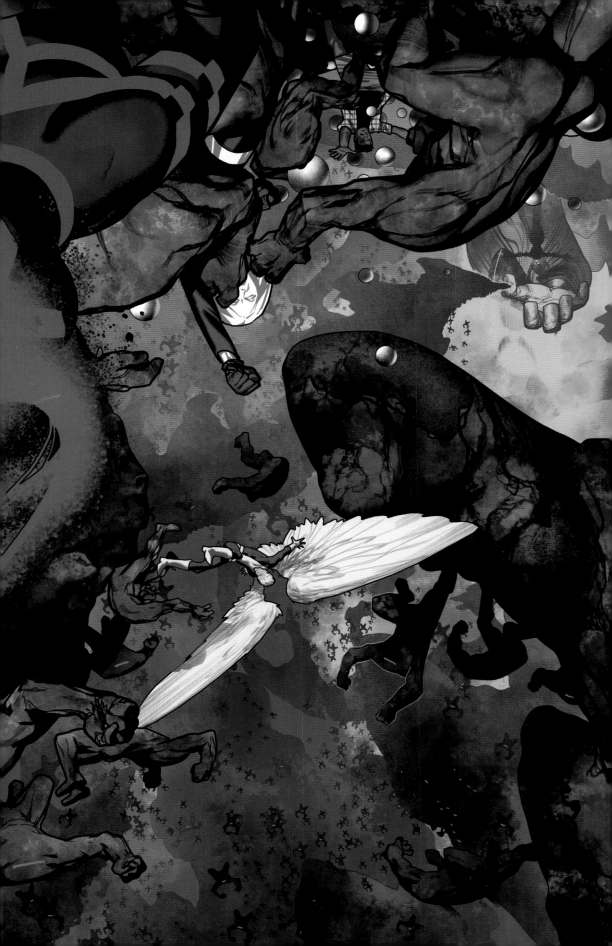

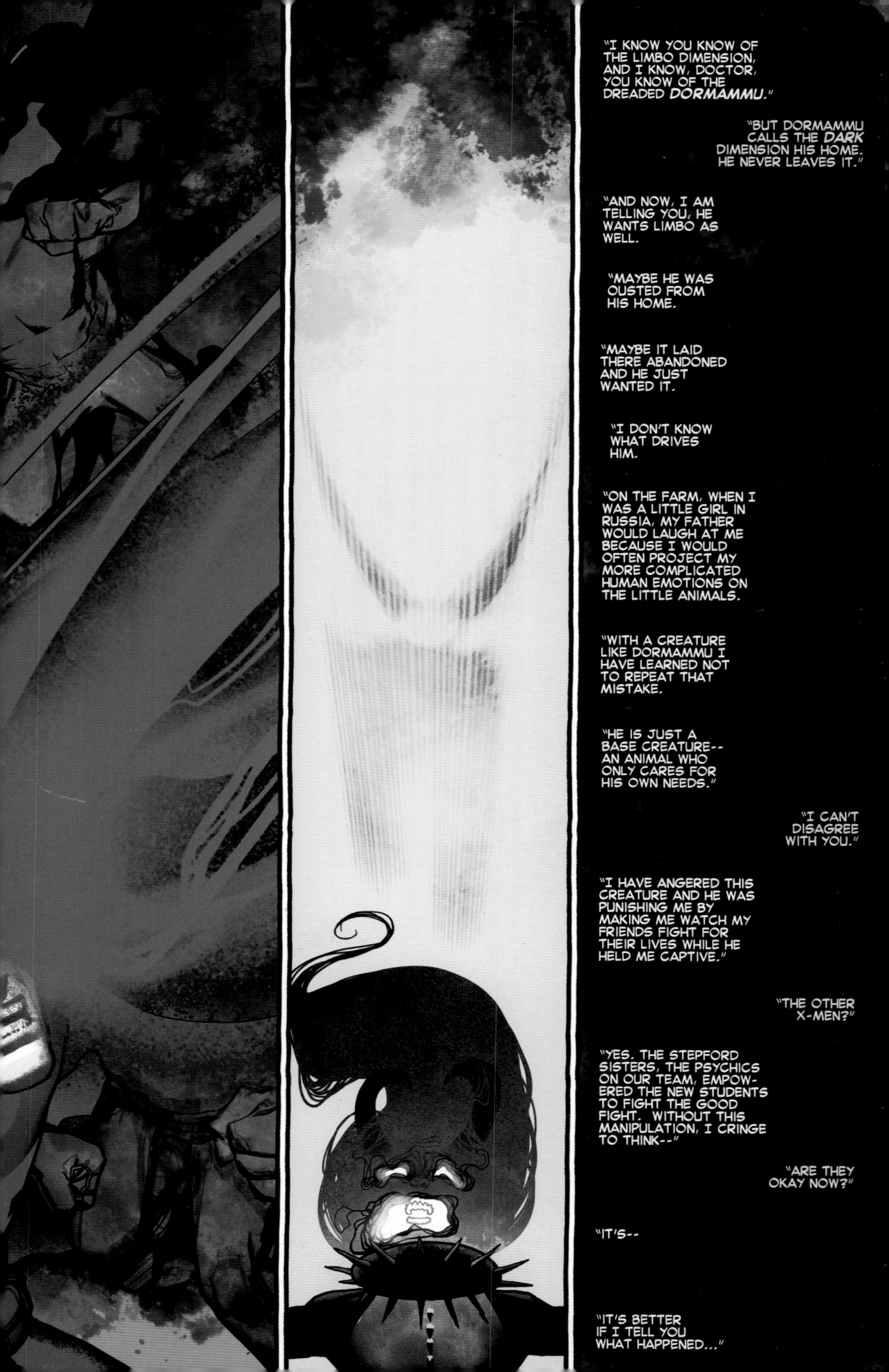
"I KNOW YOU KNOW OF THE LIMBO DIMENSION, AND I KNOW, DOCTOR, YOU KNOW OF THE DREADED *DORMAMMU.*"
"BUT DORMAMMU CALLS THE *DARK* DIMENSION HIS HOME. HE NEVER LEAVES IT."
"AND NOW, I AM TELLING YOU, HE WANTS LIMBO AS WELL.
"MAYBE HE WAS OUSTED FROM HIS HOME.
"MAYBE IT LAID THERE ABANDONED AND HE JUST WANTED IT.
"I DON'T KNOW WHAT DRIVES HIM.
"ON THE FARM, WHEN I WAS A LITTLE GIRL IN RUSSIA, MY FATHER WOULD LAUGH AT ME BECAUSE I WOULD OFTEN PROJECT MY MORE COMPLICATED HUMAN EMOTIONS ON THE LITTLE ANIMALS.
"WITH A CREATURE LIKE DORMAMMU I HAVE LEARNED NOT TO REPEAT THAT MISTAKE.
"HE IS JUST A BASE CREATURE--AN ANIMAL WHO ONLY CARES FOR HIS OWN NEEDS."
"I CAN'T DISAGREE WITH YOU."
"I HAVE ANGERED THIS CREATURE AND HE WAS PUNISHING ME BY MAKING ME WATCH MY FRIENDS FIGHT FOR THEIR LIVES WHILE HE HELD ME CAPTIVE."
"THE OTHER X-MEN?"
"YES. THE STEPFORD SISTERS, THE PSYCHICS ON OUR TEAM, EMPOWERED THE NEW STUDENTS TO FIGHT THE GOOD FIGHT. WITHOUT THIS MANIPULATION, I CRINGE TO THINK--"
"ARE THEY OKAY NOW?"
"IT'S--
"IT'S BETTER IF I TELL YOU WHAT HAPPENED..."

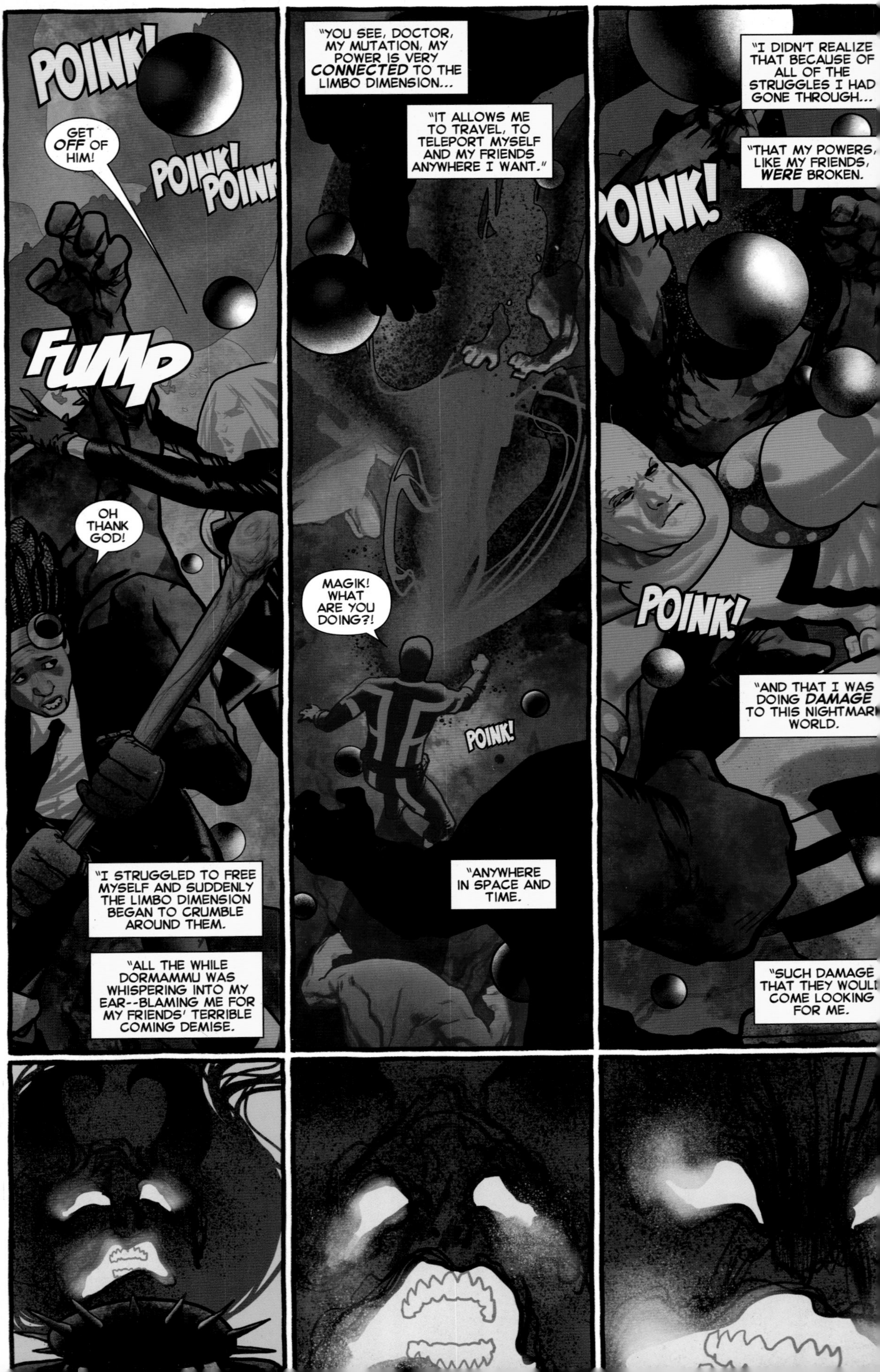
POINK!
GET OFF OF HIM!
POINK! POINK!
FUMP
OH THANK GOD!
"I STRUGGLED TO FREE MYSELF AND SUDDENLY THE LIMBO DIMENSION BEGAN TO CRUMBLE AROUND THEM.
"ALL THE WHILE DORMAMMU WAS WHISPERING INTO MY EAR--BLAMING ME FOR MY FRIENDS' TERRIBLE COMING DEMISE.
"YOU SEE, DOCTOR, MY MUTATION, MY POWER IS VERY CONNECTED TO THE LIMBO DIMENSION...
"IT ALLOWS ME TO TRAVEL, TO TELEPORT MYSELF AND MY FRIENDS ANYWHERE I WANT."
MAGIK! WHAT ARE YOU DOING?!
POINK!
"ANYWHERE IN SPACE AND TIME.
"I DIDN'T REALIZE THAT BECAUSE OF ALL OF THE STRUGGLES I HAD GONE THROUGH...
"THAT MY POWERS, LIKE MY FRIENDS, WERE BROKEN.
POINK!
POINK!
"AND THAT I WAS DOING DAMAGE TO THIS NIGHTMAR
WORLD.
"SUCH DAMAGE THAT THEY WOUL
COME LOOKING FOR ME.

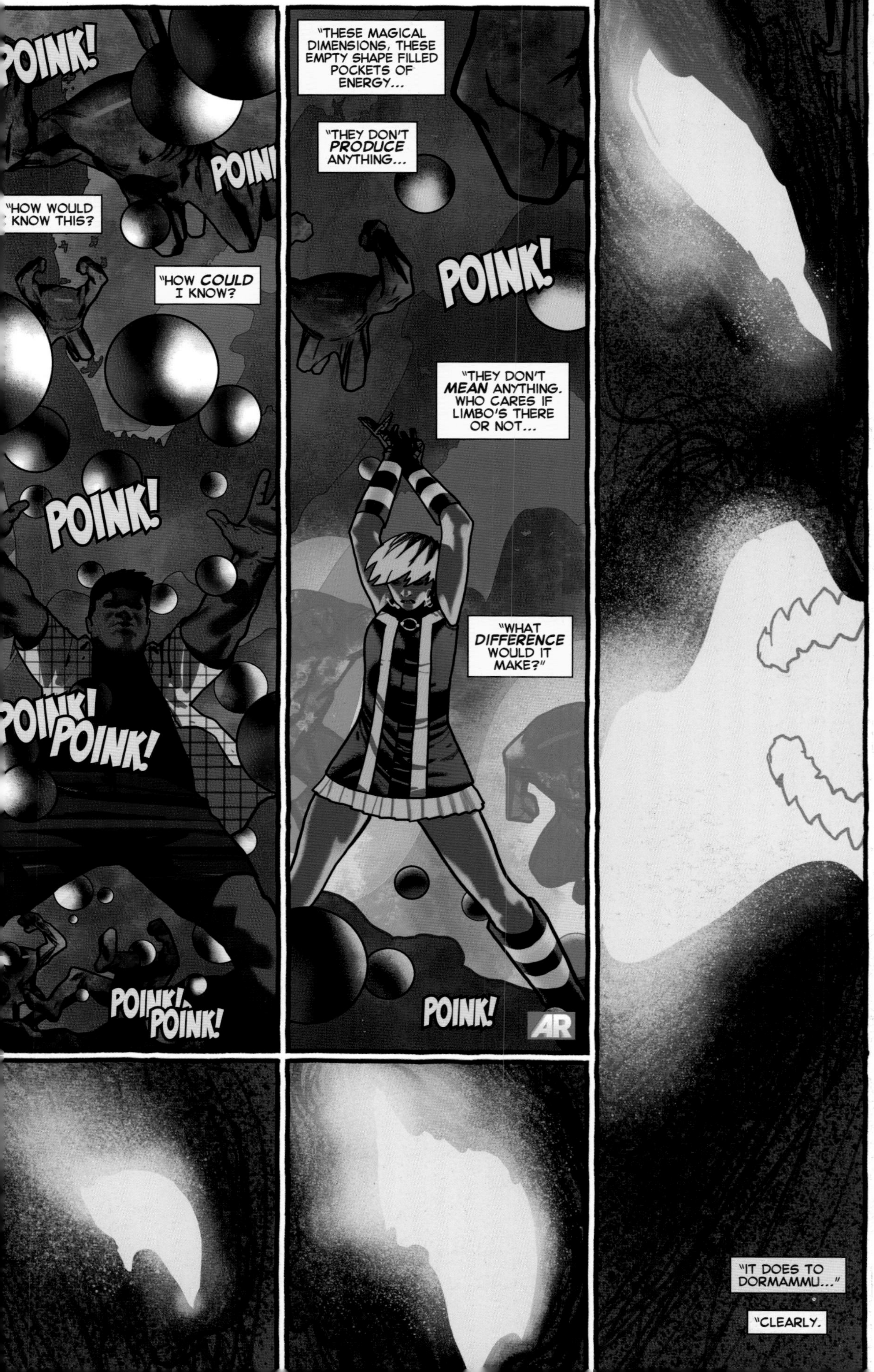
POINK!
POINK
"HOW WOULD
KNOW THIS?
"HOW COULD I KNOW?
POINK!
POINK!
POINK!
POINK!
POINK!
"THESE MAGICAL DIMENSIONS, THESE EMPTY SHAPE FILLED POCKETS OF ENERGY...
"THEY DON'T PRODUCE ANYTHING...
POINK!
"THEY DON'T MEAN ANYTHING. WHO CARES IF LIMBO'S THERE OR NOT...
"WHAT DIFFERENCE WOULD IT MAKE?"
POINK!
AR
"IT DOES TO DORMAMMU..."
"CLEARLY.

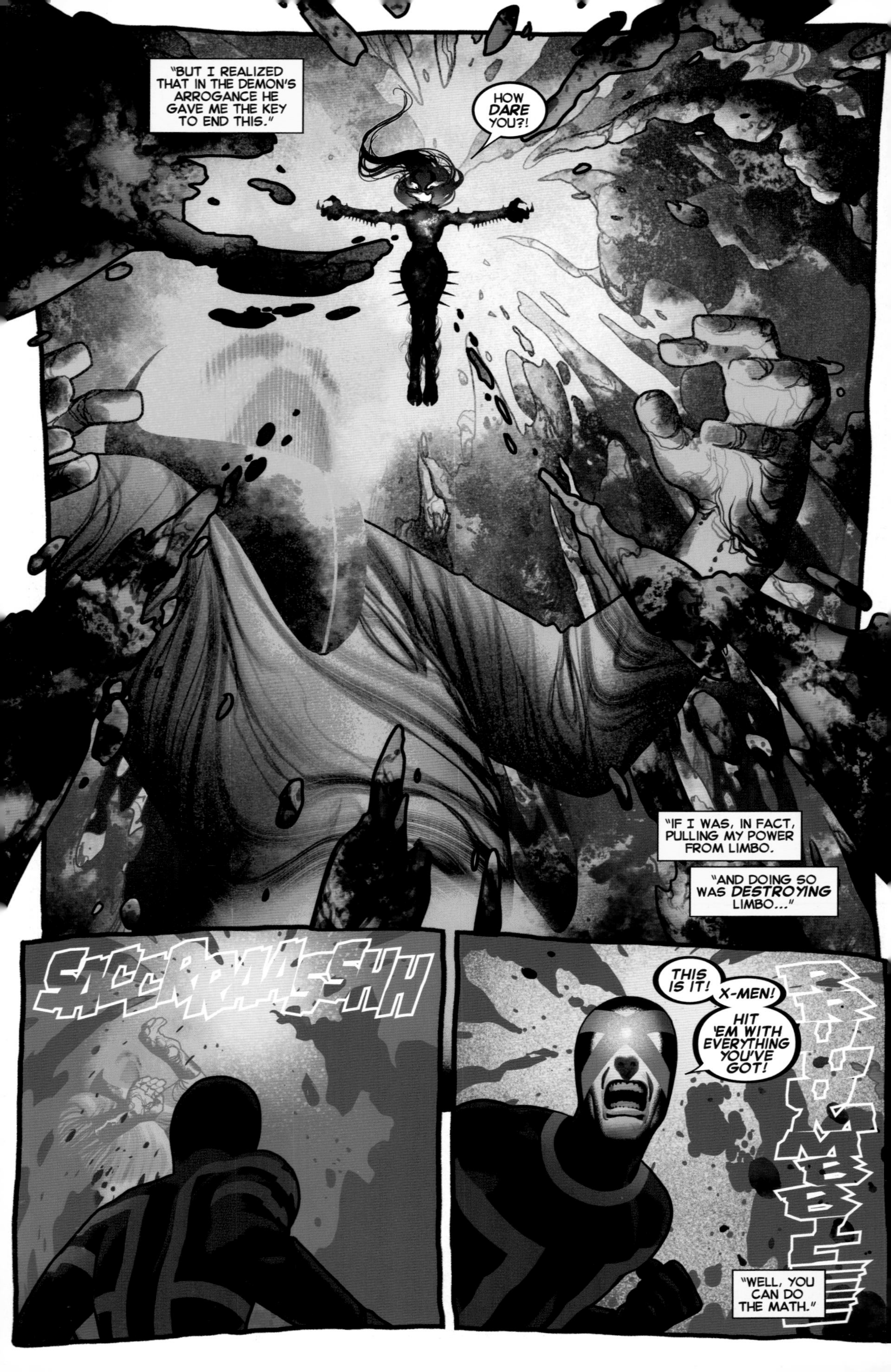
"BUT I REALIZED THAT IN THE DEMON'S ARROGANCE HE GAVE ME THE KEY TO END THIS."
HOW DARE YOU?!
"IF I WAS, IN FACT, PULLING MY POWER FROM LIMBO.
"AND DOING SO WAS DESTROYING LIMBO..."
THIS IS IT!
X-MEN!
HIT 'EM WITH EVERYTHING YOU'VE GOT!
"WELL, YOU CAN DO THE MATH."

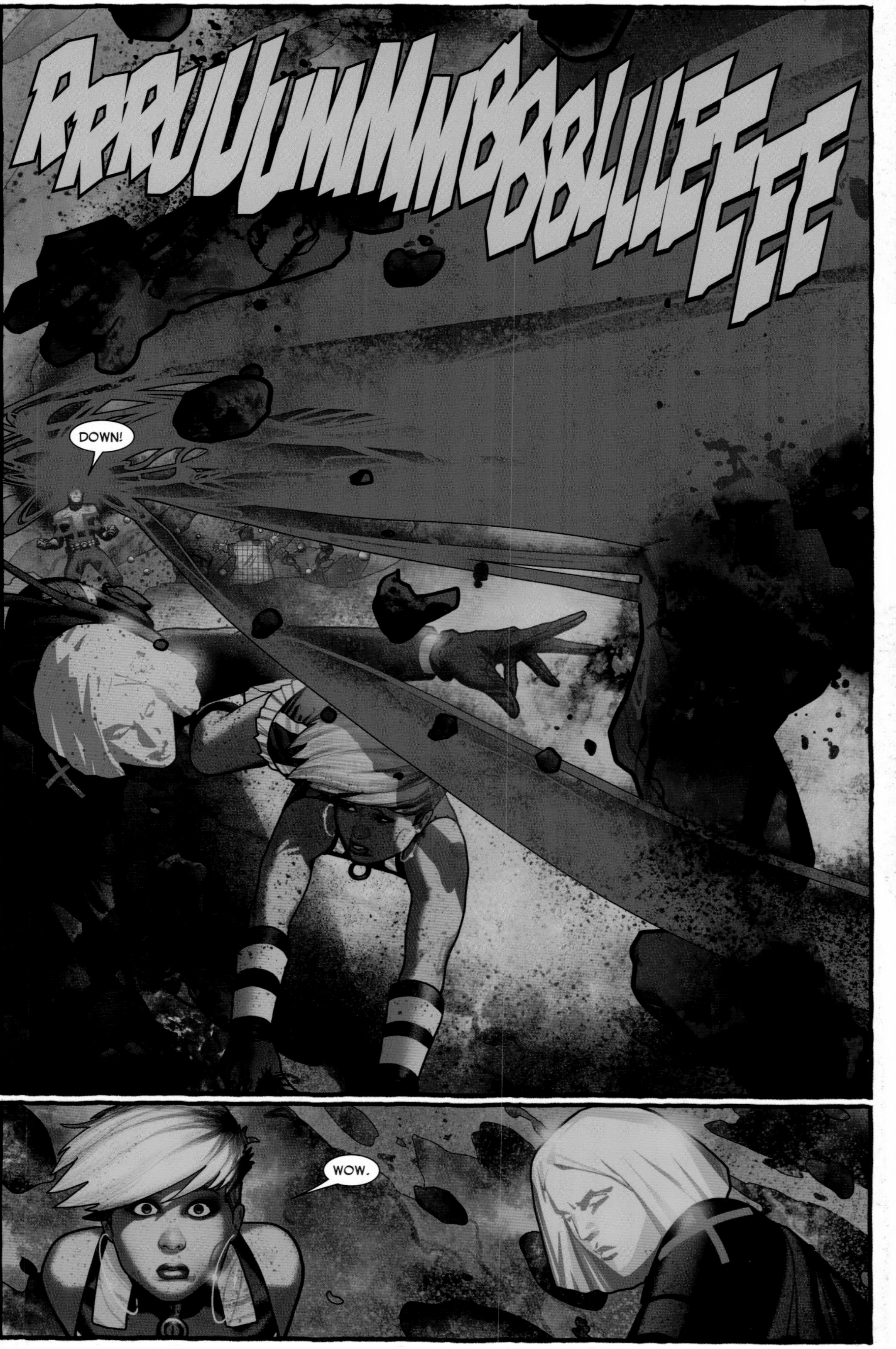
RRRUUMMMBBBLLEEEE
DOWN!
WOW.

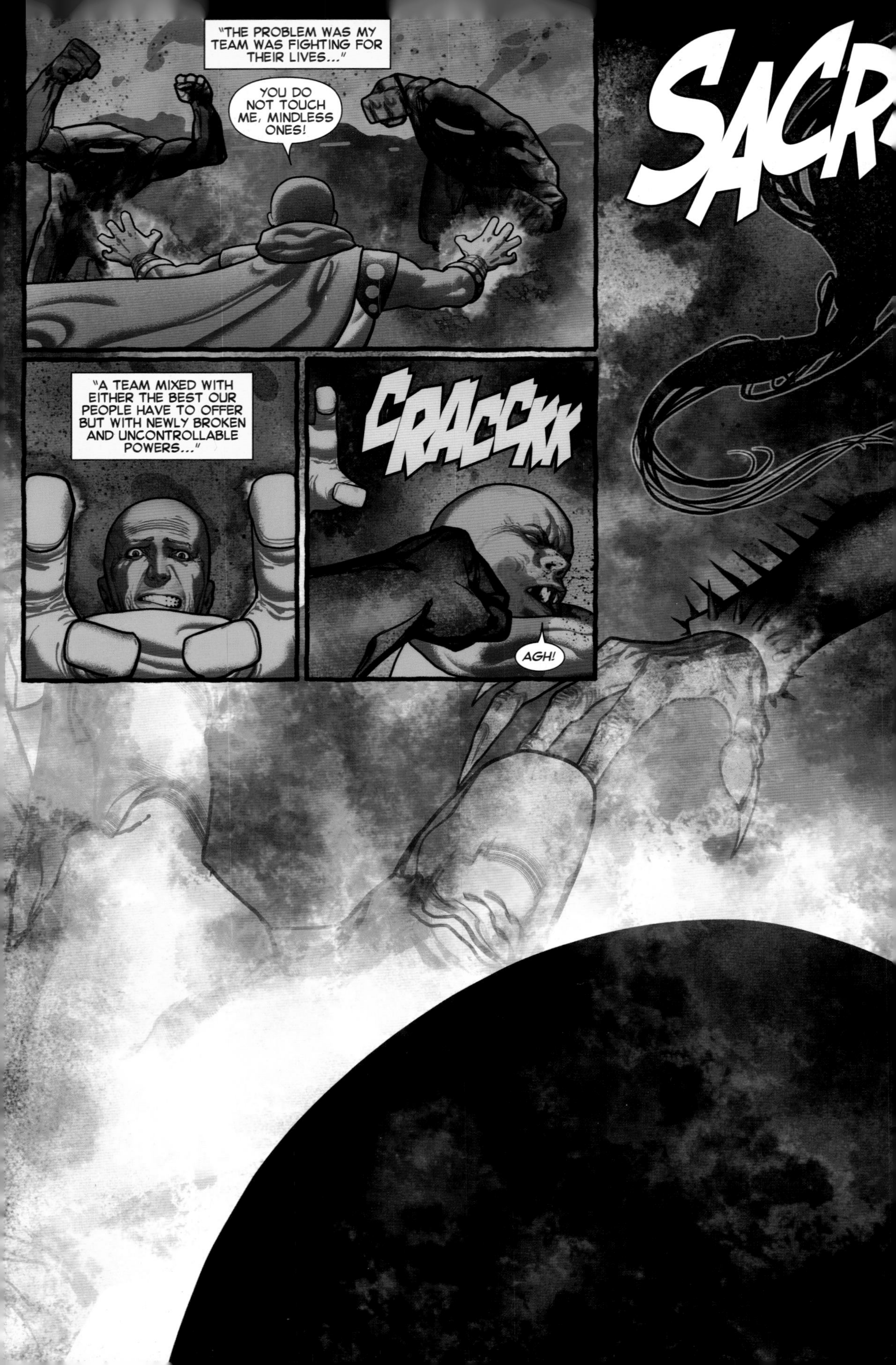
"THE PROBLEM WAS MY TEAM WAS FIGHTING FOR THEIR LIVES..."
YOU DO NOT TOUCH ME, MINDLESS ONES!
SACR
"A TEAM MIXED WITH EITHER THE BEST OUR PEOPLE HAVE TO OFFER BUT WITH NEWLY BROKEN AND UNCONTROLLABLE POWERS..."
CRACCKK
AGH!

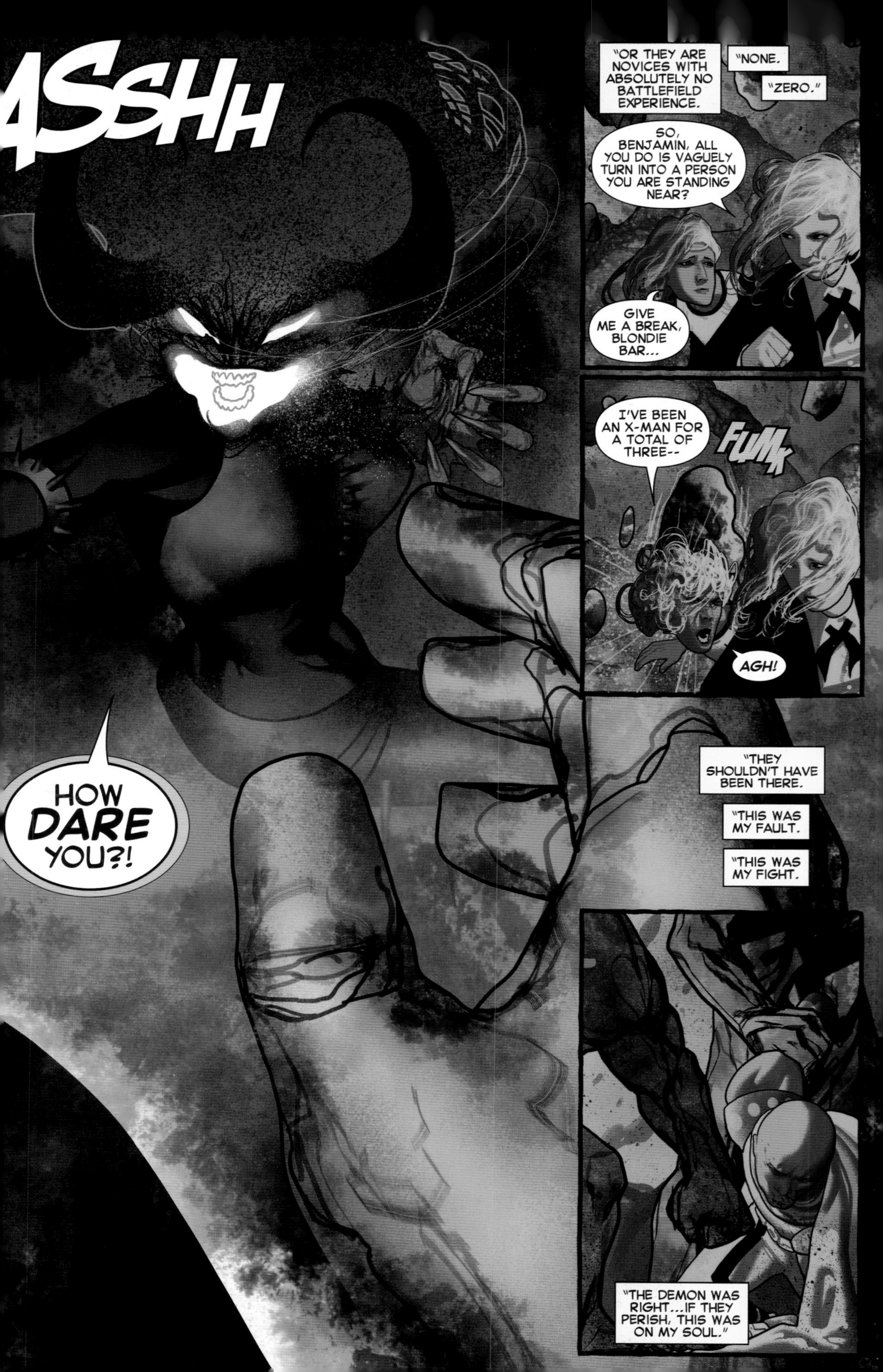
ASSHH
"OR THEY ARE NOVICES WITH ABSOLUTELY NO BATTLEFIELD EXPERIENCE.
"NONE.
"ZERO."
SO, BENJAMIN, ALL YOU DO IS VAGUELY TURN INTO A PERSON YOU ARE STANDING NEAR?
GIVE ME A BREAK, BLONDIE BAR...
I'VE BEEN AN X-MAN FOR A TOTAL OF THREE--
FUMK
AGH!
HOW DARE YOU?!
"THEY SHOULDN'T HAVE BEEN THERE.
"THIS WAS MY FAULT.
"THIS WAS MY FIGHT.
"THE DEMON WAS RIGHT...IF THEY PERISH, THIS WAS ON MY SOUL."

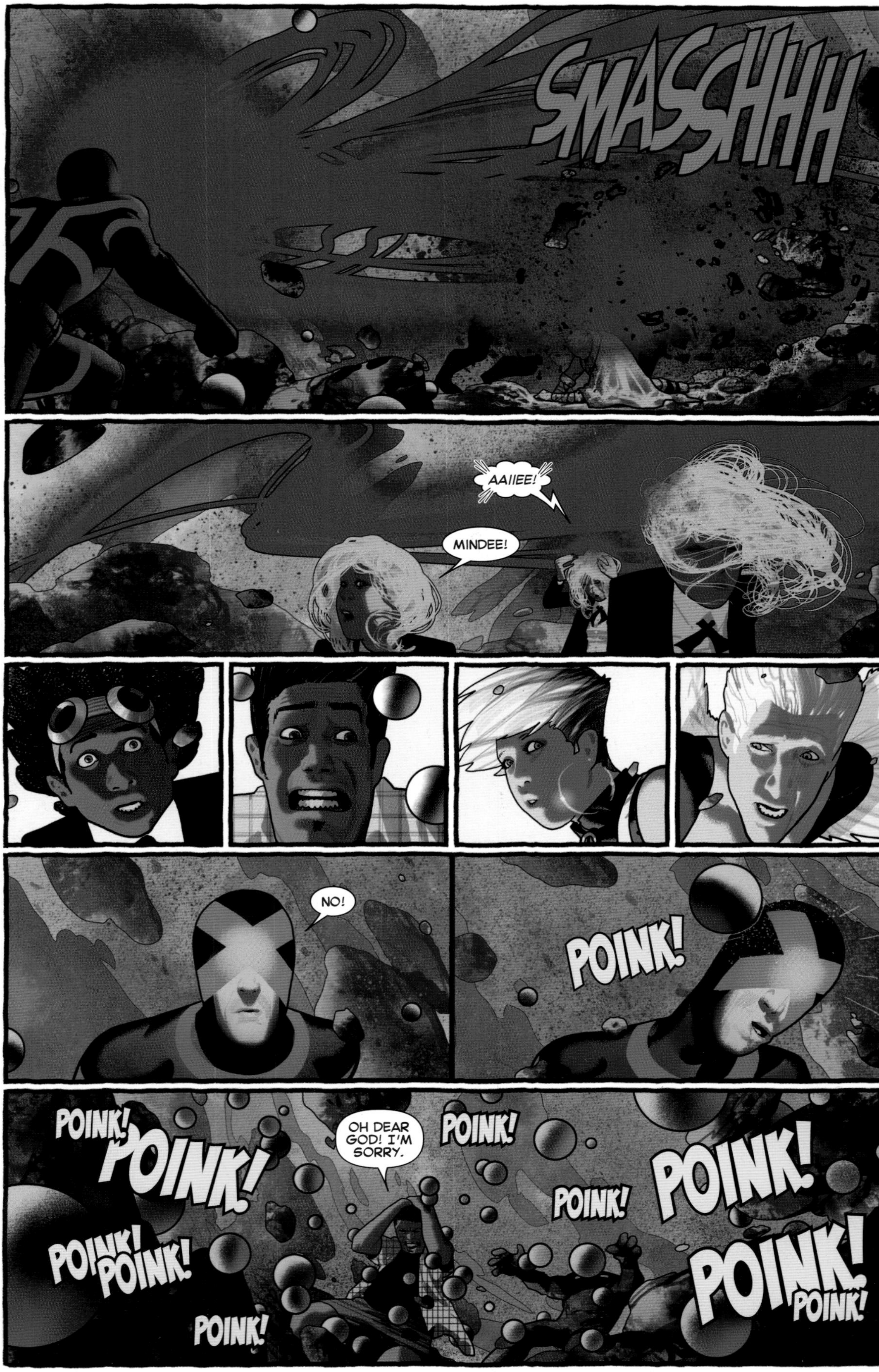
SMASSHHH
AAIIEE!
MINDEE!
NO!
POINK!
POINK!
POINK!
OH DEAR GOD! I'M SORRY.
POINK!
POINK!
POINK!
POINK!
POINK!
POINK!
POINK!
POINK!

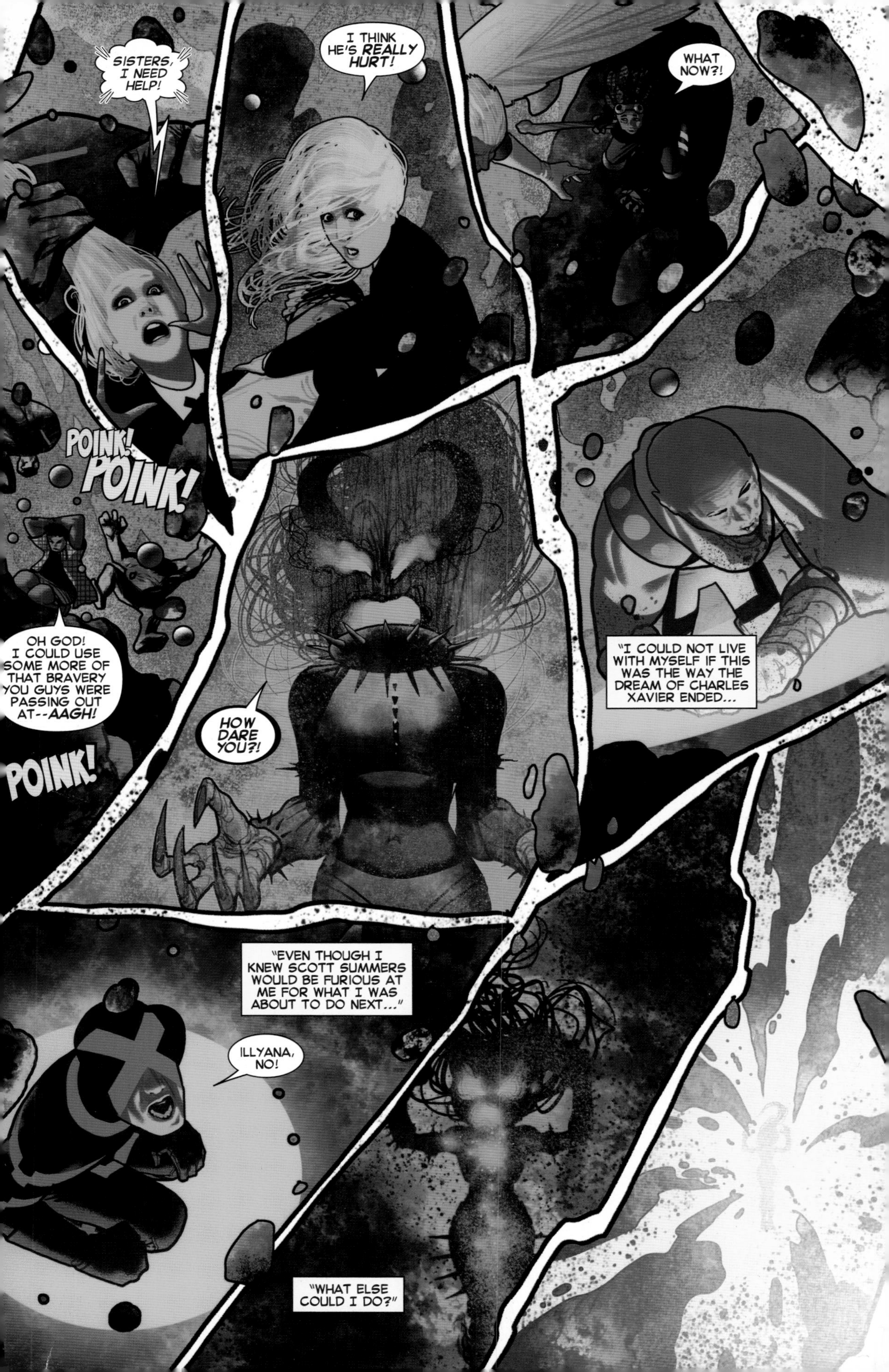
SISTERS, I NEED HELP!
I THINK HE'S REALLY HURT!
WHAT NOW?!
POINK! POINK!
OH GOD! I COULD USE SOME MORE OF THAT BRAVERY YOU GUYS WERE PASSING OUT AT--AAGH!
POINK!
HOW DARE YOU?!
"I COULD NOT LIVE WITH MYSELF IF THIS WAS THE WAY THE DREAM OF CHARLES XAVIER ENDED...
"EVEN THOUGH I KNEW SCOTT SUMMERS WOULD BE FURIOUS AT ME FOR WHAT I WAS ABOUT TO DO NEXT..."
ILLYANA, NO!
"WHAT ELSE COULD I DO?"

"I ENDED
THE LIMBO
DIMENSION.

"I TOOK
IT INSIDE
MYSELF.

"EVERY
PART.

"IT MAY HAVE
BEEN OVERREACHING
BUT SOMETIMES YOU
DON'T KNOW WHAT
YOU CAN DO TILL
YOU TRY."

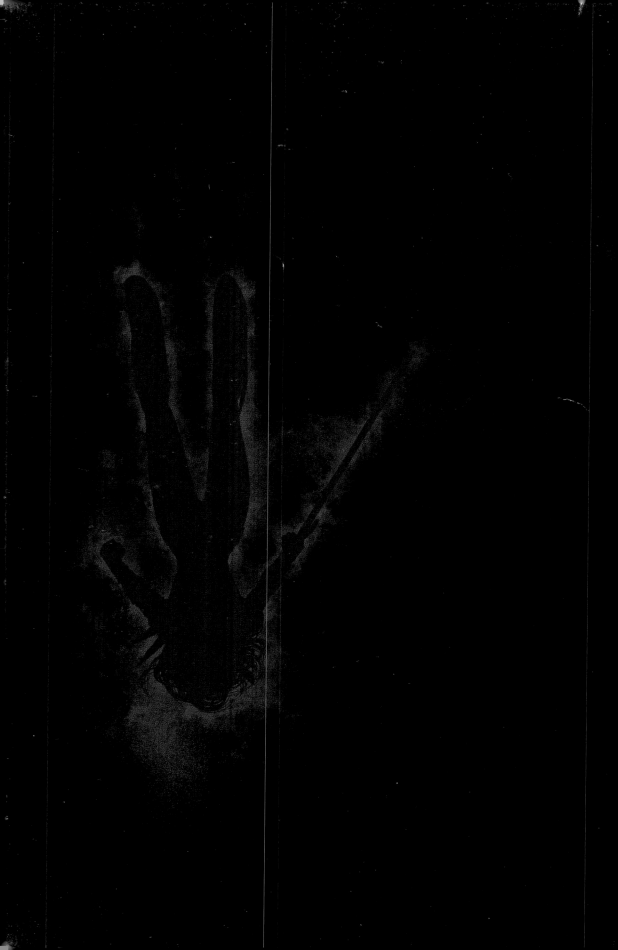

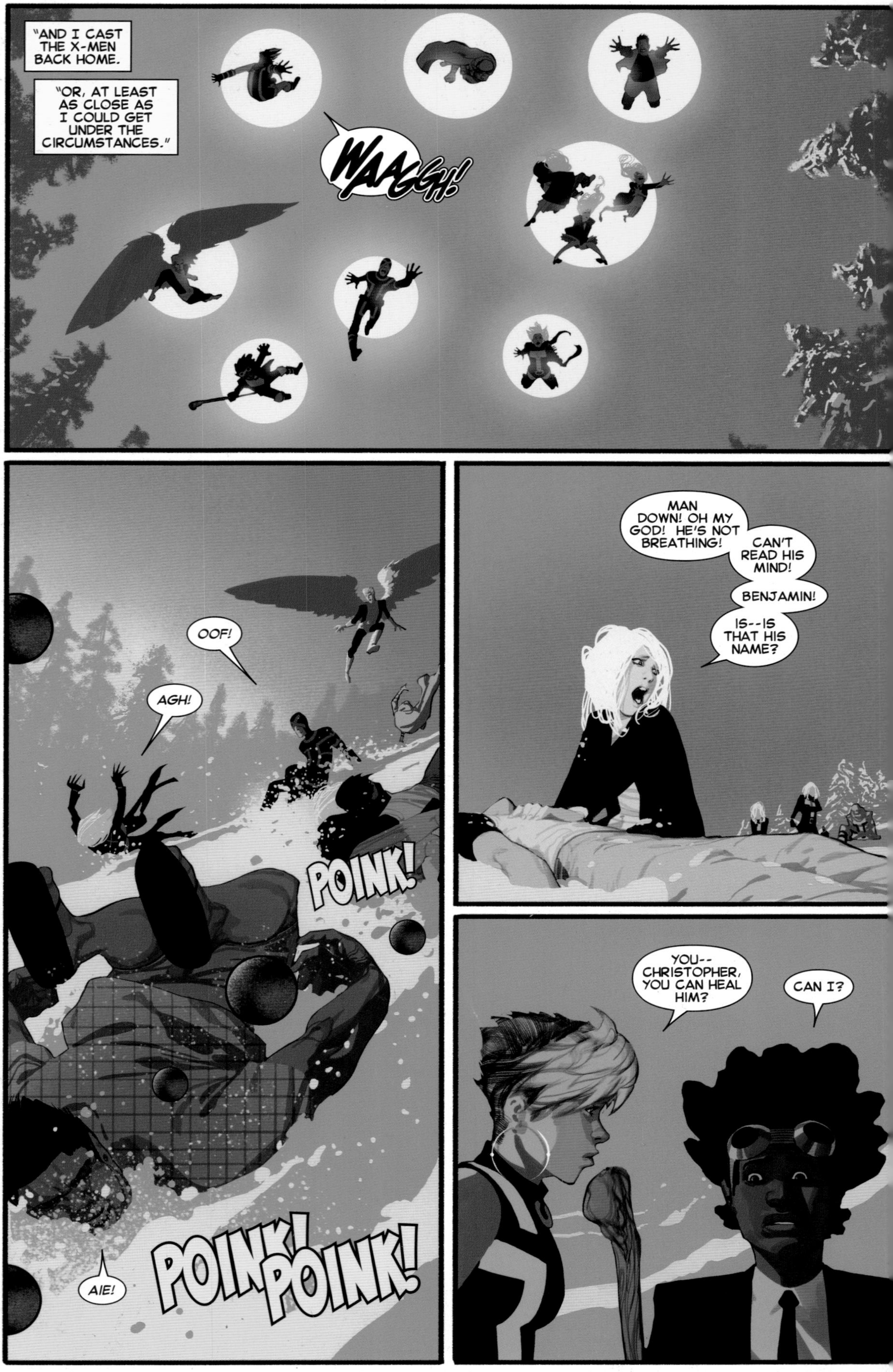
"AND I CAST THE X-MEN BACK HOME.
"OR, AT LEAST AS CLOSE AS I COULD GET UNDER THE CIRCUMSTANCES."
WAAGGH!
OOF!
AGH!
POINK!
AIE!
POINK! POINK!
MAN DOWN! OH MY GOD! HE'S NOT BREATHING!
CAN'T READ HIS MIND!
BENJAMIN!
IS--IS THAT HIS NAME?
YOU-- CHRISTOPHER, YOU CAN HEAL HIM?
CAN I?

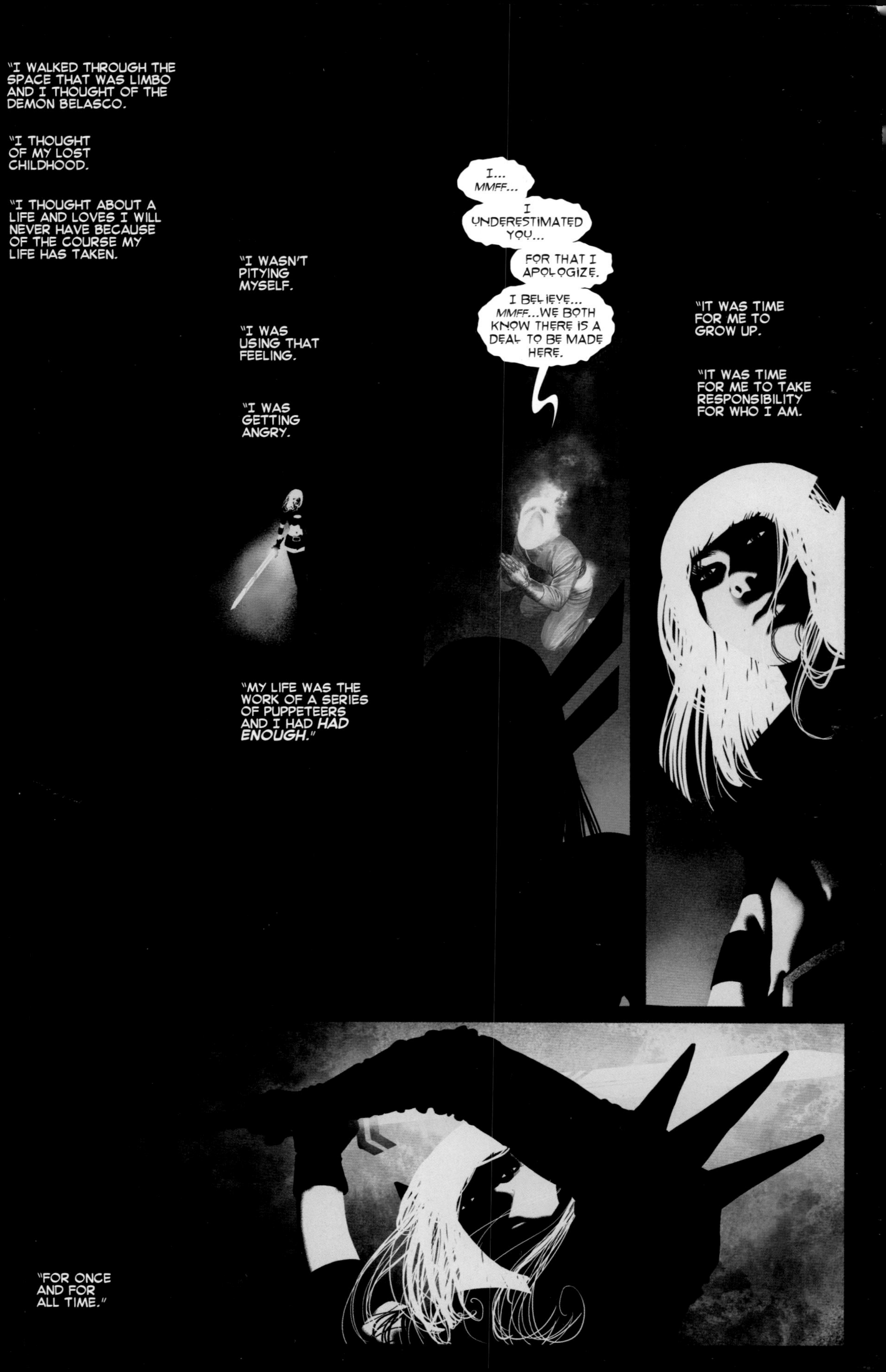
"I WALKED THROUGH THE SPACE THAT WAS LIMBO AND I THOUGHT OF THE DEMON BELASCO.
"I THOUGHT OF MY LOST CHILDHOOD.
"I THOUGHT ABOUT A LIFE AND LOVES I WILL NEVER HAVE BECAUSE OF THE COURSE MY LIFE HAS TAKEN.
"I WASN'T PITYING MYSELF.
"I WAS USING THAT FEELING.
"I WAS GETTING ANGRY.
"MY LIFE WAS THE WORK OF A SERIES OF PUPPETEERS AND I HAD *HAD ENOUGH*."
I... MMFF...
I UNDERESTIMATED YOU...
FOR THAT I APOLOGIZE.
I BELIEVE... MMFF...WE BOTH KNOW THERE IS A DEAL TO BE MADE HERE.
"IT WAS TIME FOR ME TO GROW UP.
"IT WAS TIME FOR ME TO TAKE RESPONSIBILITY FOR WHO I AM.
"FOR ONCE AND FOR ALL TIME."

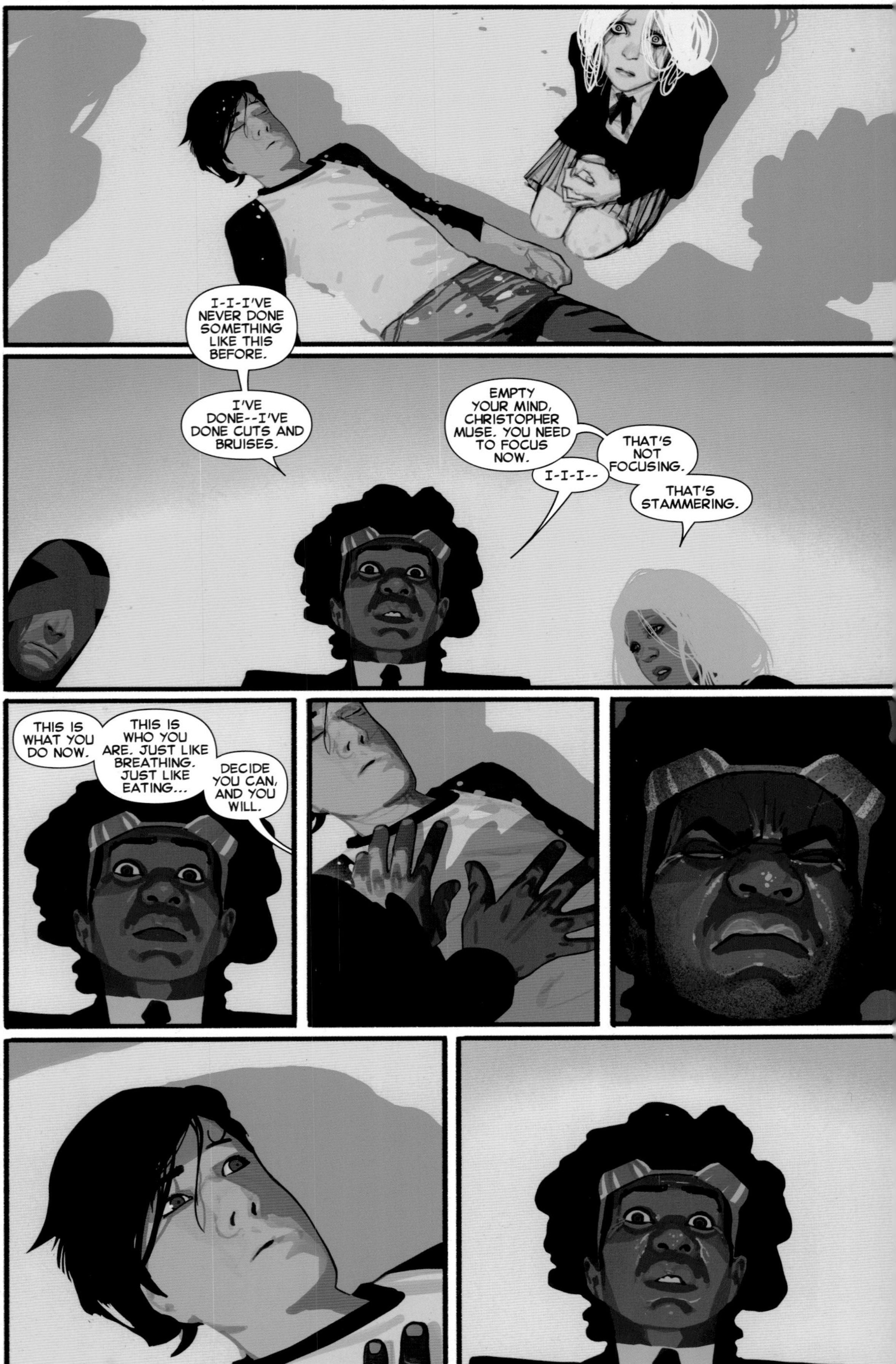
I-I-I'VE NEVER DONE SOMETHING LIKE THIS BEFORE.
I'VE DONE--I'VE DONE CUTS AND BRUISES.
EMPTY YOUR MIND, CHRISTOPHER MUSE. YOU NEED TO FOCUS NOW.
I-I-I--
THAT'S NOT FOCUSING.
THAT'S STAMMERING.
THIS IS WHAT YOU DO NOW.
THIS IS WHO YOU ARE. JUST LIKE BREATHING. JUST LIKE EATING...
DECIDE YOU CAN, AND YOU WILL.

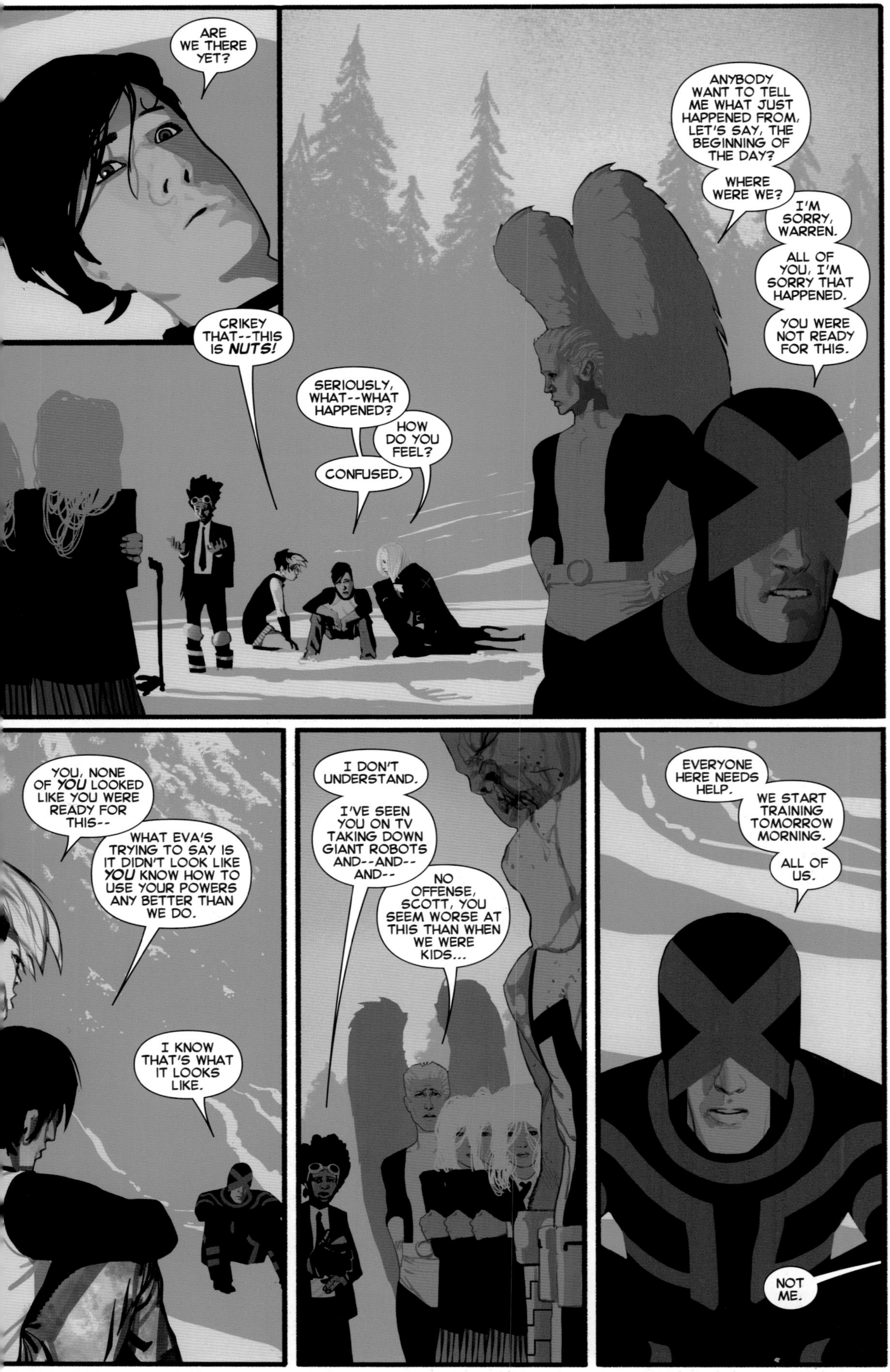
ARE WE THERE YET?
ANYBODY WANT TO TELL ME WHAT JUST HAPPENED FROM, LET'S SAY, THE BEGINNING OF THE DAY?
WHERE WERE WE?
I'M SORRY, WARREN.
ALL OF YOU, I'M SORRY THAT HAPPENED.
YOU WERE NOT READY FOR THIS.
CRIKEY THAT--THIS IS NUTS!
SERIOUSLY, WHAT--WHAT HAPPENED?
HOW DO YOU FEEL?
CONFUSED.
YOU, NONE OF YOU LOOKED LIKE YOU WERE READY FOR THIS--
WHAT EVA'S TRYING TO SAY IS IT DIDN'T LOOK LIKE YOU KNOW HOW TO USE YOUR POWERS ANY BETTER THAN WE DO.
I KNOW THAT'S WHAT IT LOOKS LIKE.
I DON'T UNDERSTAND.
I'VE SEEN YOU ON TV TAKING DOWN GIANT ROBOTS AND--AND--AND--
NO OFFENSE, SCOTT, YOU SEEM WORSE AT THIS THAN WHEN WE WERE KIDS...
EVERYONE HERE NEEDS HELP.
WE START TRAINING TOMORROW MORNING.
ALL OF US.
NOT ME.

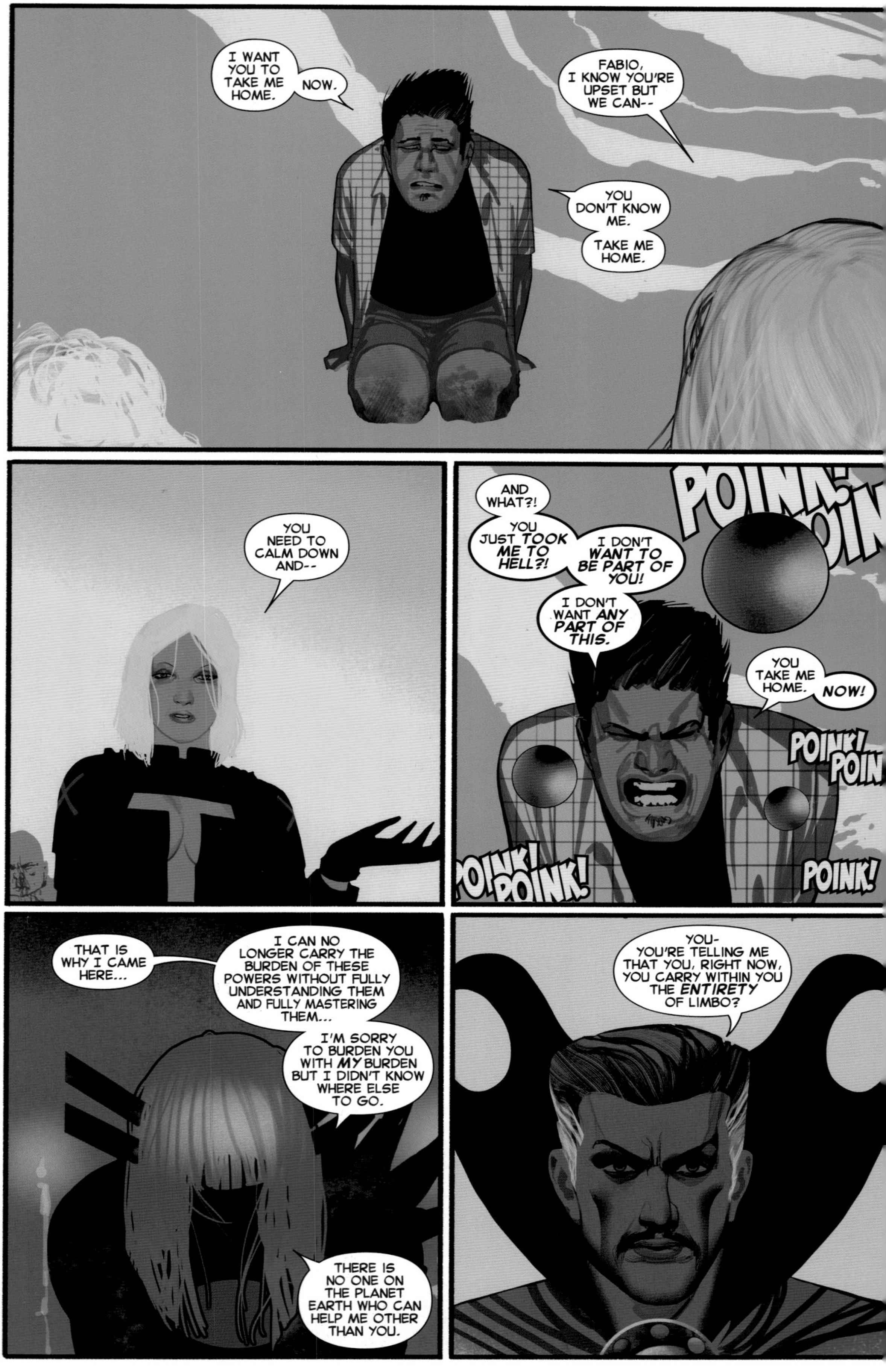
I WANT YOU TO TAKE ME HOME.
NOW.
FABIO, I KNOW YOU'RE UPSET BUT WE CAN--
YOU DON'T KNOW ME.
TAKE ME HOME.
YOU NEED TO CALM DOWN AND--
AND WHAT?!
YOU JUST *TOOK ME TO HELL?!*
I DON'T *WANT TO BE PART OF YOU!*
I DON'T WANT *ANY PART OF THIS.*
YOU TAKE ME HOME.
NOW!
POINK!
POINK! POIN
POINK! POINK!
POINK!
THAT IS WHY I CAME HERE...
I CAN NO LONGER CARRY THE BURDEN OF THESE POWERS WITHOUT FULLY UNDERSTANDING THEM AND FULLY MASTERING THEM...
I'M SORRY TO BURDEN YOU WITH *MY* BURDEN BUT I DIDN'T KNOW WHERE ELSE TO GO.
THERE IS NO ONE ON THE PLANET EARTH WHO CAN HELP ME OTHER THAN YOU.
YOU- YOU'RE TELLING ME THAT YOU, RIGHT NOW, YOU CARRY WITHIN YOU THE *ENTIRETY* OF LIMBO?

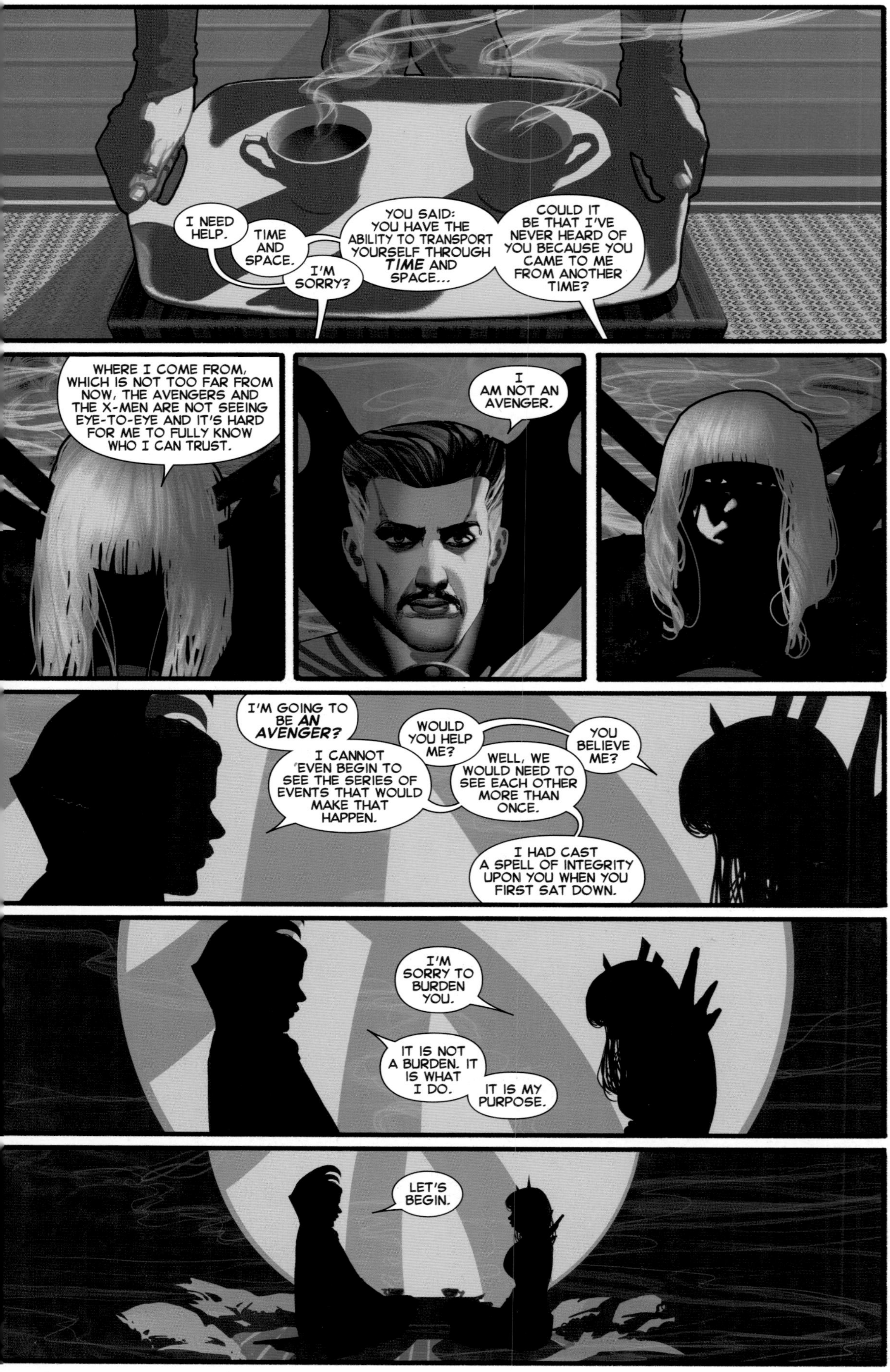
I NEED HELP.
TIME AND SPACE.
I'M SORRY?
YOU SAID: YOU HAVE THE ABILITY TO TRANSPORT YOURSELF THROUGH *TIME* AND SPACE...
COULD IT BE THAT I'VE NEVER HEARD OF YOU BECAUSE YOU CAME TO ME FROM ANOTHER TIME?
WHERE I COME FROM, WHICH IS NOT TOO FAR FROM NOW, THE AVENGERS AND THE X-MEN ARE NOT SEEING EYE-TO-EYE AND IT'S HARD FOR ME TO FULLY KNOW WHO I CAN TRUST.
I AM NOT AN AVENGER.
I'M GOING TO BE ***AN AVENGER?***
I CANNOT EVEN BEGIN TO SEE THE SERIES OF EVENTS THAT WOULD MAKE THAT HAPPEN.
WOULD YOU HELP ME?
WELL, WE WOULD NEED TO SEE EACH OTHER MORE THAN ONCE.
YOU BELIEVE ME?
I HAD CAST A SPELL OF INTEGRITY UPON YOU WHEN YOU FIRST SAT DOWN.
I'M SORRY TO BURDEN YOU.
IT IS NOT A BURDEN. IT IS WHAT I DO.
IT IS MY PURPOSE.
LET'S BEGIN.

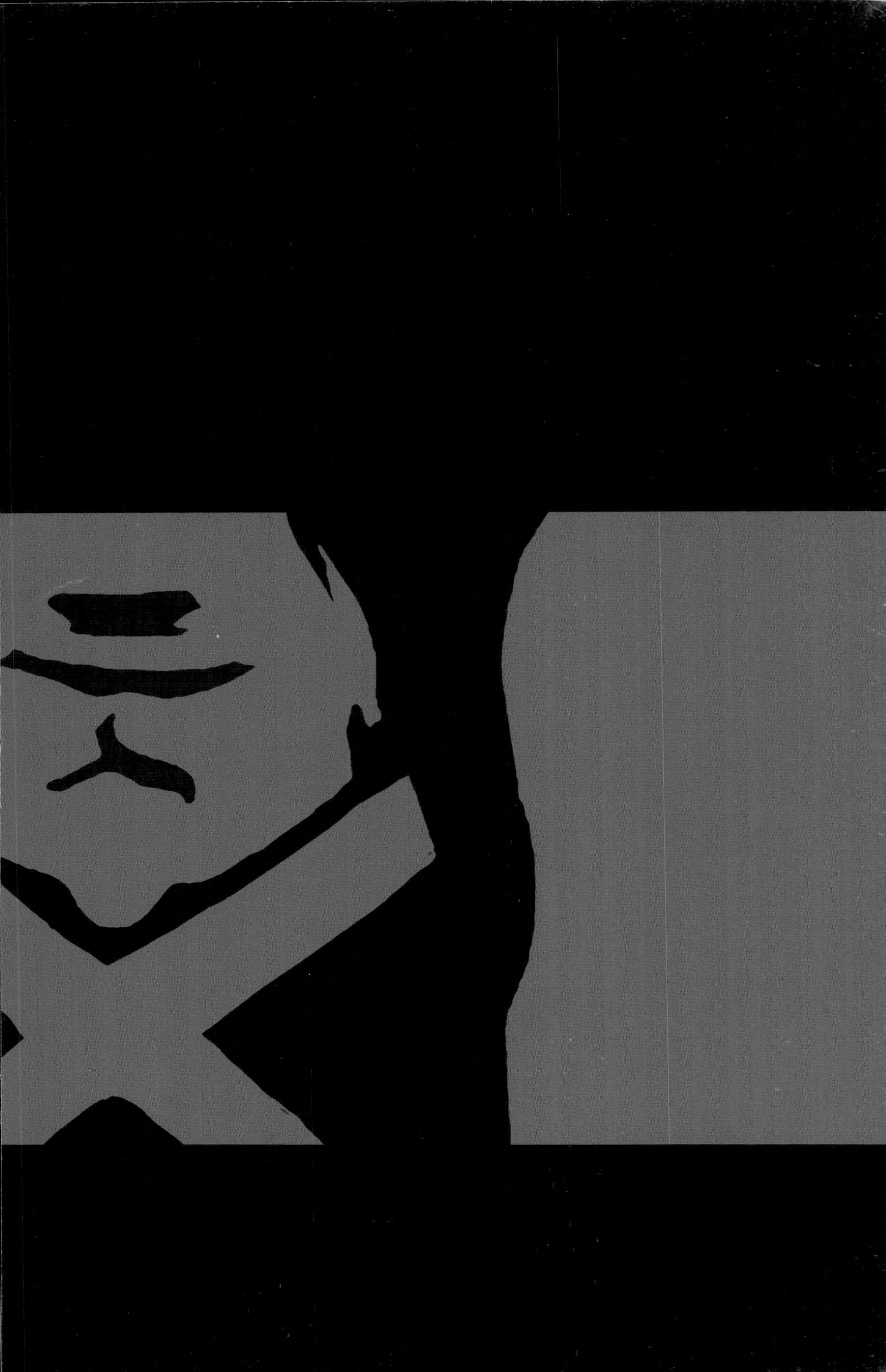

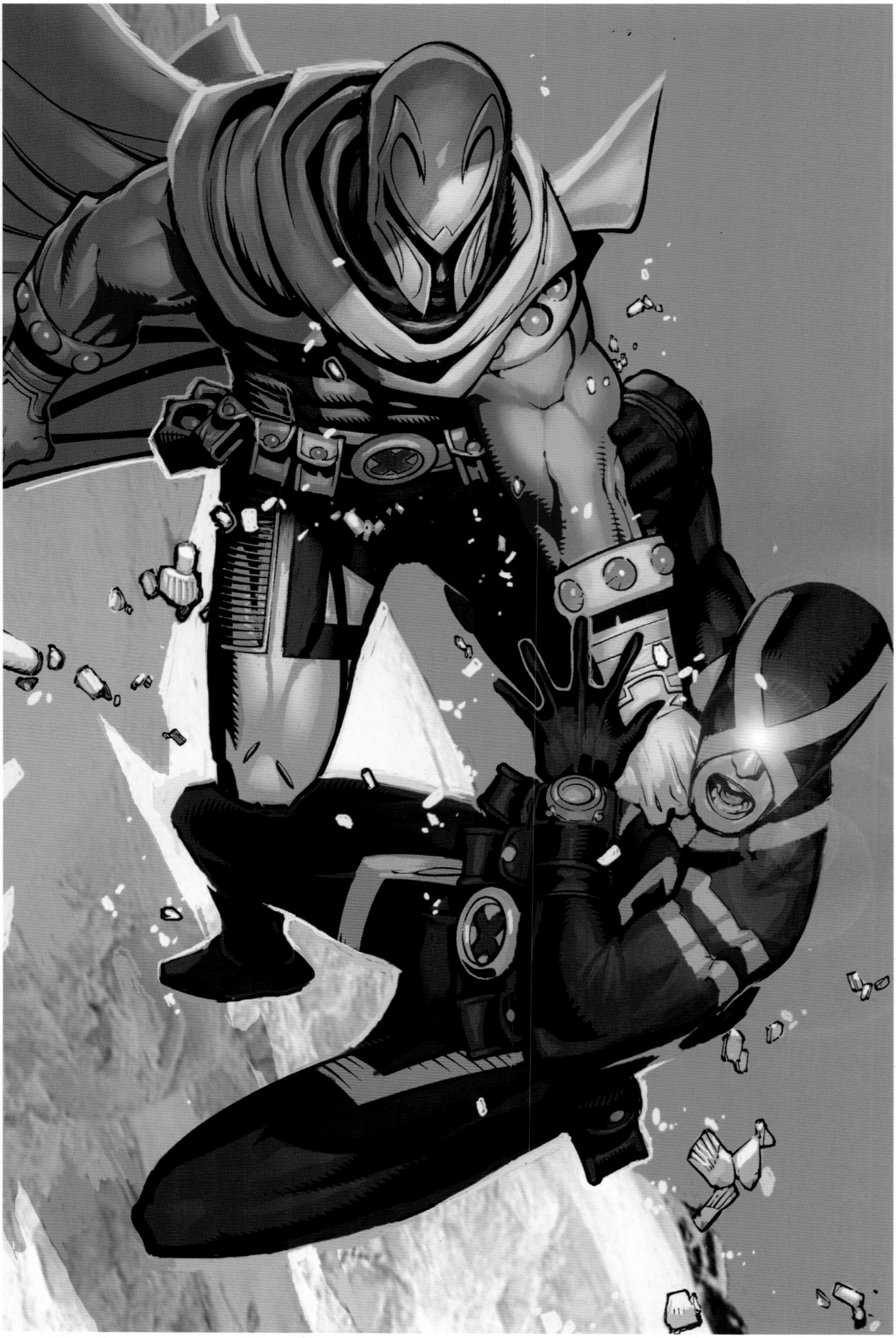

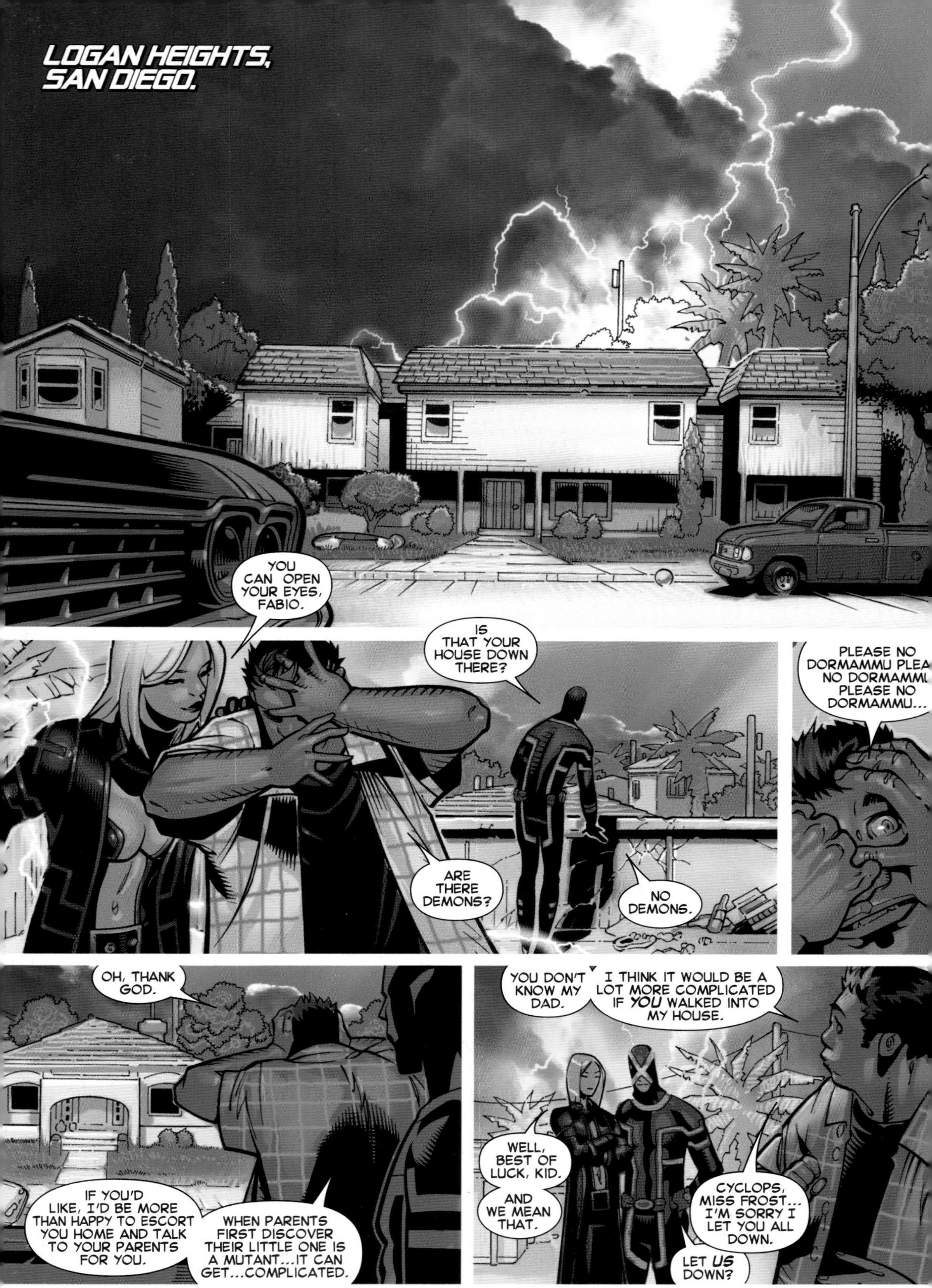
LOGAN HEIGHTS, SAN DIEGO.
YOU CAN OPEN YOUR EYES, FABIO.
IS THAT YOUR HOUSE DOWN THERE?
ARE THERE DEMONS?
NO DEMONS.
PLEASE NO DORMAMMU PLEA NO DORMAMMU PLEASE NO DORMAMMU...
OH, THANK GOD.
IF YOU'D LIKE, I'D BE MORE THAN HAPPY TO ESCORT YOU HOME AND TALK TO YOUR PARENTS FOR YOU.
WHEN PARENTS FIRST DISCOVER THEIR LITTLE ONE IS A MUTANT...IT CAN GET...COMPLICATED.
YOU DON'T KNOW MY DAD.
I THINK IT WOULD BE A LOT MORE COMPLICATED IF *YOU* WALKED INTO MY HOUSE.
WELL, BEST OF LUCK, KID.
AND WE MEAN THAT.
CYCLOPS, MISS FROST... I'M SORRY I LET YOU ALL DOWN.
LET *US* DOWN?

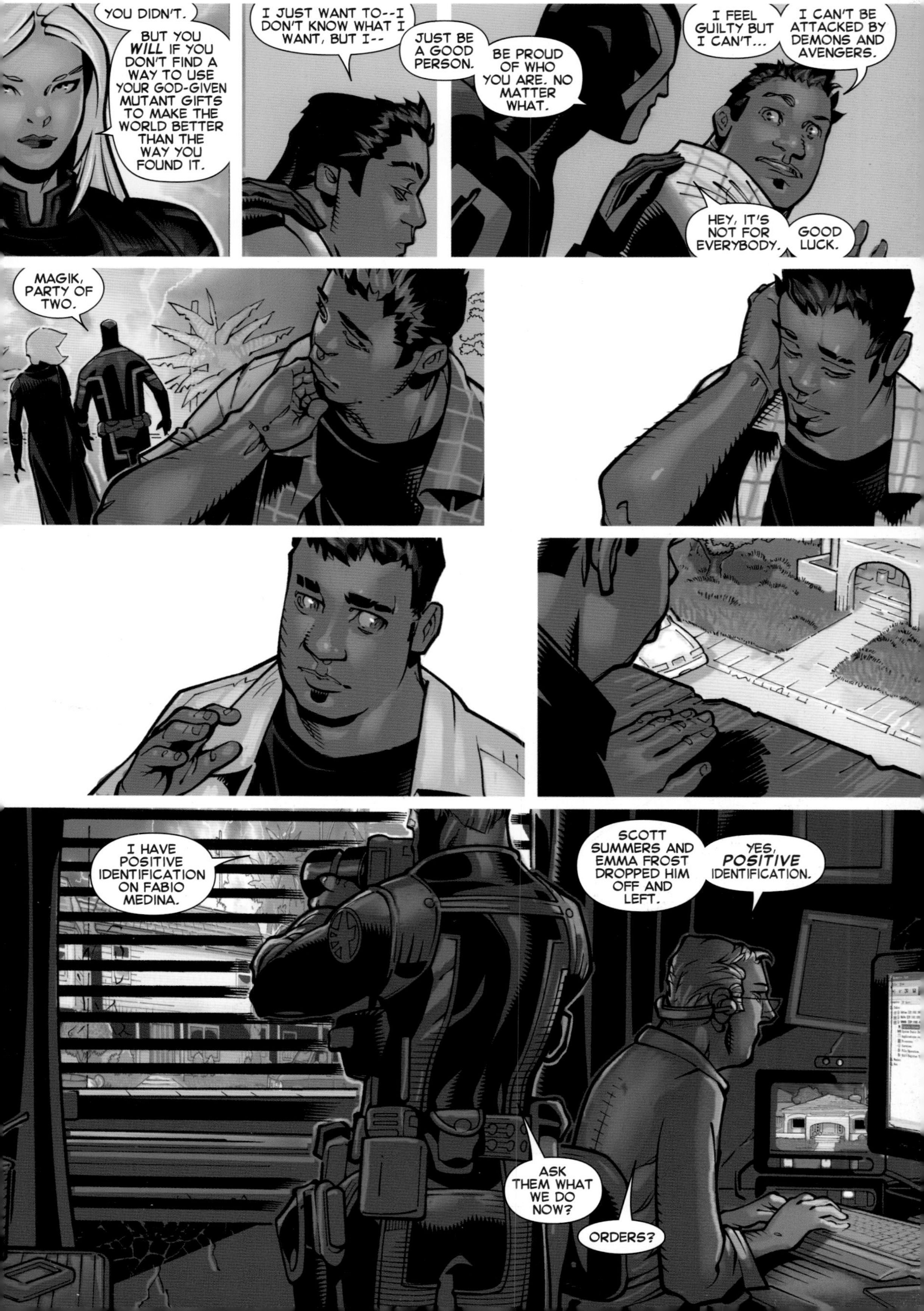
YOU DIDN'T.
BUT YOU *WILL* IF YOU DON'T FIND A WAY TO USE YOUR GOD-GIVEN MUTANT GIFTS TO MAKE THE WORLD BETTER THAN THE WAY YOU FOUND IT.
I JUST WANT TO--I DON'T KNOW WHAT I WANT, BUT I--
JUST BE A GOOD PERSON.
BE PROUD OF WHO YOU ARE. NO MATTER WHAT.
I FEEL GUILTY BUT I CAN'T...
I CAN'T BE ATTACKED BY DEMONS AND AVENGERS.
HEY, IT'S NOT FOR EVERYBODY.
GOOD LUCK.
MAGIK, PARTY OF TWO.
I HAVE POSITIVE IDENTIFICATION ON FABIO MEDINA.
SCOTT SUMMERS AND EMMA FROST DROPPED HIM OFF AND LEFT.
YES, *POSITIVE* IDENTIFICATION.
ASK THEM WHAT WE DO NOW?
ORDERS?

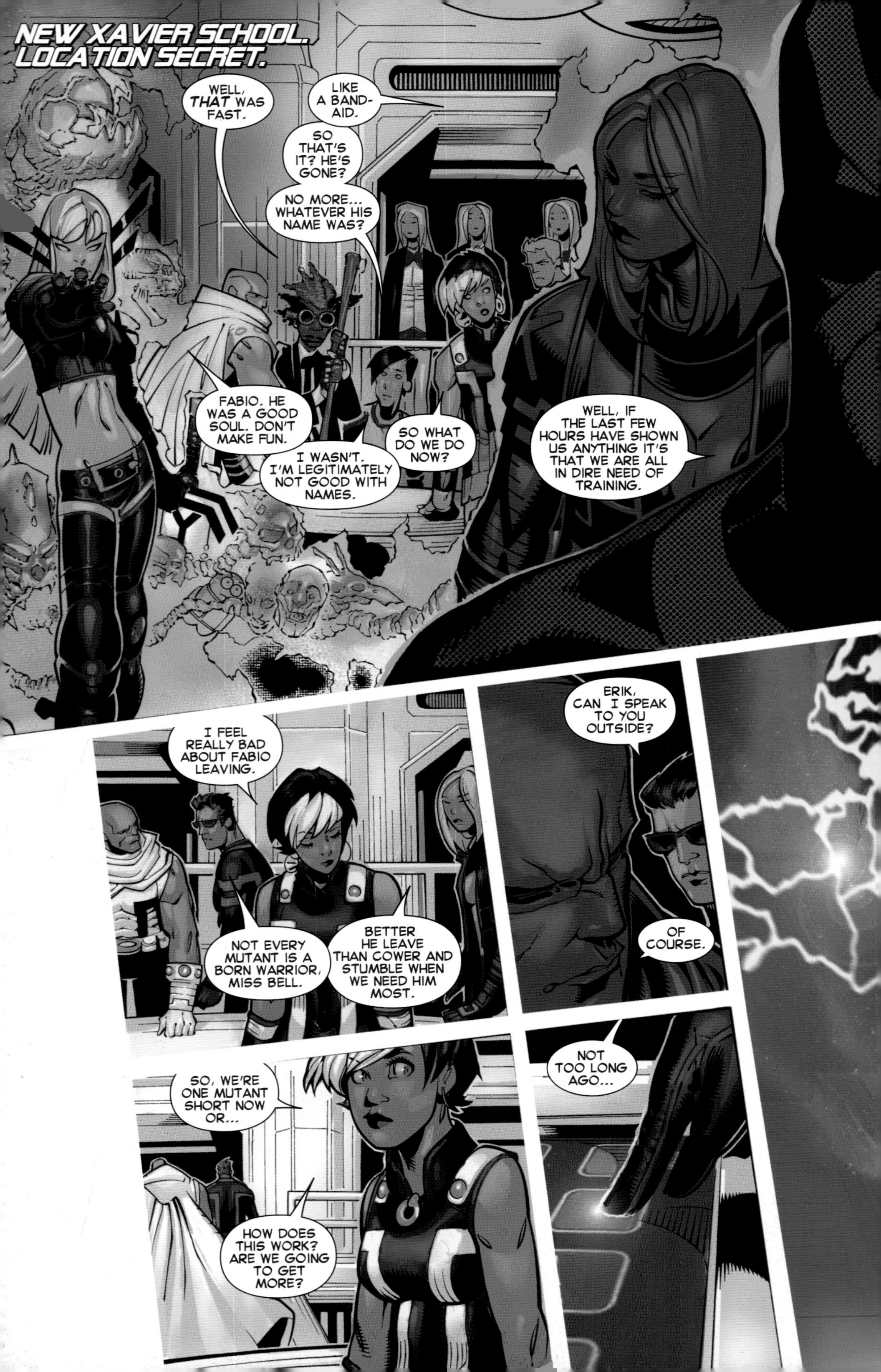
NEW XAVIER SCHOOL. LOCATION SECRET.
WELL, THAT WAS FAST.
LIKE A BAND-AID.
SO THAT'S IT? HE'S GONE?
NO MORE... WHATEVER HIS NAME WAS?
FABIO. HE WAS A GOOD SOUL. DON'T MAKE FUN.
I WASN'T. I'M LEGITIMATELY NOT GOOD WITH NAMES.
SO WHAT DO WE DO NOW?
WELL, IF THE LAST FEW HOURS HAVE SHOWN US ANYTHING IT'S THAT WE ARE ALL IN DIRE NEED OF TRAINING.
I FEEL REALLY BAD ABOUT FABIO LEAVING.
NOT EVERY MUTANT IS A BORN WARRIOR, MISS BELL.
BETTER HE LEAVE THAN COWER AND STUMBLE WHEN WE NEED HIM MOST.
ERIK, CAN I SPEAK TO YOU OUTSIDE?
OF COURSE.
SO, WE'RE ONE MUTANT SHORT NOW OR...
HOW DOES THIS WORK? ARE WE GOING TO GET MORE?
NOT TOO LONG AGO...

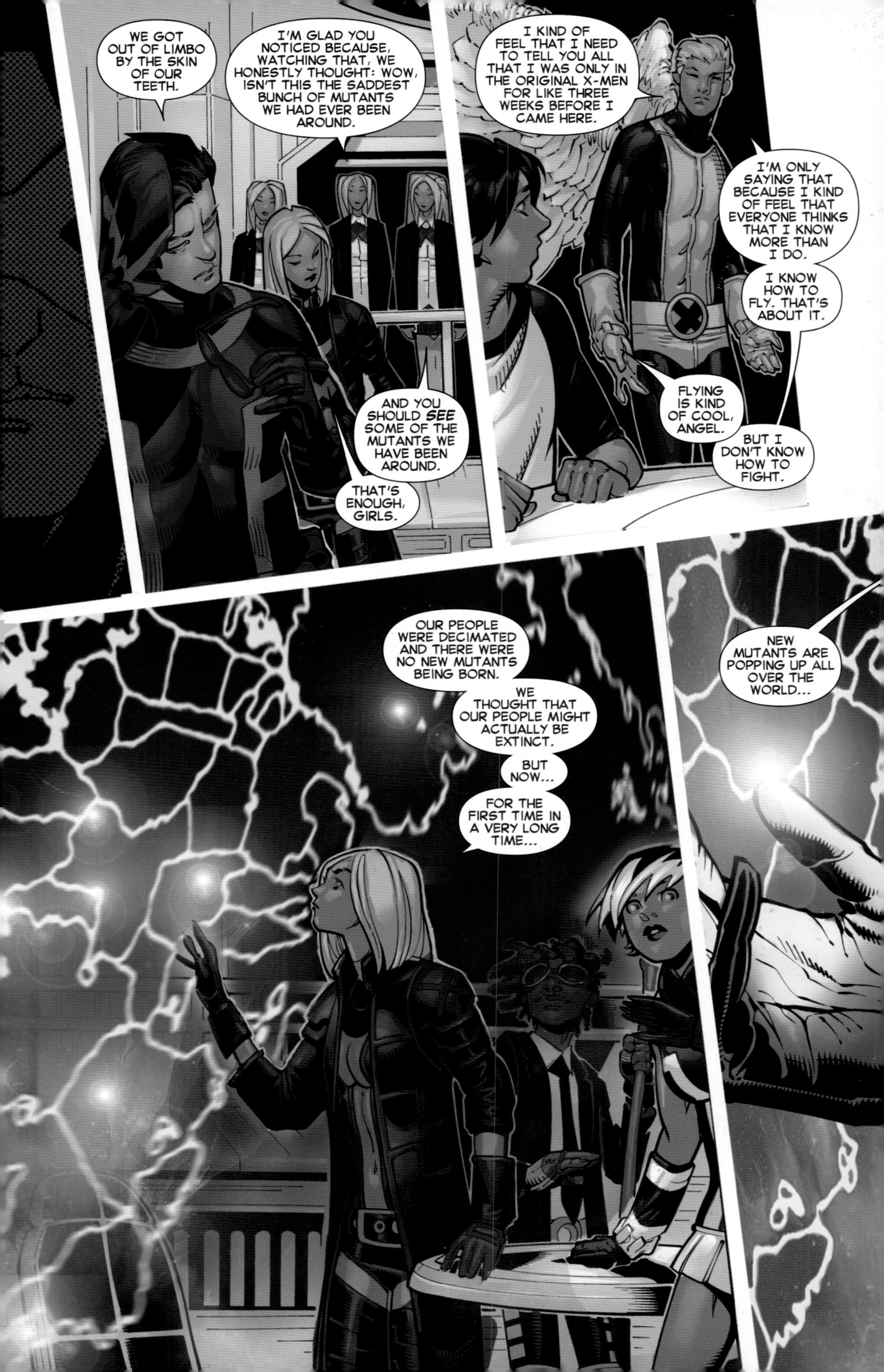
WE GOT OUT OF LIMBO BY THE SKIN OF OUR TEETH.
I'M GLAD YOU NOTICED BECAUSE, WATCHING THAT, WE HONESTLY THOUGHT: WOW, ISN'T THIS THE SADDEST BUNCH OF MUTANTS WE HAD EVER BEEN AROUND.
AND YOU SHOULD **SEE** SOME OF THE MUTANTS WE HAVE BEEN AROUND.
THAT'S ENOUGH, GIRLS.
I KIND OF FEEL THAT I NEED TO TELL YOU ALL THAT I WAS ONLY IN THE ORIGINAL X-MEN FOR LIKE THREE WEEKS BEFORE I CAME HERE.
I'M ONLY SAYING THAT BECAUSE I KIND OF FEEL THAT EVERYONE THINKS THAT I KNOW MORE THAN I DO.
I KNOW HOW TO FLY. THAT'S ABOUT IT.
FLYING IS KIND OF COOL, ANGEL.
BUT I DON'T KNOW HOW TO FIGHT.
OUR PEOPLE WERE DECIMATED AND THERE WERE NO NEW MUTANTS BEING BORN.
WE THOUGHT THAT OUR PEOPLE MIGHT ACTUALLY BE EXTINCT.
BUT NOW...
FOR THE FIRST TIME IN A VERY LONG TIME...
NEW MUTANTS ARE POPPING UP ALL OVER THE WORLD...

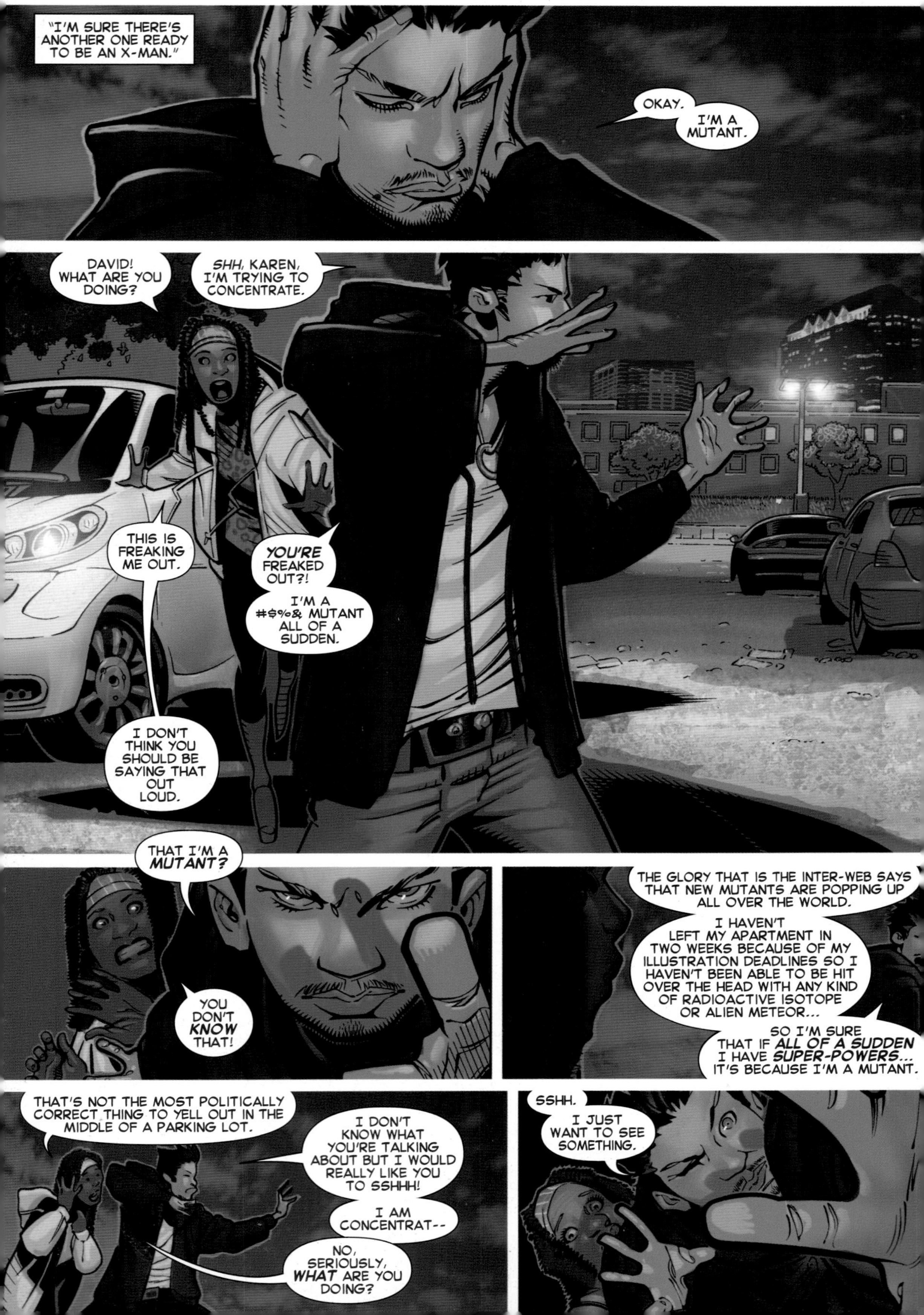
"I'M SURE THERE'S ANOTHER ONE READY TO BE AN X-MAN."
OKAY. I'M A MUTANT.
DAVID! WHAT ARE YOU DOING?
SHH, KAREN, I'M TRYING TO CONCENTRATE.
THIS IS FREAKING ME OUT.
YOU'RE FREAKED OUT?!
I'M A #$%& MUTANT ALL OF A SUDDEN.
I DON'T THINK YOU SHOULD BE SAYING THAT OUT LOUD.
THAT I'M A MUTANT?
YOU DON'T KNOW THAT!
THE GLORY THAT IS THE INTER-WEB SAYS THAT NEW MUTANTS ARE POPPING UP ALL OVER THE WORLD.
I HAVEN'T LEFT MY APARTMENT IN TWO WEEKS BECAUSE OF MY ILLUSTRATION DEADLINES SO I HAVEN'T BEEN ABLE TO BE HIT OVER THE HEAD WITH ANY KIND OF RADIOACTIVE ISOTOPE OR ALIEN METEOR...
SO I'M SURE THAT IF ALL OF A SUDDEN I HAVE SUPER-POWERS... IT'S BECAUSE I'M A MUTANT.
THAT'S NOT THE MOST POLITICALLY CORRECT THING TO YELL OUT IN THE MIDDLE OF A PARKING LOT.
I DON'T KNOW WHAT YOU'RE TALKING ABOUT BUT I WOULD REALLY LIKE YOU TO SSHHH!
I AM CONCENTRAT--
NO, SERIOUSLY, WHAT ARE YOU DOING?
SSHH.
I JUST WANT TO SEE SOMETHING.

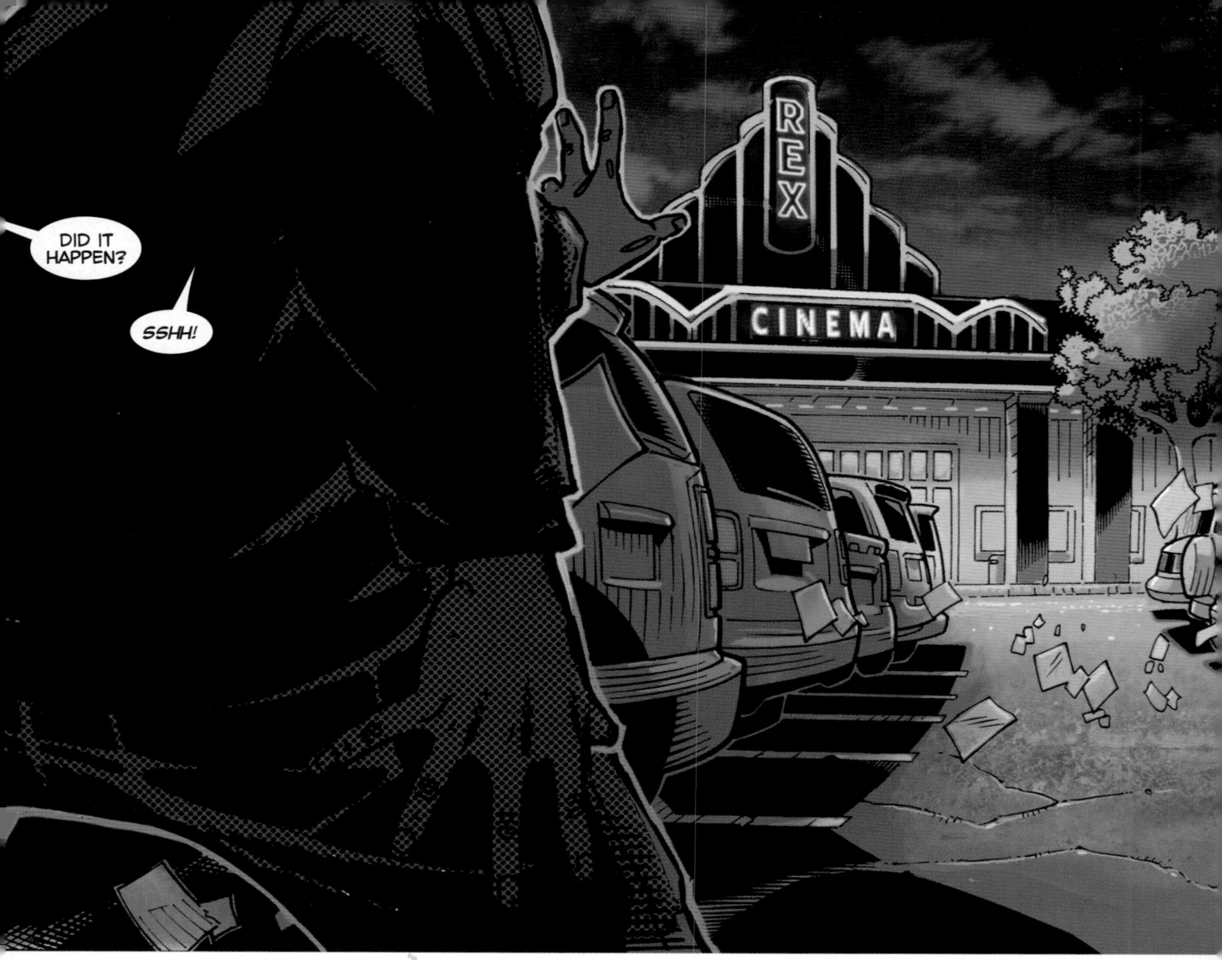
REX
CINEMA
DID IT HAPPEN?
SSHH!
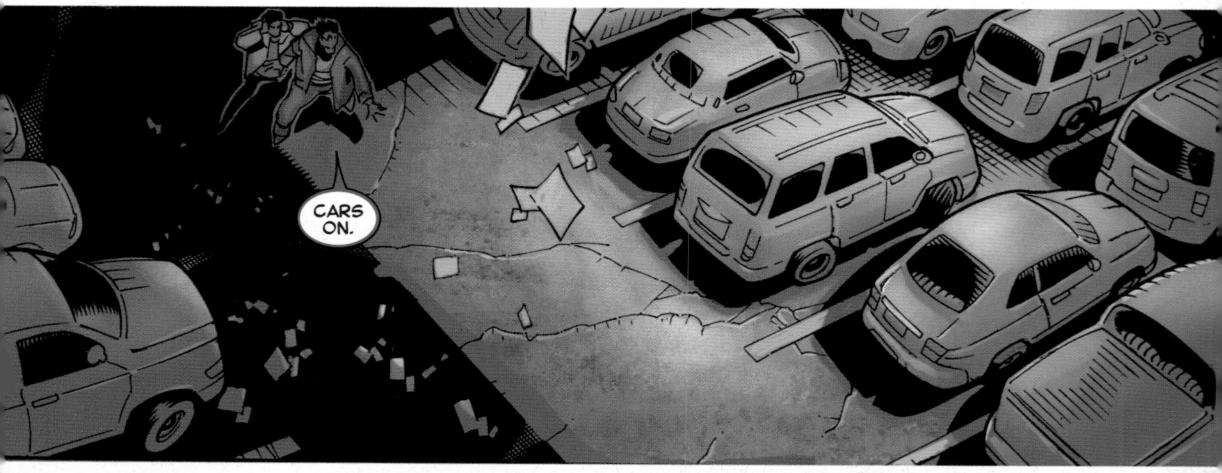
CARS ON.
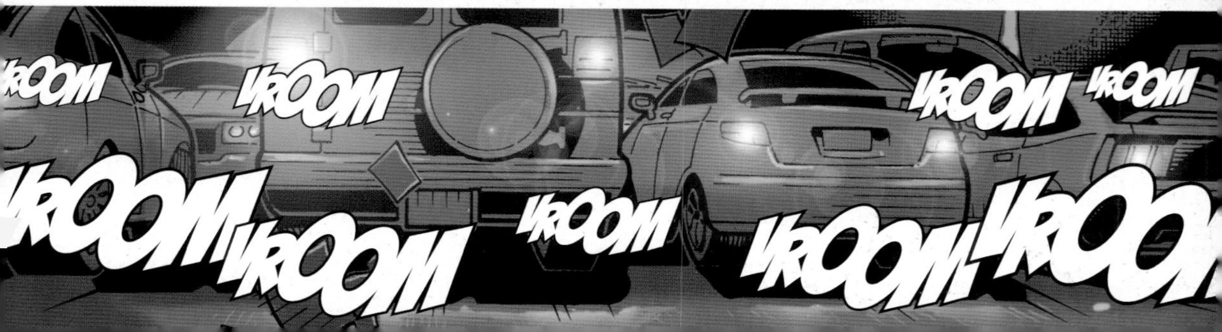
VROOM
VROOM
VROOM
VROOM
VROOM
VROOM
VROOM
VROOM
VROOM

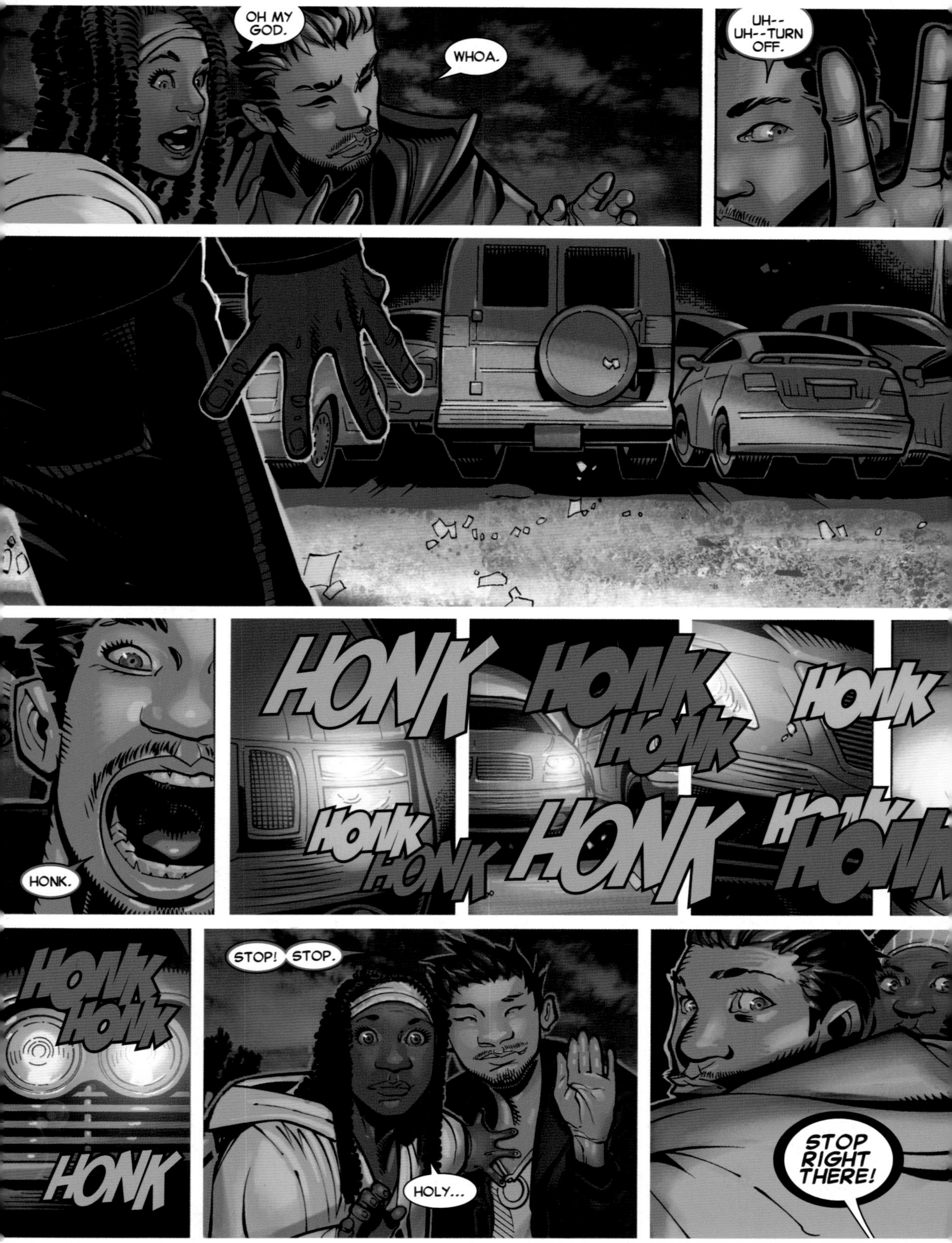
OH MY GOD.
WHOA.
UH-- UH--TURN OFF.
HONK.
HONK
HONK HONK
HONK HONK
HONK
HONK
HONK HONK
HONK HONK
HONK
STOP! STOP.
HOLY...
STOP RIGHT THERE!

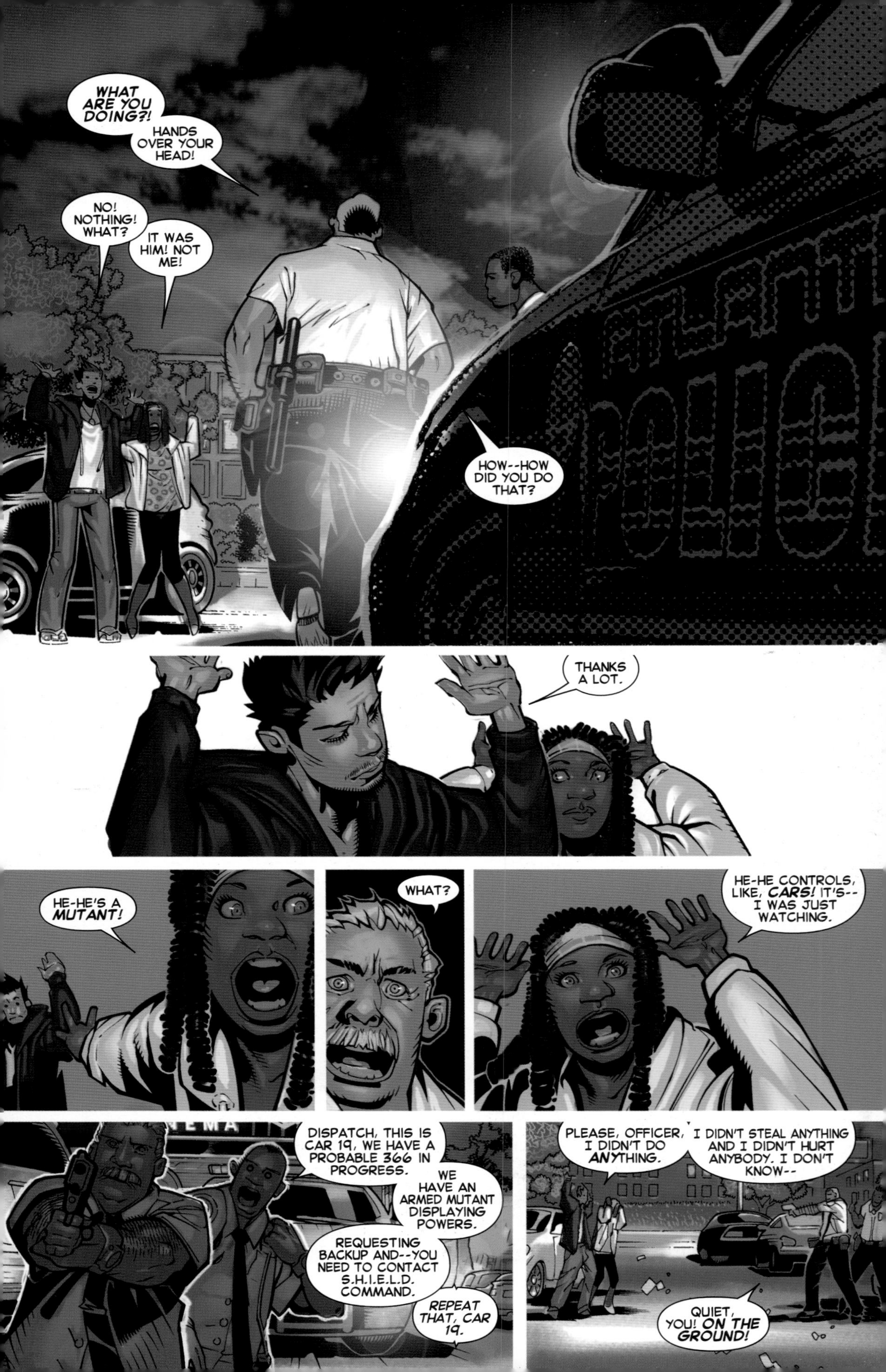
WHAT ARE YOU DOING?!
HANDS OVER YOUR HEAD!
NO! NOTHING! WHAT?
IT WAS HIM! NOT ME!
HOW--HOW DID YOU DO THAT?
THANKS A LOT.
HE-HE'S A MUTANT!
WHAT?
HE-HE CONTROLS, LIKE, CARS! IT'S-- I WAS JUST WATCHING.
DISPATCH, THIS IS CAR 19, WE HAVE A PROBABLE 366 IN PROGRESS.
WE HAVE AN ARMED MUTANT DISPLAYING POWERS.
REQUESTING BACKUP AND--YOU NEED TO CONTACT S.H.I.E.L.D. COMMAND.
REPEAT THAT, CAR 19.
PLEASE, OFFICER, I DIDN'T DO ANYTHING.
I DIDN'T STEAL ANYTHING AND I DIDN'T HURT ANYBODY. I DON'T KNOW--
QUIET, YOU! ON THE GROUND!

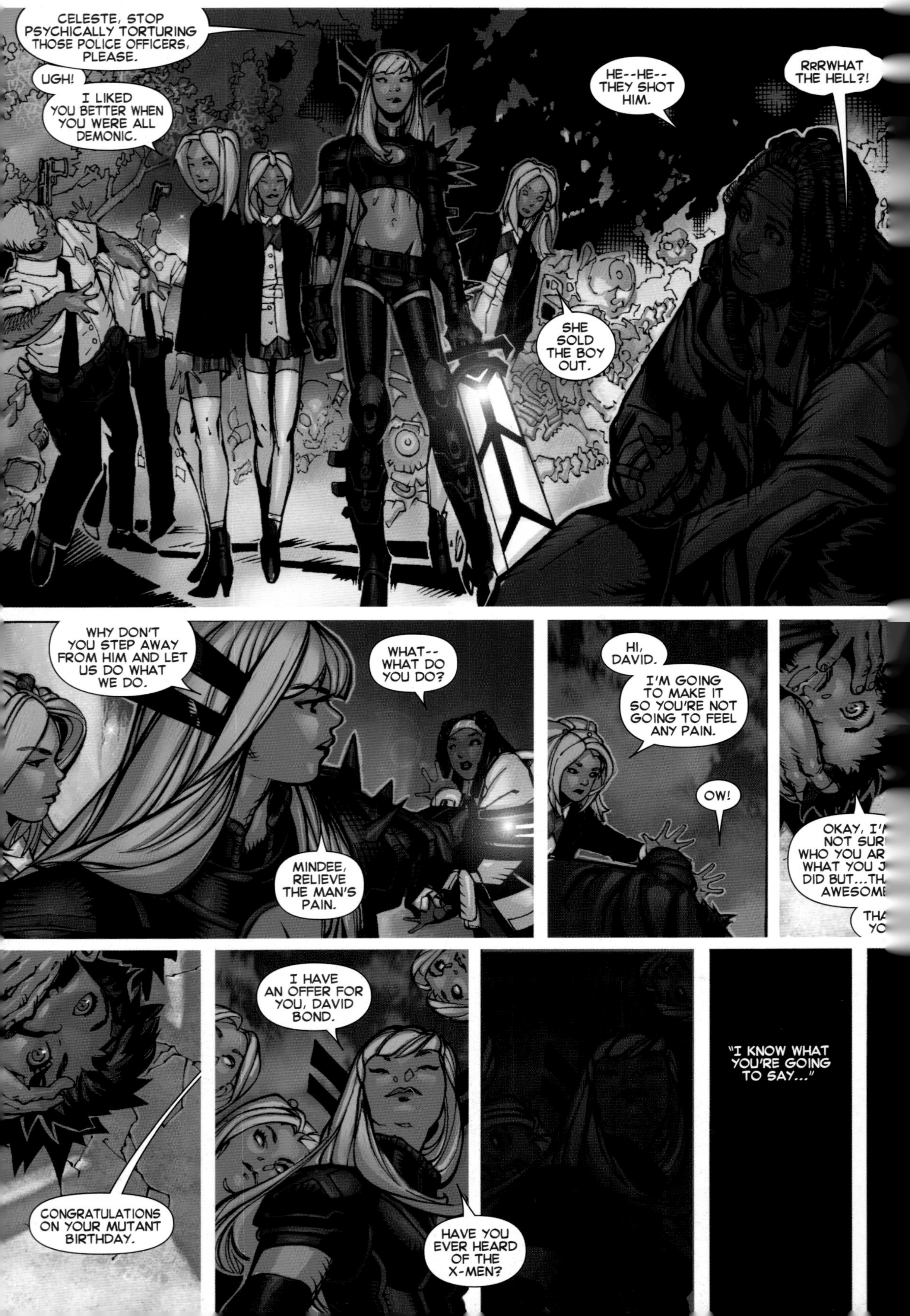
CELESTE, STOP PSYCHICALLY TORTURING THOSE POLICE OFFICERS, PLEASE.
UGH!
I LIKED YOU BETTER WHEN YOU WERE ALL DEMONIC.
HE--HE--THEY SHOT HIM.
RRRWHAT THE HELL?!
SHE SOLD THE BOY OUT.
WHY DON'T YOU STEP AWAY FROM HIM AND LET US DO WHAT WE DO.
WHAT--WHAT DO YOU DO?
MINDEE, RELIEVE THE MAN'S PAIN.
HI, DAVID.
I'M GOING TO MAKE IT SO YOU'RE NOT GOING TO FEEL ANY PAIN.
OW!
CONGRATULATIONS ON YOUR MUTANT BIRTHDAY.
I HAVE AN OFFER FOR YOU, DAVID BOND.
HAVE YOU EVER HEARD OF THE X-MEN?
"I KNOW WHAT YOU'RE GOING TO SAY..."

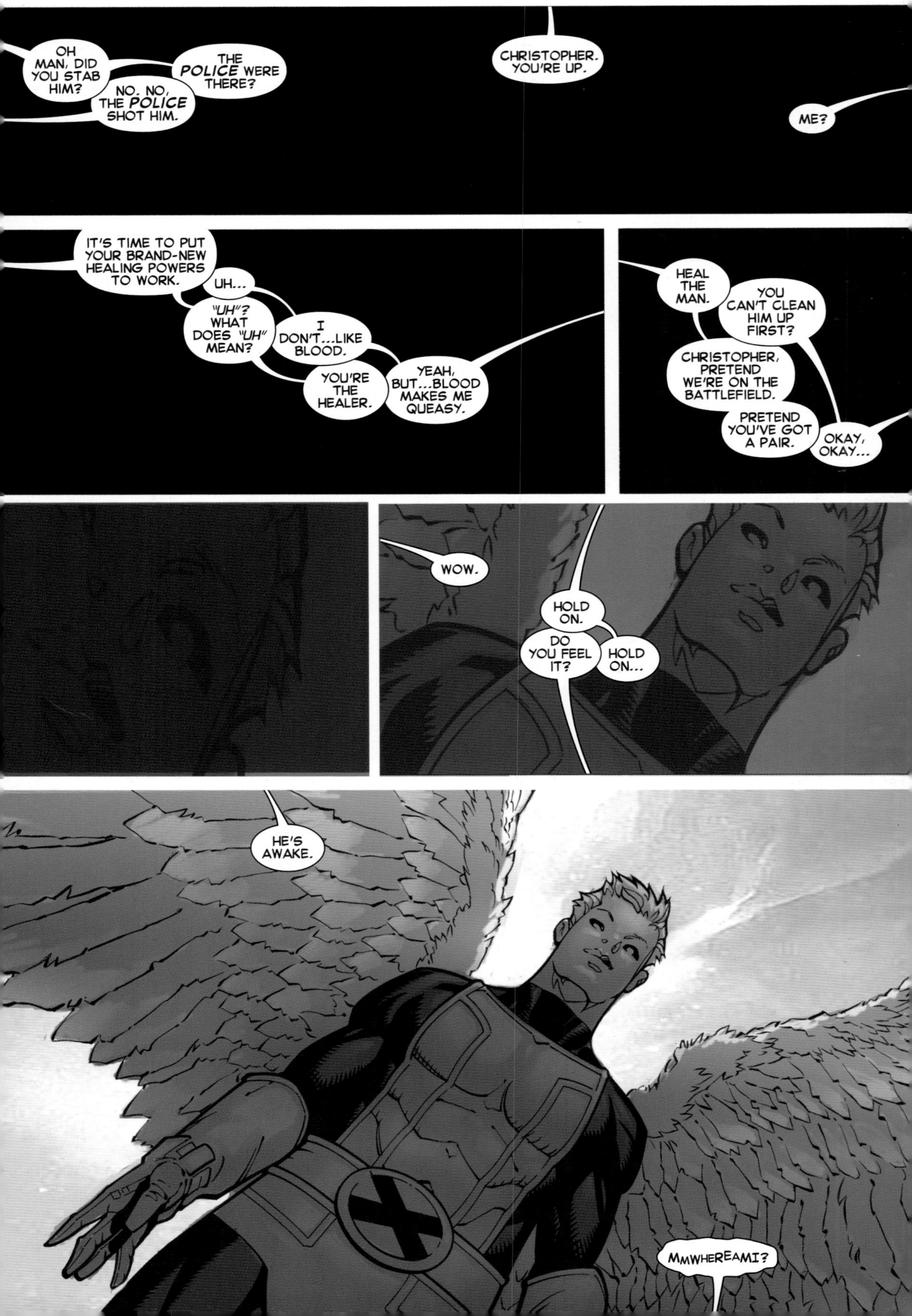
OH MAN, DID YOU STAB HIM?
THE *POLICE* WERE THERE?
NO. NO, THE *POLICE* SHOT HIM.
CHRISTOPHER. YOU'RE UP.
ME?
IT'S TIME TO PUT YOUR BRAND-NEW HEALING POWERS TO WORK.
UH...
"UH"? WHAT DOES "UH" MEAN?
I DON'T...LIKE BLOOD.
YOU'RE THE HEALER.
YEAH, BUT...BLOOD MAKES ME QUEASY.
HEAL THE MAN.
YOU CAN'T CLEAN HIM UP FIRST?
CHRISTOPHER, PRETEND WE'RE ON THE BATTLEFIELD.
PRETEND YOU'VE GOT A PAIR.
OKAY, OKAY...
WOW.
HOLD ON.
DO YOU FEEL IT?
HOLD ON...
HE'S AWAKE.
MMWHEREAMI?

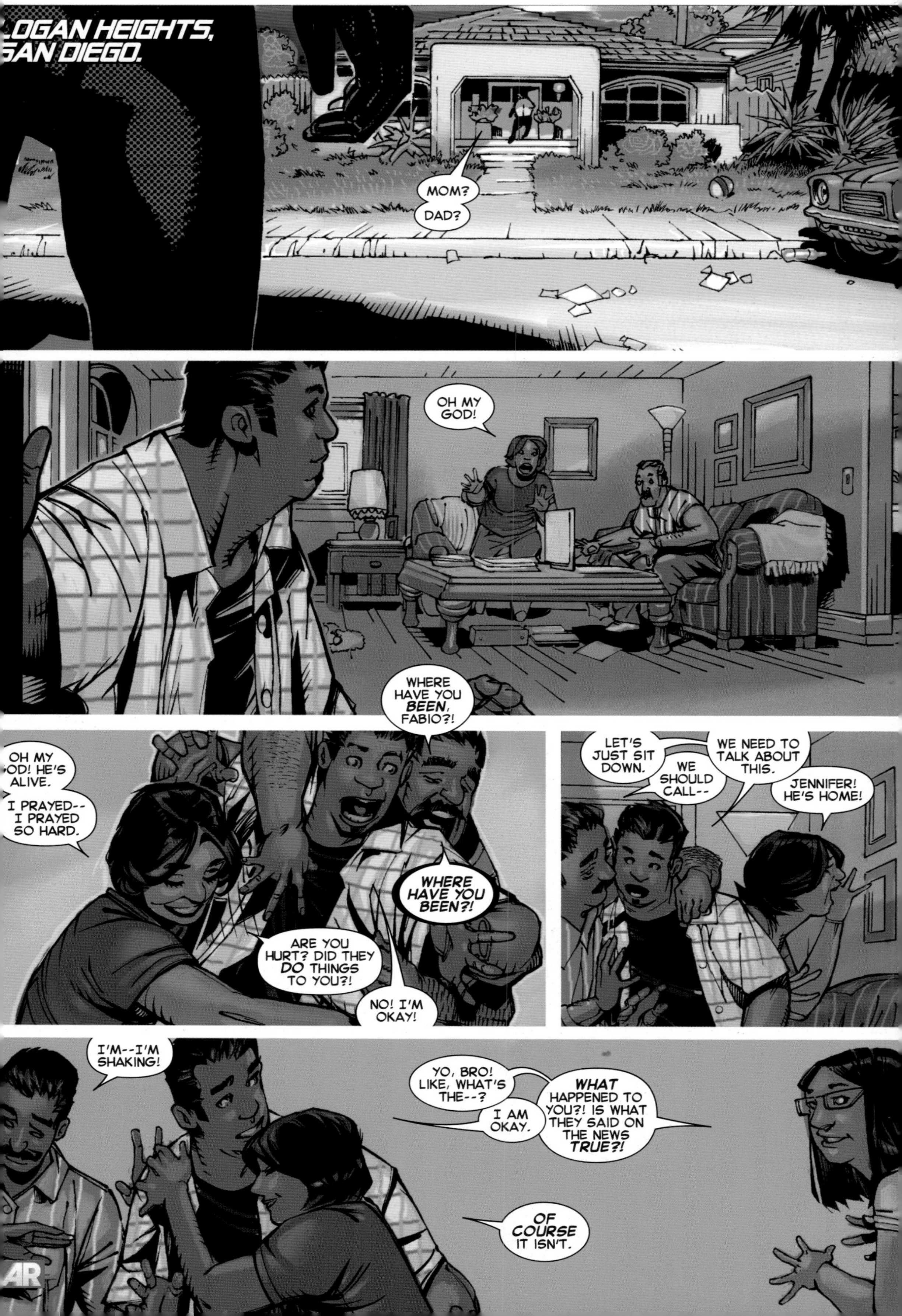

LOGAN HEIGHTS, SAN DIEGO.
MOM?
DAD?
OH MY GOD!
WHERE HAVE YOU BEEN, FABIO?!
OH MY GOD! HE'S ALIVE.
I PRAYED-- I PRAYED SO HARD.
WHERE HAVE YOU BEEN?!
ARE YOU HURT? DID THEY DO THINGS TO YOU?!
NO! I'M OKAY!
LET'S JUST SIT DOWN.
WE SHOULD CALL--
WE NEED TO TALK ABOUT THIS.
JENNIFER! HE'S HOME!
I'M--I'M SHAKING!
YO, BRO! LIKE, WHAT'S THE--?
I AM OKAY.
WHAT HAPPENED TO YOU?! IS WHAT THEY SAID ON THE NEWS TRUE?!
OF COURSE IT ISN'T.

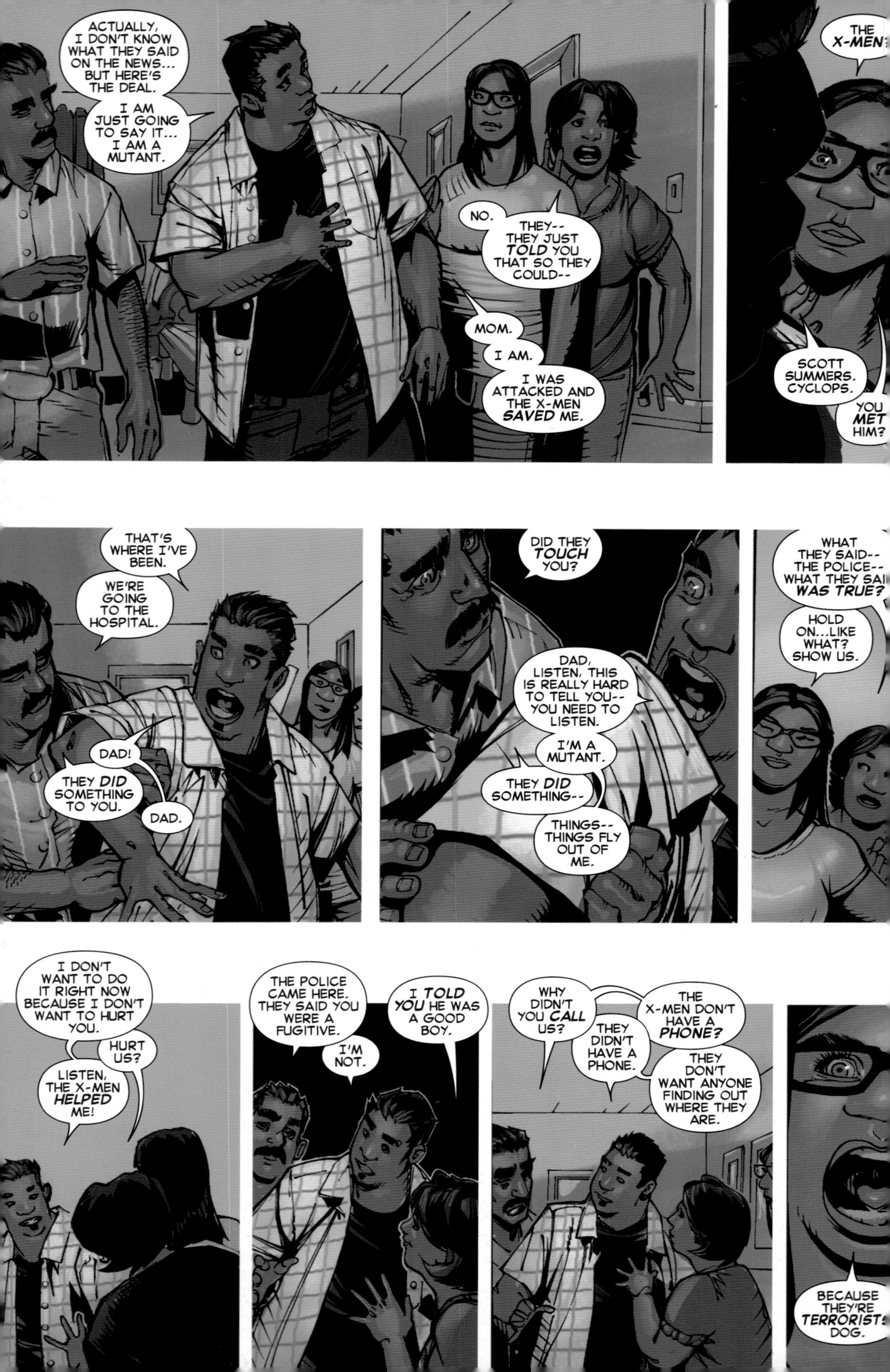
ACTUALLY, I DON'T KNOW WHAT THEY SAID ON THE NEWS... BUT HERE'S THE DEAL.
I AM JUST GOING TO SAY IT... I AM A MUTANT.
NO.
THEY-- THEY JUST **TOLD** YOU THAT SO THEY COULD--
MOM.
I AM.
I WAS ATTACKED AND THE X-MEN **SAVED** ME.
THE **X-MEN**
SCOTT SUMMERS. CYCLOPS.
YOU **MET** HIM?
THAT'S WHERE I'VE BEEN.
WE'RE GOING TO THE HOSPITAL.
DAD!
THEY **DID** SOMETHING TO YOU.
DAD.
DID THEY **TOUCH** YOU?
DAD, LISTEN, THIS IS REALLY HARD TO TELL YOU-- YOU NEED TO LISTEN.
I'M A MUTANT.
THEY **DID** SOMETHING--
THINGS-- THINGS FLY OUT OF ME.
WHAT THEY SAID-- THE POLICE-- WHAT THEY SAI **WAS TRUE?**
HOLD ON...LIKE WHAT? SHOW US.
I DON'T WANT TO DO IT RIGHT NOW BECAUSE I DON'T WANT TO HURT YOU.
HURT US?
LISTEN, THE X-MEN **HELPED** ME!
THE POLICE CAME HERE. THEY SAID YOU WERE A FUGITIVE.
I'M NOT.
I **TOLD YOU** HE WAS A GOOD BOY.
WHY DIDN'T YOU **CALL** US?
THE X-MEN DON'T HAVE A **PHONE?**
THEY DIDN'T HAVE A PHONE.
THEY DON'T WANT ANYONE FINDING OUT WHERE THEY ARE.
BECAUSE THEY'RE **TERRORISTS** DOG.

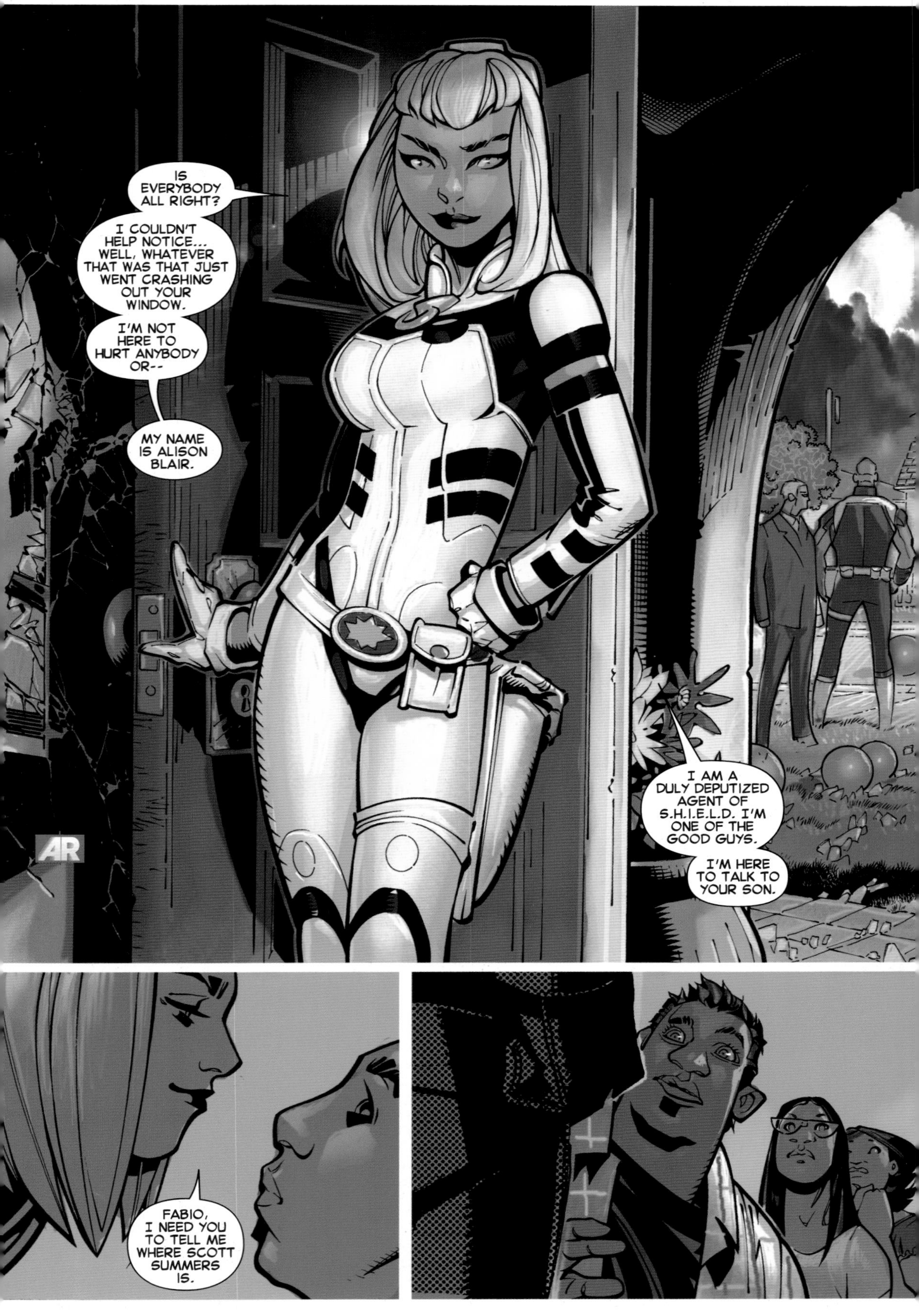
IS EVERYBODY ALL RIGHT?
I COULDN'T HELP NOTICE... WELL, WHATEVER THAT WAS THAT JUST WENT CRASHING OUT YOUR WINDOW.
I'M NOT HERE TO HURT ANYBODY OR--
MY NAME IS ALISON BLAIR.
I AM A DULY DEPUTIZED AGENT OF S.H.I.E.L.D. I'M ONE OF THE GOOD GUYS.
I'M HERE TO TALK TO YOUR SON.
AR
FABIO, I NEED YOU TO TELL ME WHERE SCOTT SUMMERS IS.

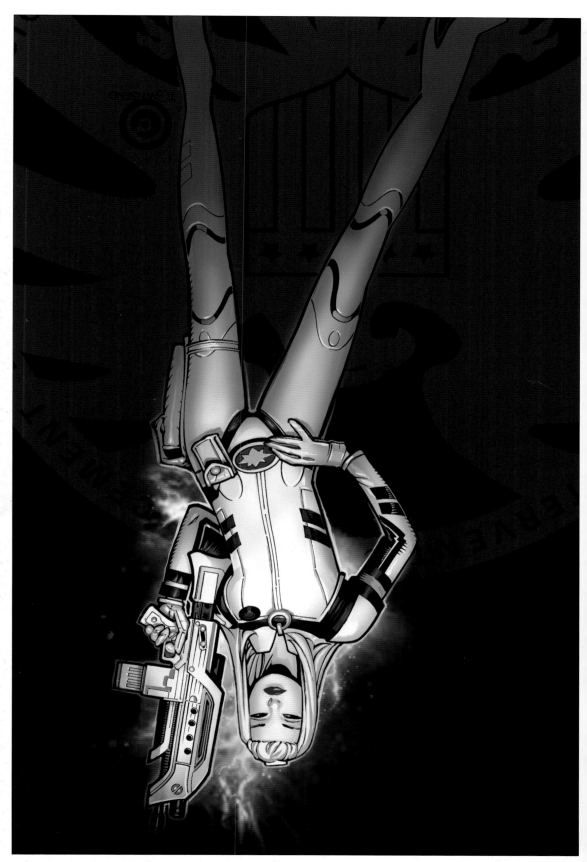

UNCANNY X-MEN #9

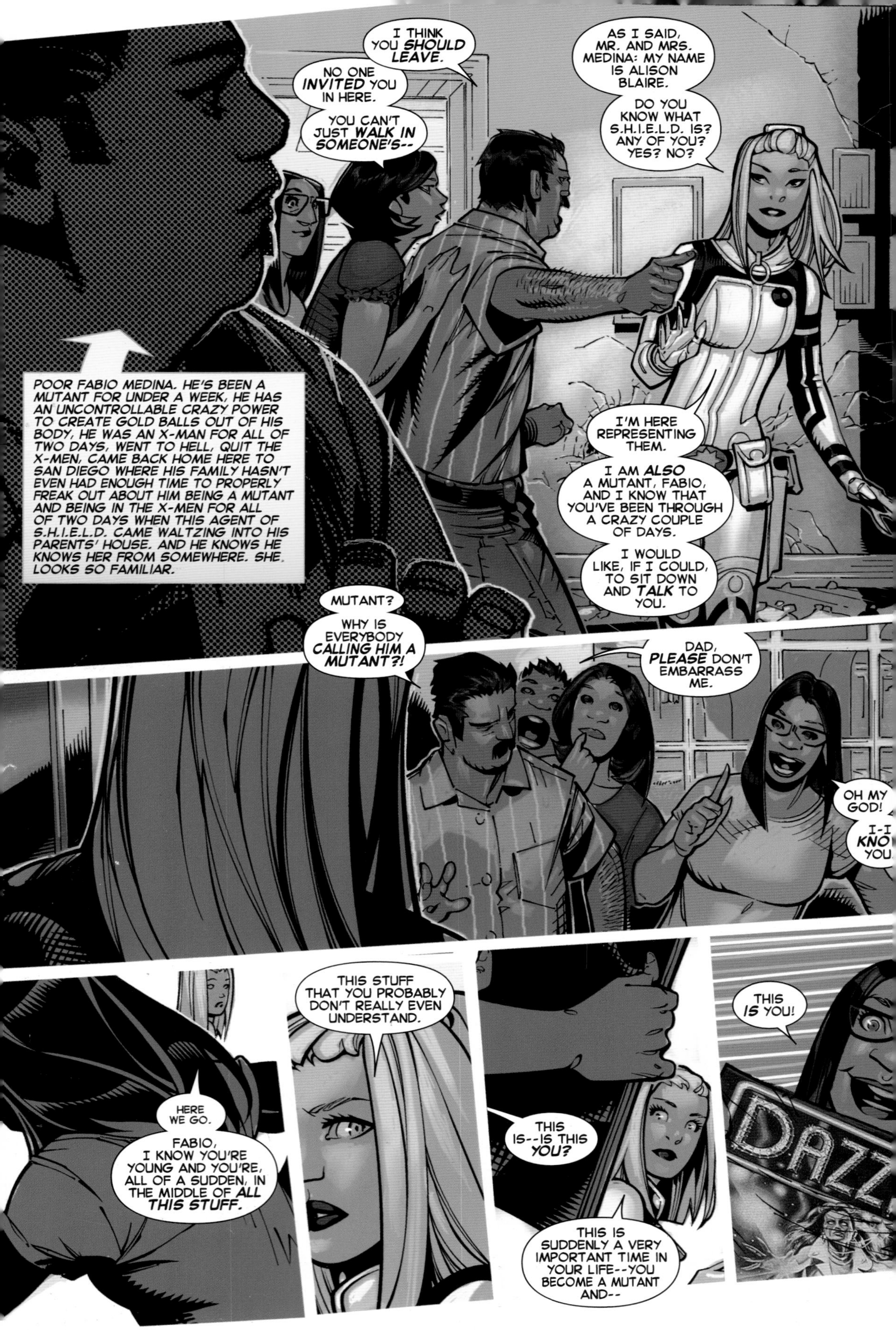

POOR FABIO MEDINA. HE'S BEEN A MUTANT FOR UNDER A WEEK, HE HAS AN UNCONTROLLABLE CRAZY POWER TO CREATE GOLD BALLS OUT OF HIS BODY, HE WAS AN X-MAN FOR ALL OF TWO DAYS, WENT TO HELL, QUIT THE X-MEN, CAME BACK HOME HERE TO SAN DIEGO WHERE HIS FAMILY HASN'T EVEN HAD ENOUGH TIME TO PROPERLY FREAK OUT ABOUT HIM BEING A MUTANT AND BEING IN THE X-MEN FOR ALL OF TWO DAYS WHEN THIS AGENT OF S.H.I.E.L.D. CAME WALTZING INTO HIS PARENTS' HOUSE. AND HE KNOWS HE KNOWS HER FROM SOMEWHERE. SHE LOOKS SO FAMILIAR.
I THINK YOU SHOULD LEAVE.
NO ONE INVITED YOU IN HERE.
YOU CAN'T JUST WALK IN SOMEONE'S--
AS I SAID, MR. AND MRS. MEDINA: MY NAME IS ALISON BLAIRE.
DO YOU KNOW WHAT S.H.I.E.L.D. IS? ANY OF YOU? YES? NO?
I'M HERE REPRESENTING THEM.
I AM ALSO A MUTANT, FABIO, AND I KNOW THAT YOU'VE BEEN THROUGH A CRAZY COUPLE OF DAYS.
I WOULD LIKE, IF I COULD, TO SIT DOWN AND TALK TO YOU.
MUTANT?
WHY IS EVERYBODY CALLING HIM A MUTANT?!
DAD, PLEASE DON'T EMBARRASS ME.
OH MY GOD!
I-I KNO YOU.
HERE WE GO.
FABIO, I KNOW YOU'RE YOUNG AND YOU'RE, ALL OF A SUDDEN, IN THE MIDDLE OF ALL THIS STUFF.
THIS STUFF THAT YOU PROBABLY DON'T REALLY EVEN UNDERSTAND.
THIS IS--IS THIS YOU?
THIS IS SUDDENLY A VERY IMPORTANT TIME IN YOUR LIFE--YOU BECOME A MUTANT AND--
THIS IS YOU!
DAZZ

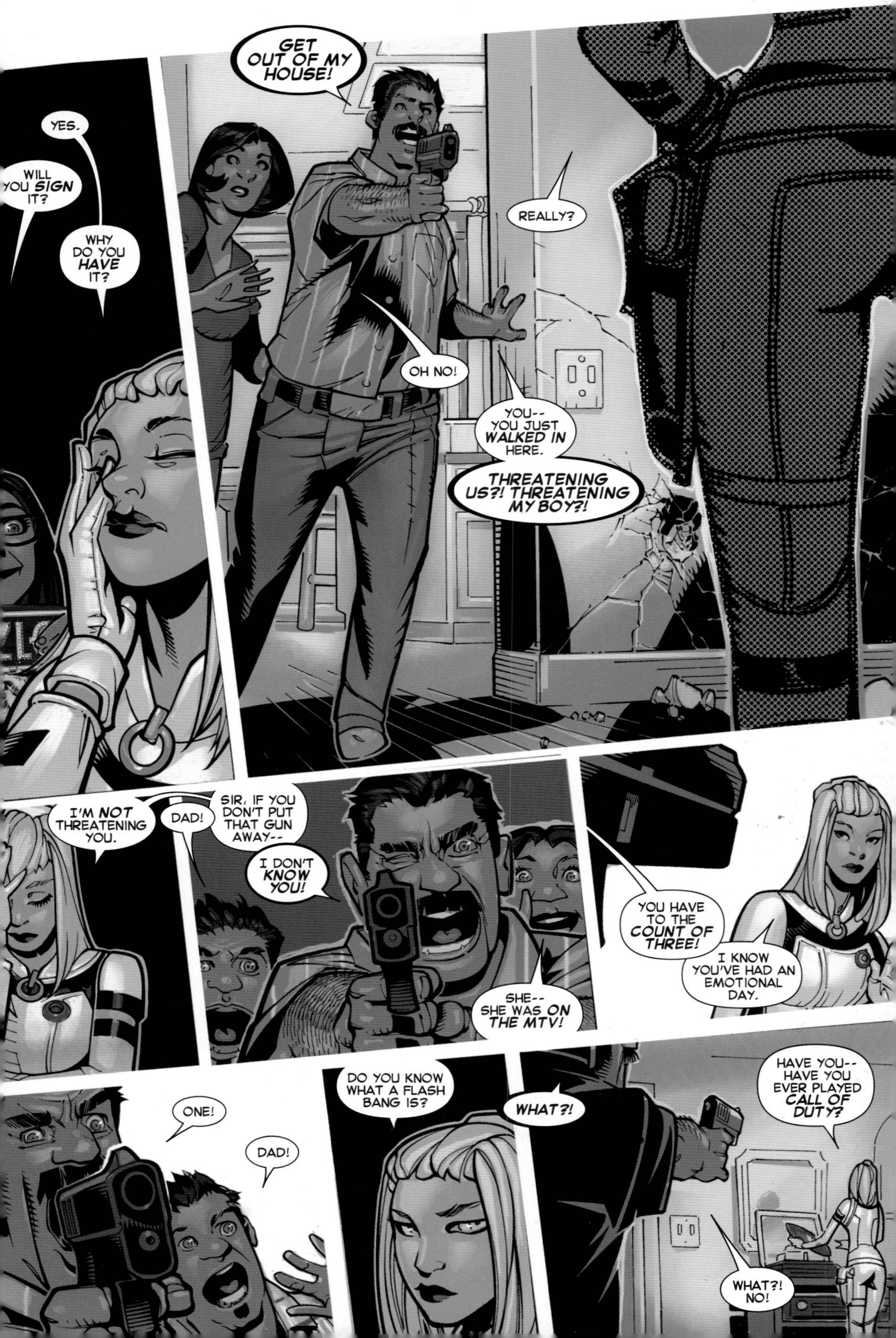
WILL YOU SIGN IT?
YES.
WHY DO YOU HAVE IT?
GET OUT OF MY HOUSE!
OH NO!
REALLY?
YOU-- YOU JUST WALKED IN HERE.
THREATENING US?! THREATENING MY BOY?!
I'M NOT THREATENING YOU.
DAD!
SIR, IF YOU DON'T PUT THAT GUN AWAY--
I DON'T KNOW YOU!
SHE-- SHE WAS ON THE MTV!
YOU HAVE TO THE COUNT OF THREE!
I KNOW YOU'VE HAD AN EMOTIONAL DAY.
ONE!
DAD!
DO YOU KNOW WHAT A FLASH BANG IS?
WHAT?!
HAVE YOU-- HAVE YOU EVER PLAYED CALL OF DUTY?
WHAT?! NO!

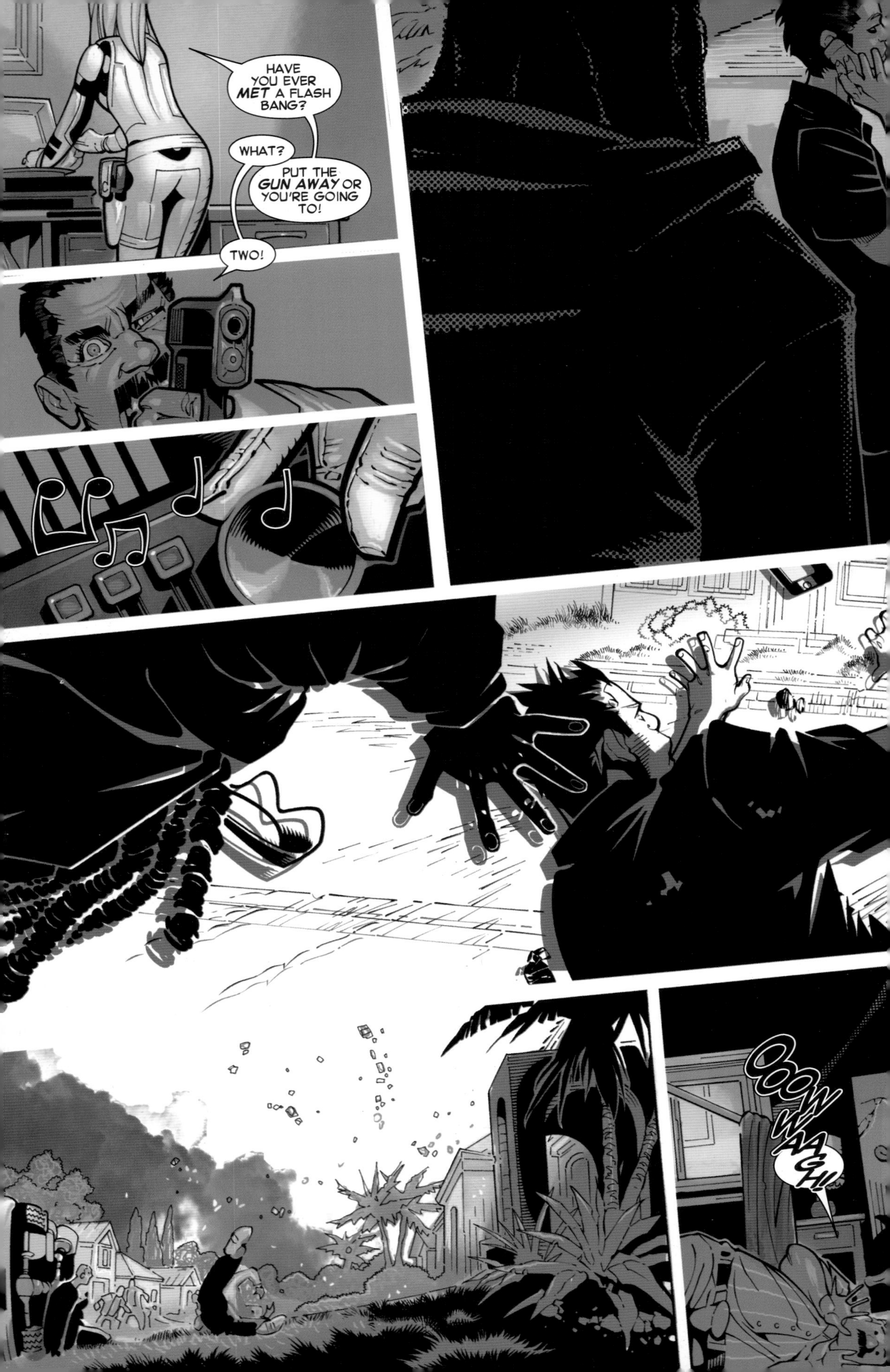
HAVE YOU EVER MET A FLASH BANG?
WHAT?
PUT THE GUN AWAY OR YOU'RE GOING TO!
TWO!
OOOWWAAGH!!

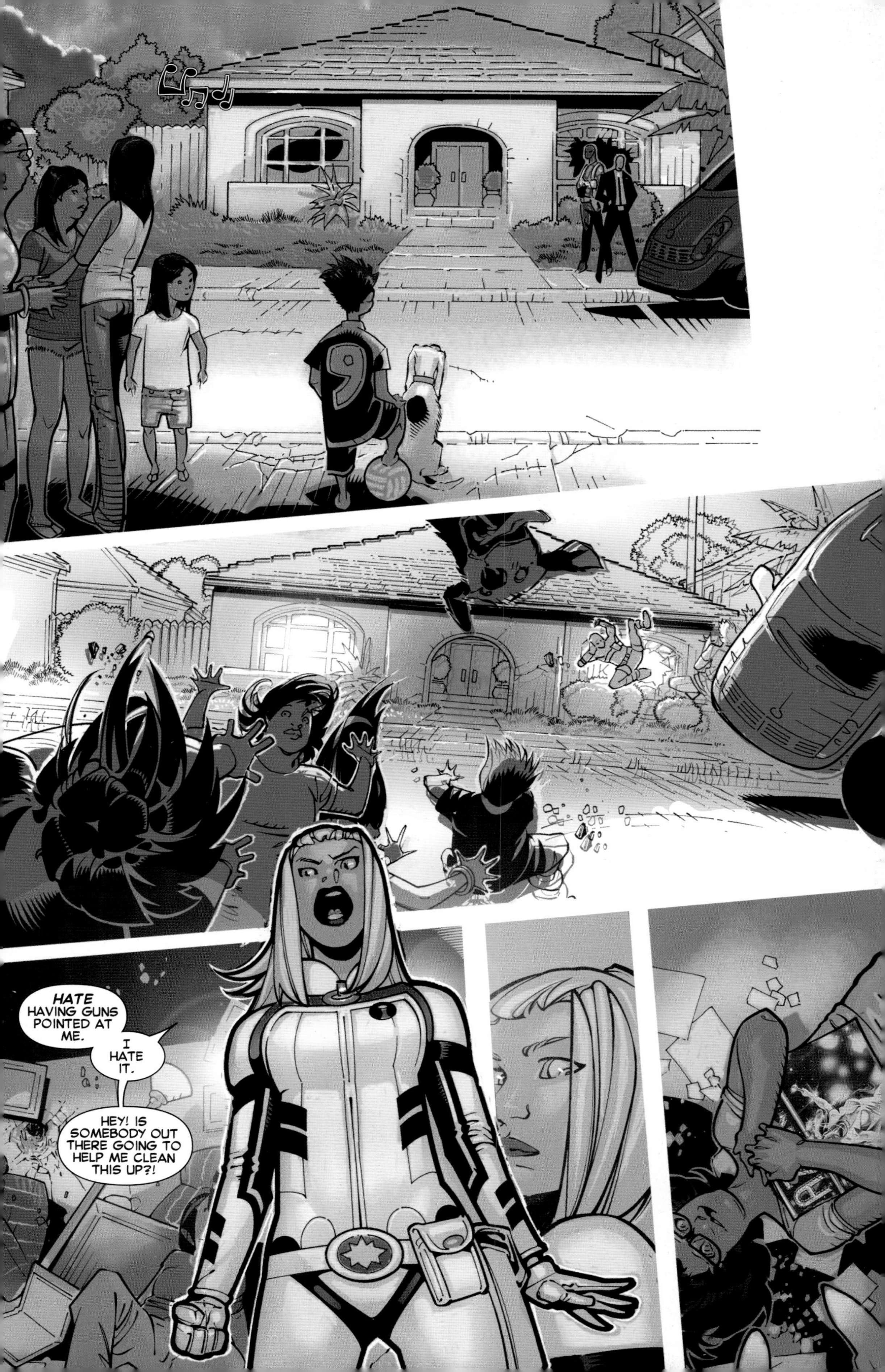
HATE HAVING GUNS POINTED AT ME.
I HATE IT.
HEY! IS SOMEBODY OUT THERE GOING TO HELP ME CLEAN THIS UP?!

AAAND
RELEASE.

WE TALKED
ABOUT THIS, MS.
FROST.

NOT EVERY
MUTANT IS
CUT OUT FOR
THIS LINE OF
WORK.

WORK?

AS IN
WE'RE GETTING
PAID?

HE'S THE
REAL DEAL,
SCOTT.

SHOW
ME.

SHOW
HIM.

⸢SIGH.⸣

UM, THE
PLANE?

SURE.

OKAY, UH, BIG
PLANE!

TURN
ON AND, UH,
GO UP.

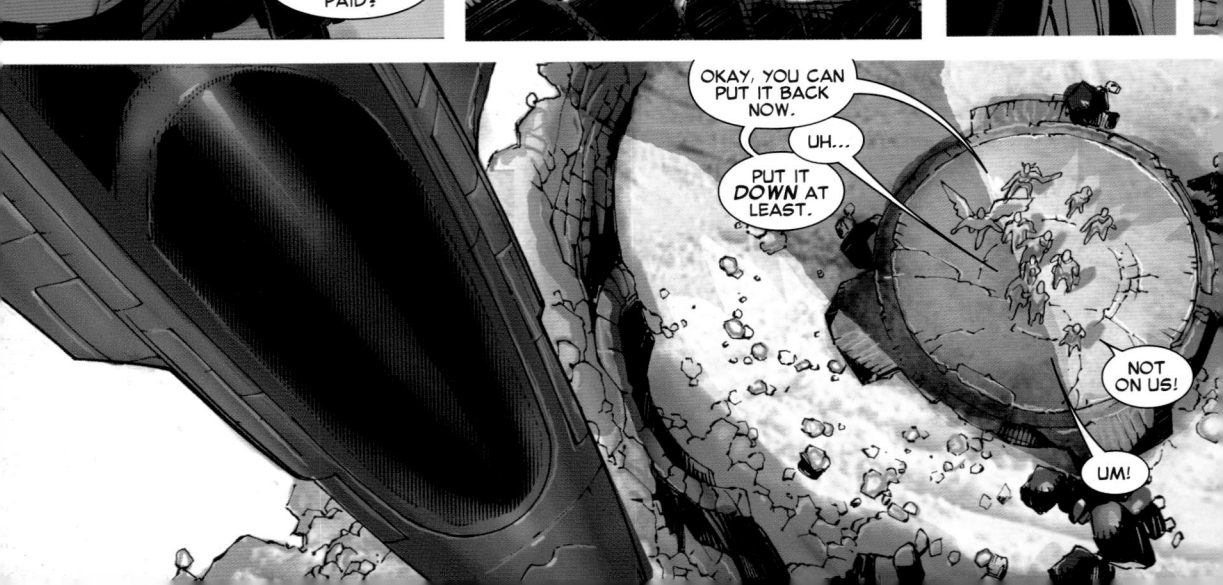

OKAY, YOU CAN
PUT IT BACK
NOW.

UH...

PUT IT
DOWN AT
LEAST.

NOT
ON US!

UM!

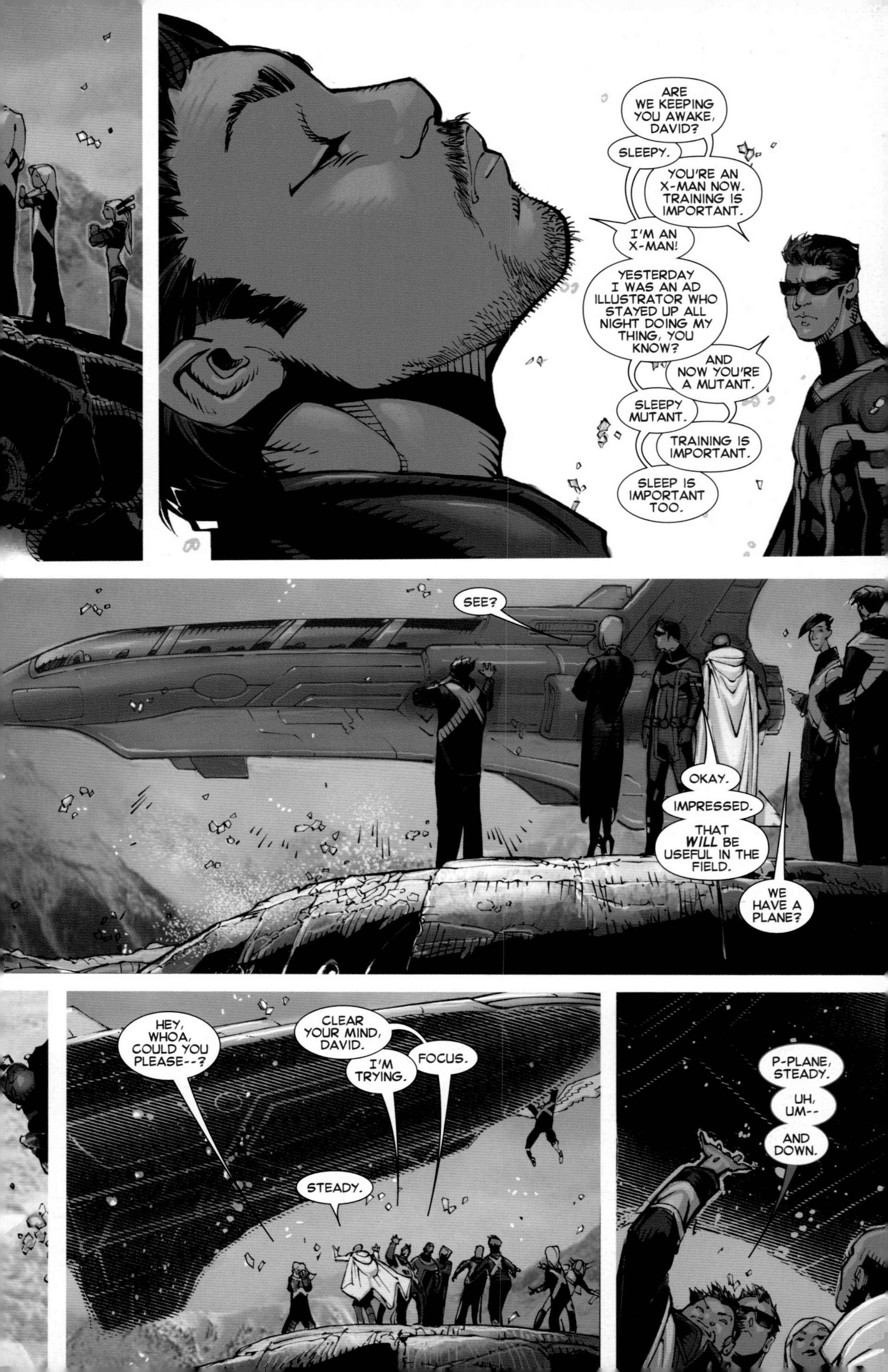
ARE WE KEEPING YOU AWAKE, DAVID?
SLEEPY.
YOU'RE AN X-MAN NOW. TRAINING IS IMPORTANT.
I'M AN X-MAN!
YESTERDAY I WAS AN AD ILLUSTRATOR WHO STAYED UP ALL NIGHT DOING MY THING, YOU KNOW?
AND NOW YOU'RE A MUTANT.
SLEEPY MUTANT.
TRAINING IS IMPORTANT.
SLEEP IS IMPORTANT TOO.
SEE?
OKAY.
IMPRESSED.
THAT WILL BE USEFUL IN THE FIELD.
WE HAVE A PLANE?
HEY, WHOA, COULD YOU PLEASE--?
CLEAR YOUR MIND, DAVID.
I'M TRYING.
FOCUS.
STEADY.
P-PLANE, STEADY.
UH, UM--
AND DOWN.

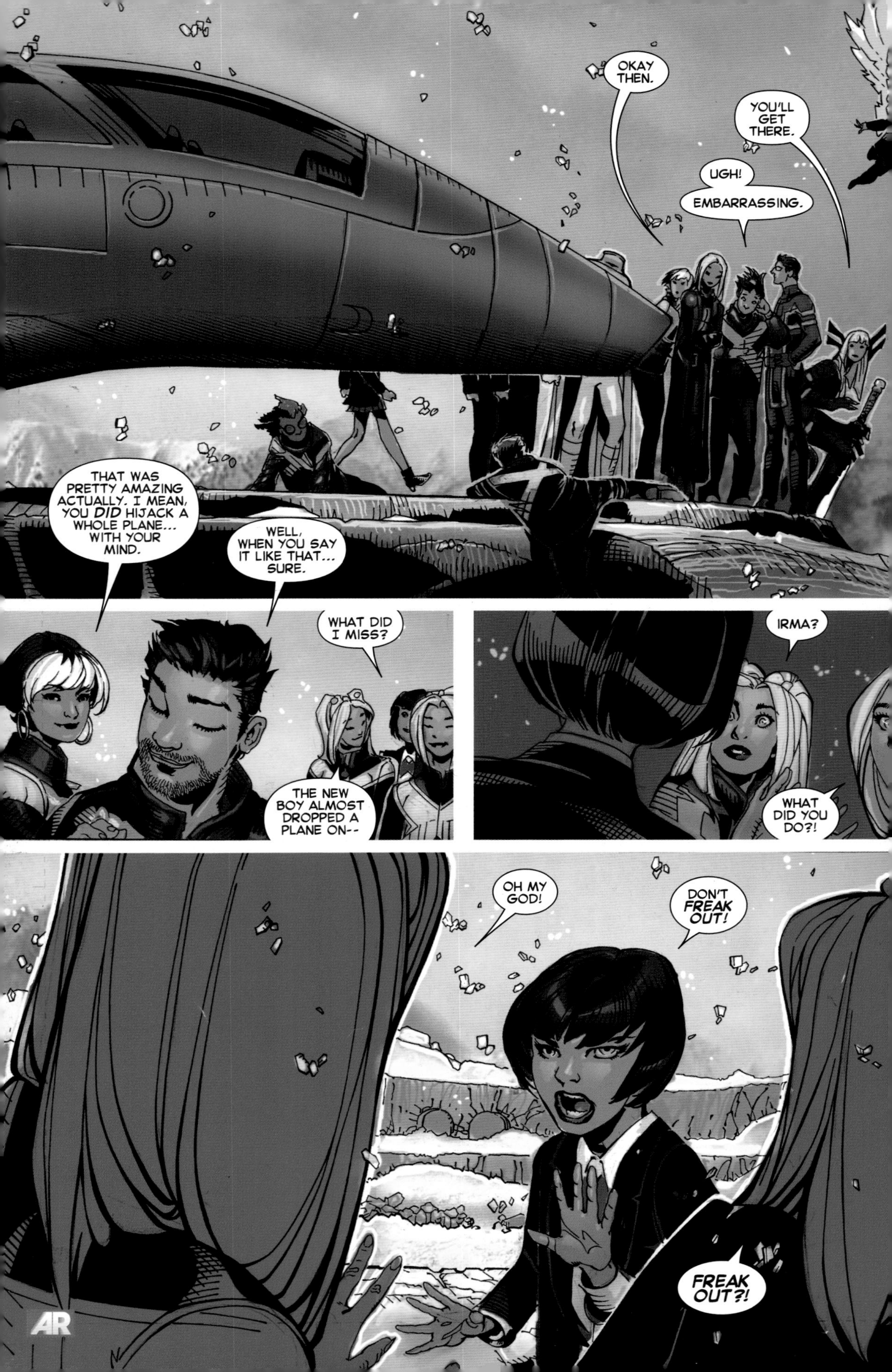
OKAY THEN.
YOU'LL GET THERE.
UGH!
EMBARRASSING.
THAT WAS PRETTY AMAZING ACTUALLY. I MEAN, YOU *DID* HIJACK A WHOLE PLANE... WITH YOUR MIND.
WELL, WHEN YOU SAY IT LIKE THAT... SURE.
WHAT DID I MISS?
THE NEW BOY ALMOST DROPPED A PLANE ON--
IRMA?
WHAT DID YOU DO?!
OH MY GOD!
DON'T *FREAK* OUT!
FREAK OUT?!
AR

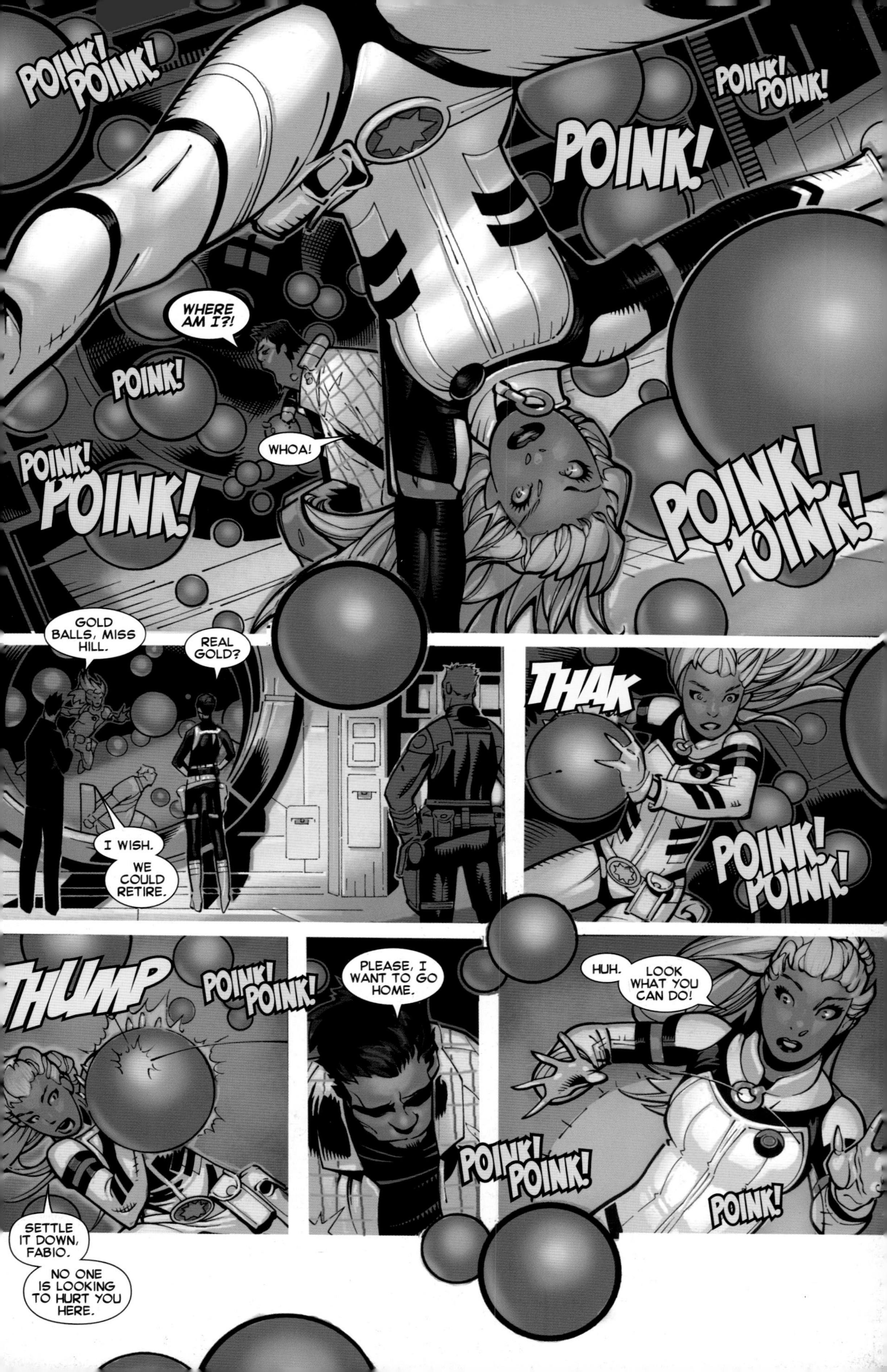
POINK! POINK!
POINK!
POINK! POINK!
WHERE AM I?!
POINK!
WHOA!
POINK! POINK!
POINK! POINK!
GOLD BALLS, MISS HILL.
REAL GOLD?
I WISH.
WE COULD RETIRE.
THAK
POINK! POINK!
THUMP
POINK! POINK!
SETTLE IT DOWN, FABIO.
NO ONE IS LOOKING TO HURT YOU HERE.
PLEASE, I WANT TO GO HOME.
POINK! POINK!
HUH.
LOOK WHAT YOU CAN DO!
POINK!

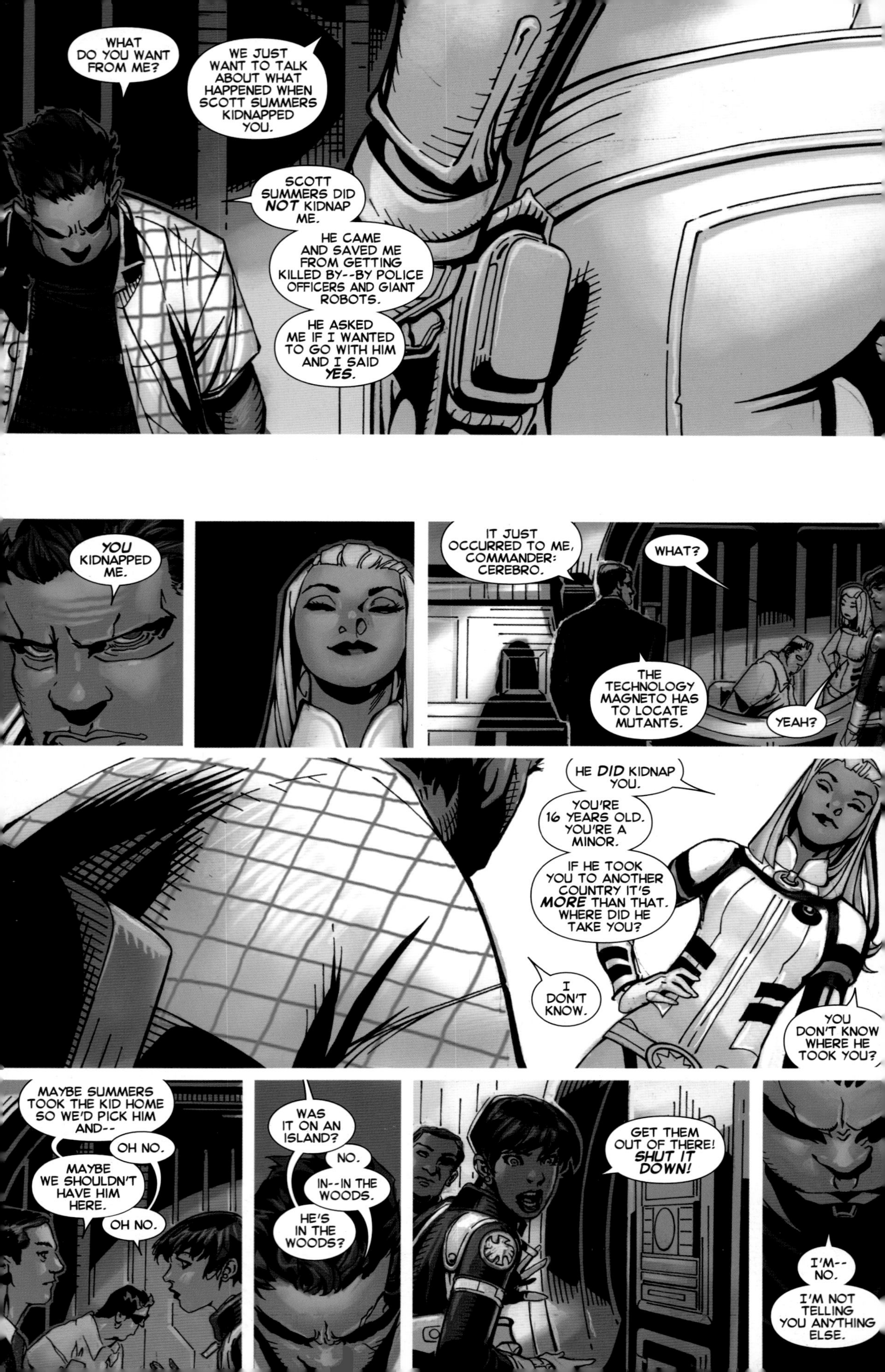
WHAT DO YOU WANT FROM ME?
WE JUST WANT TO TALK ABOUT WHAT HAPPENED WHEN SCOTT SUMMERS KIDNAPPED YOU.
SCOTT SUMMERS DID *NOT* KIDNAP ME.
HE CAME AND SAVED ME FROM GETTING KILLED BY--BY POLICE OFFICERS AND GIANT ROBOTS.
HE ASKED ME IF I WANTED TO GO WITH HIM AND I SAID *YES.*
YOU KIDNAPPED ME.
IT JUST OCCURRED TO ME, COMMANDER: CEREBRO.
WHAT?
THE TECHNOLOGY MAGNETO HAS TO LOCATE MUTANTS.
YEAH?
HE *DID* KIDNAP YOU.
YOU'RE 16 YEARS OLD. YOU'RE A MINOR.
IF HE TOOK YOU TO ANOTHER COUNTRY IT'S *MORE* THAN THAT. WHERE DID HE TAKE YOU?
I DON'T KNOW.
YOU DON'T KNOW WHERE HE TOOK YOU?
MAYBE SUMMERS TOOK THE KID HOME SO WE'D PICK HIM AND--
OH NO.
MAYBE WE SHOULDN'T HAVE HIM HERE.
OH NO.
WAS IT ON AN ISLAND?
NO.
IN--IN THE WOODS.
HE'S IN THE WOODS?
GET THEM OUT OF THERE! *SHUT IT DOWN!*
I'M-- NO.
I'M NOT TELLING YOU ANYTHING ELSE.

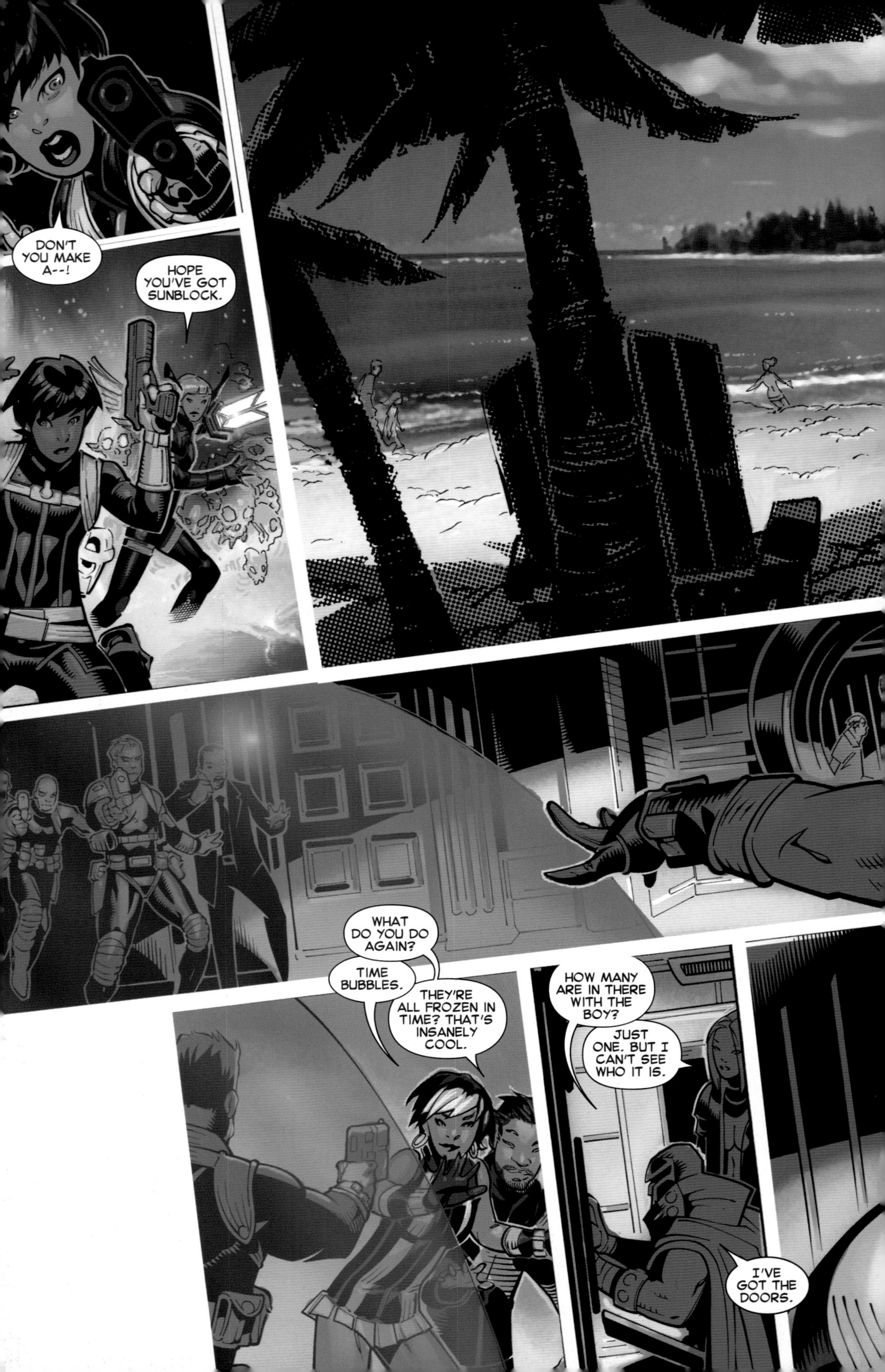
DON'T YOU MAKE A--!
HOPE YOU'VE GOT SUNBLOCK.
WHAT DO YOU DO AGAIN?
TIME BUBBLES.
THEY'RE ALL FROZEN IN TIME? THAT'S INSANELY COOL.
HOW MANY ARE IN THERE WITH THE BOY?
JUST ONE. BUT I CAN'T SEE WHO IT IS.
I'VE GOT THE DOORS.

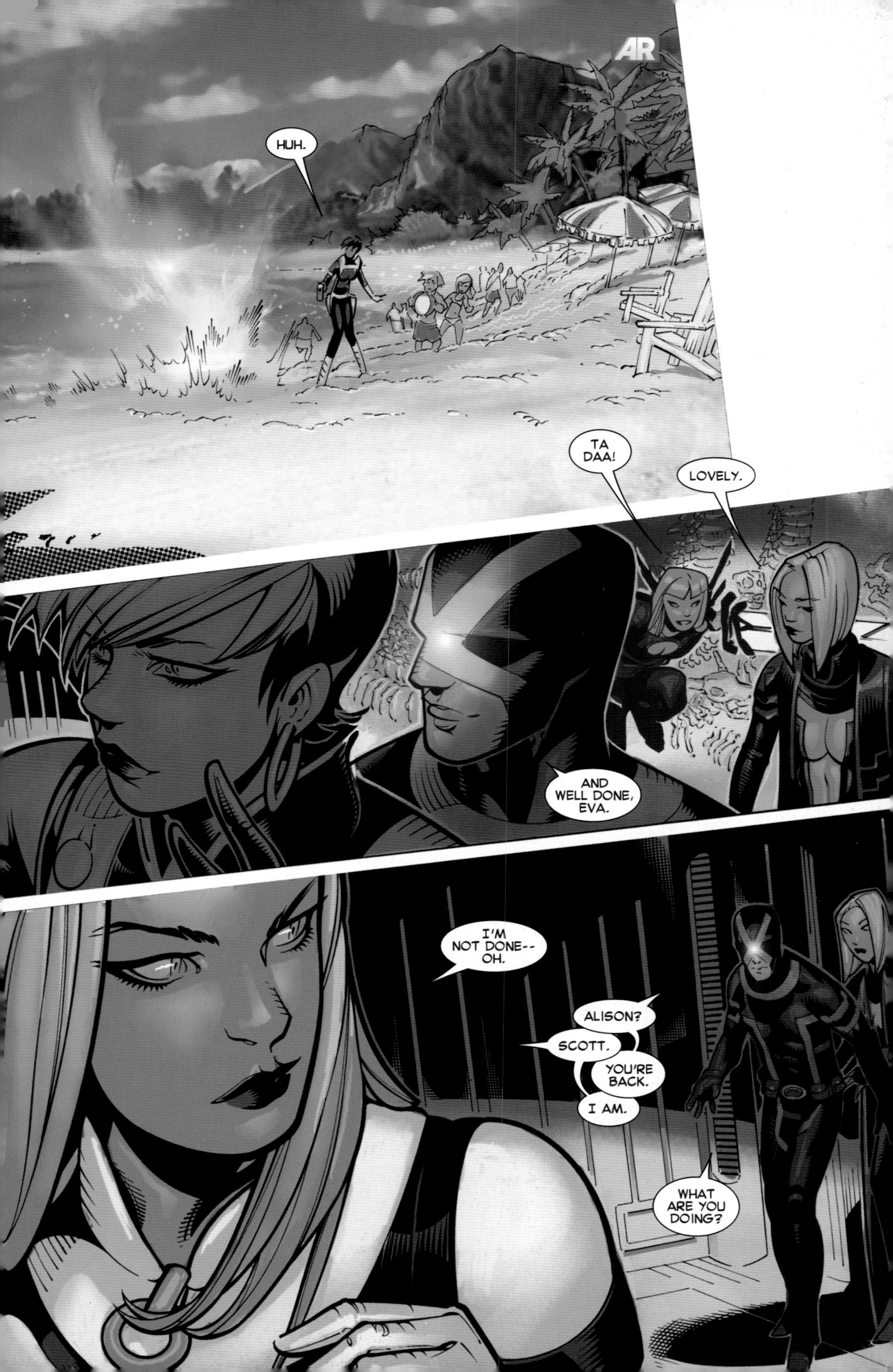
HUH.
TA DAA!
LOVELY.
AND WELL DONE, EVA.
I'M NOT DONE-- OH.
ALISON?
SCOTT.
YOU'RE BACK.
I AM.
WHAT ARE YOU DOING?

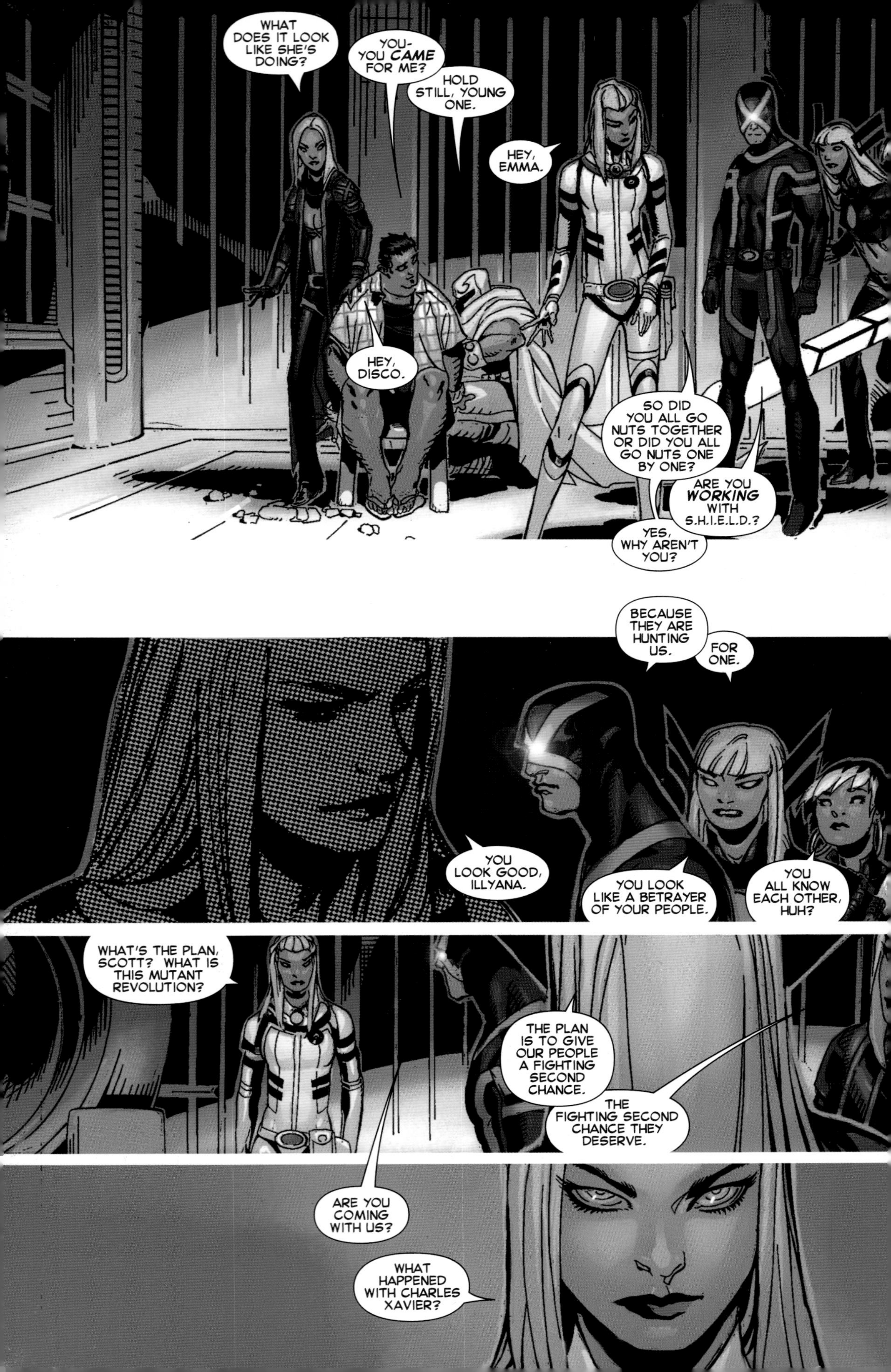
WHAT DOES IT LOOK LIKE SHE'S DOING?
YOU- YOU *CAME* FOR ME?
HOLD STILL, YOUNG ONE.
HEY, EMMA.
HEY, DISCO.
SO DID YOU ALL GO NUTS TOGETHER OR DID YOU ALL GO NUTS ONE BY ONE?
ARE YOU *WORKING* WITH S.H.I.E.L.D.?
YES, WHY AREN'T YOU?
BECAUSE THEY ARE HUNTING US.
FOR ONE.
YOU LOOK GOOD, ILLYANA.
YOU LOOK LIKE A BETRAYER OF YOUR PEOPLE.
YOU ALL KNOW EACH OTHER, HUH?
WHAT'S THE PLAN, SCOTT? WHAT IS THIS MUTANT REVOLUTION?
THE PLAN IS TO GIVE OUR PEOPLE A FIGHTING SECOND CHANCE.
THE FIGHTING SECOND CHANCE THEY DESERVE.
ARE YOU COMING WITH US?
WHAT HAPPENED WITH CHARLES XAVIER?

YOU KNOW, RIGHT NOW, YOU LOOK LIKE THE UNCLE TOM OF THE MUTANTS.

IT'S TERRIBLE AND IT'S COMPLICATED.

COME ON...

YOU THINK I'M COMING WITH *YOU?*

AND THAT WOULD MAKE YOU WHAT?

THE SIRHAN SIRHAN OF THE MUTANTS?

THAT WASN'T VERY NICE.

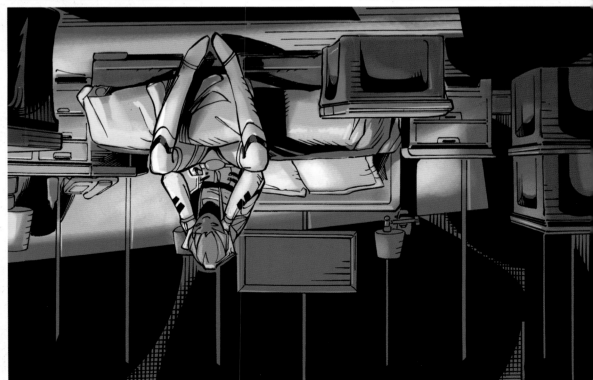

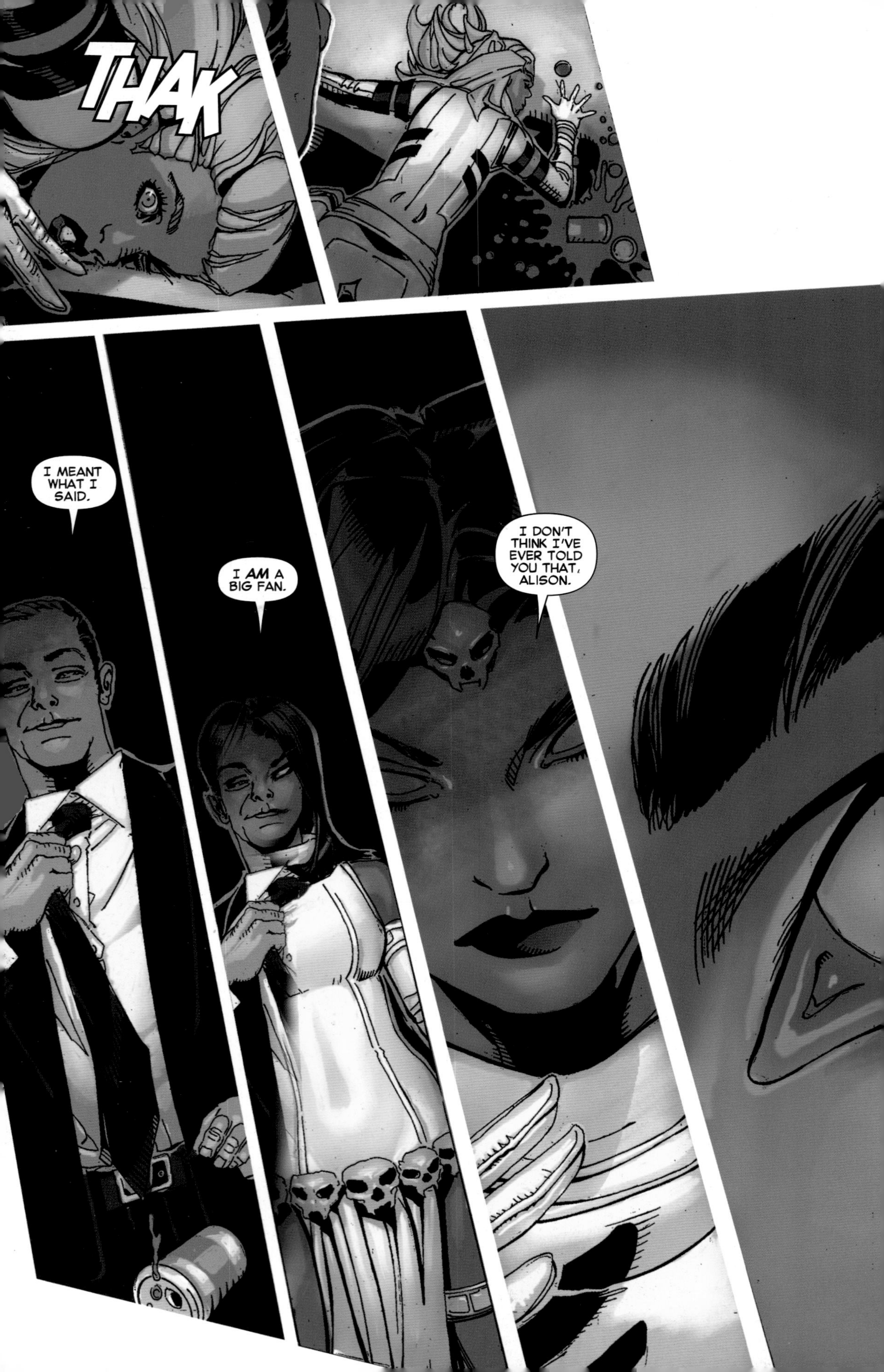
THAK
I MEANT WHAT I SAID.
I AM A BIG FAN.
I DON'T THINK I'VE EVER TOLD YOU THAT, ALISON.

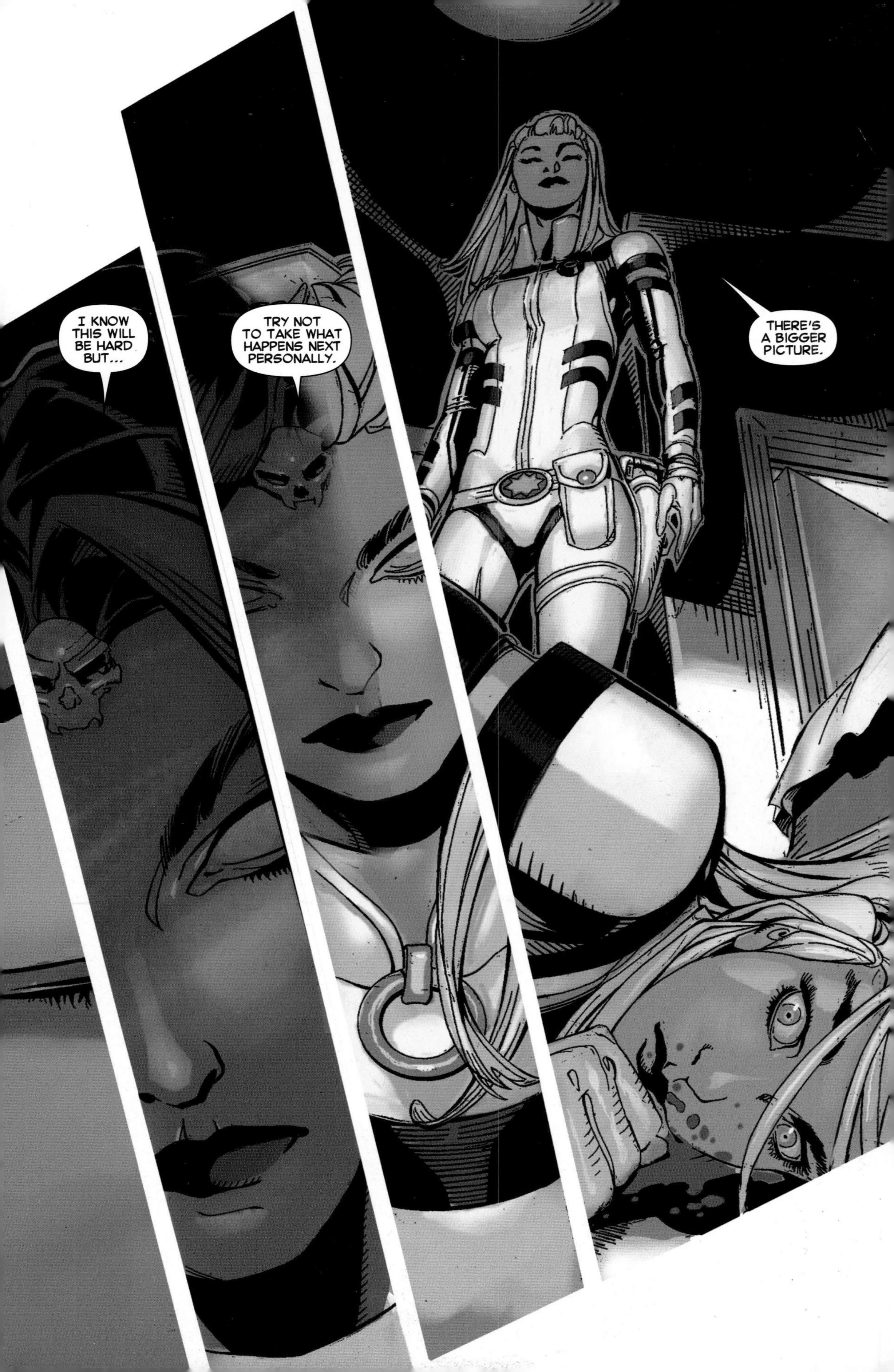
I KNOW THIS WILL BE HARD BUT...
TRY NOT TO TAKE WHAT HAPPENS NEXT PERSONALLY.
THERE'S A BIGGER PICTURE.

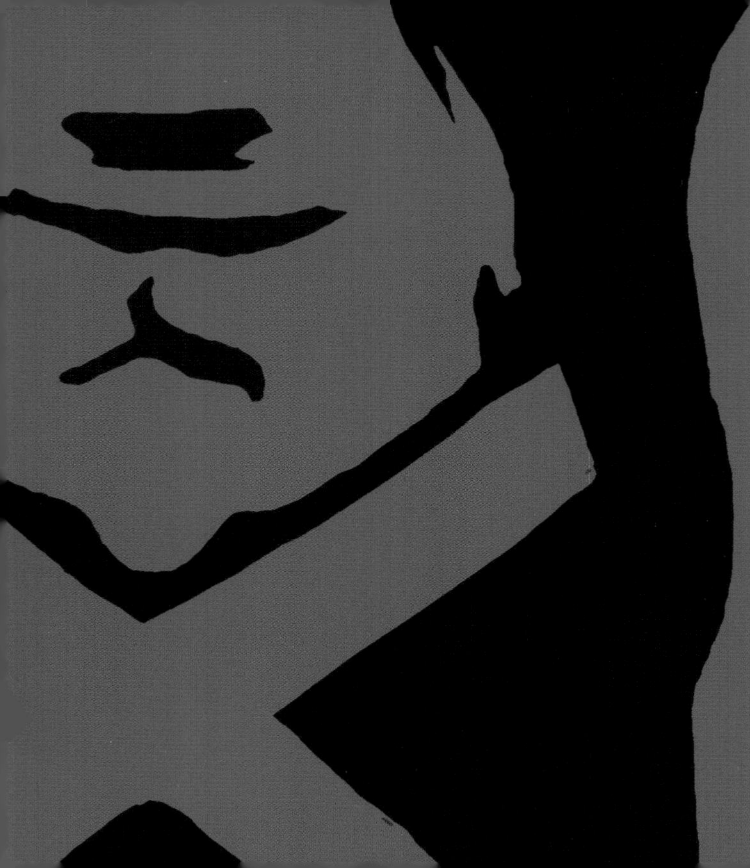

UNCANNY X-MEN #10

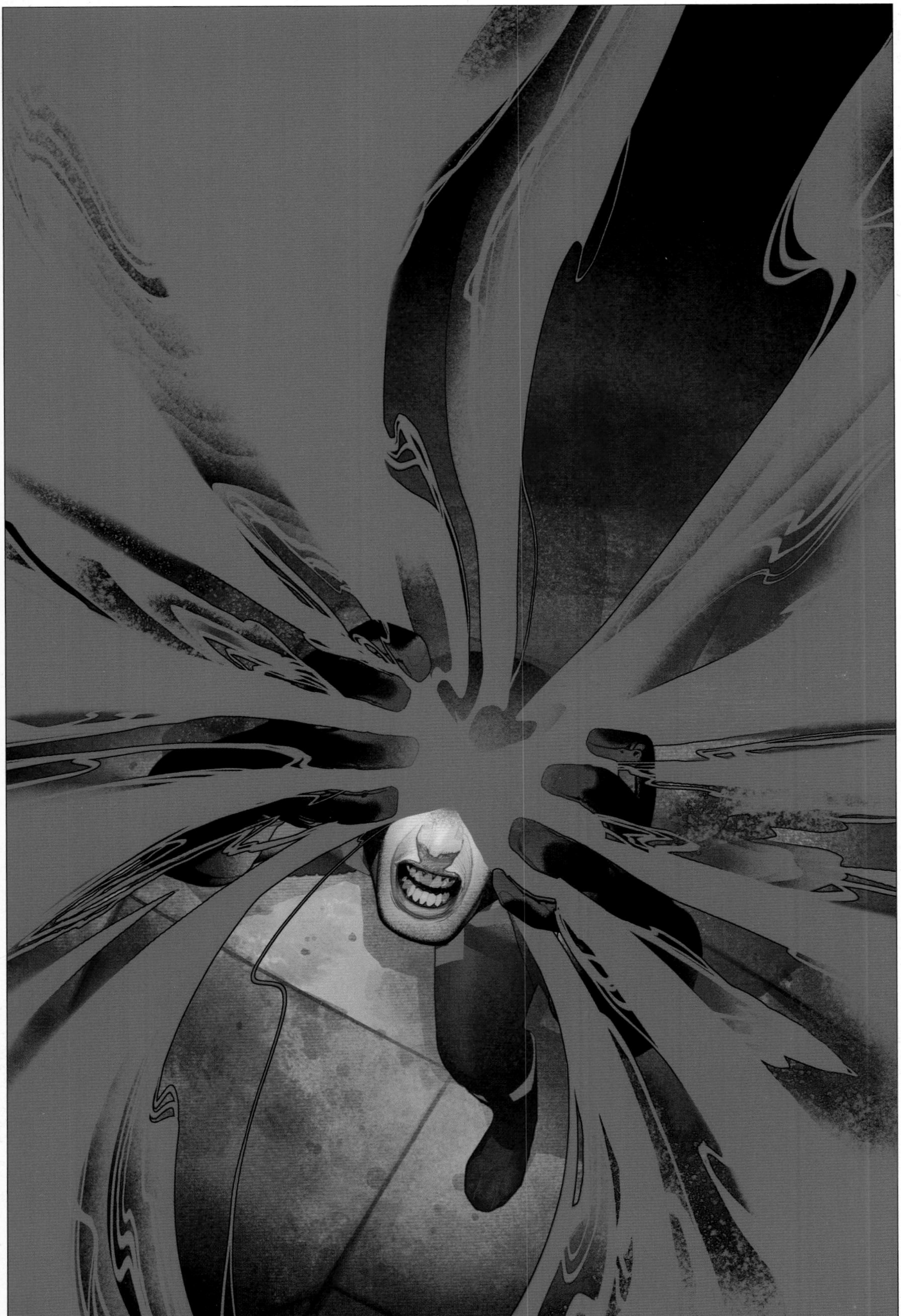

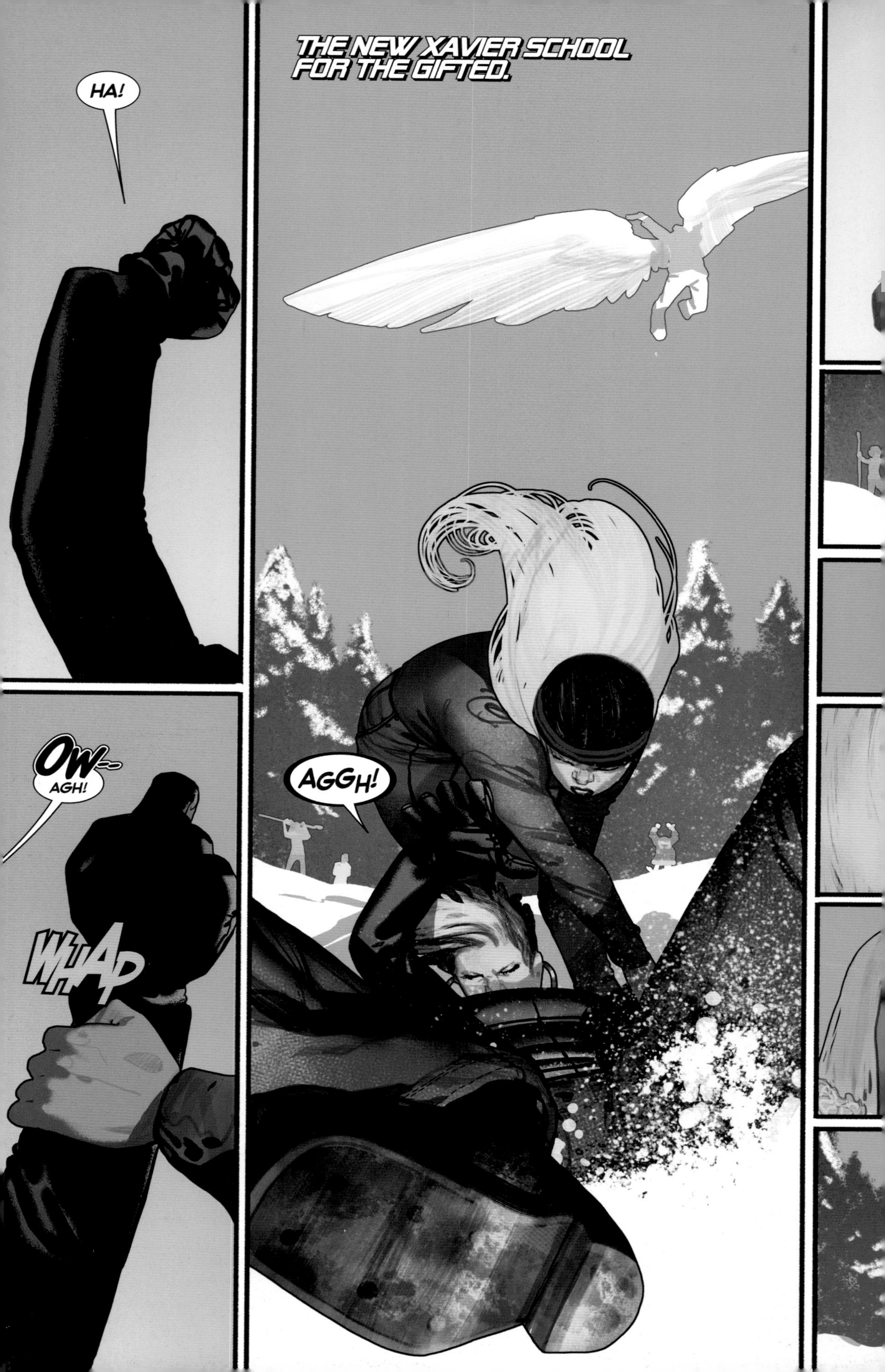
THE NEW XAVIER SCHOOL FOR THE GIFTED.
HA!
AGGH!
OW--
AGH!
WHAP

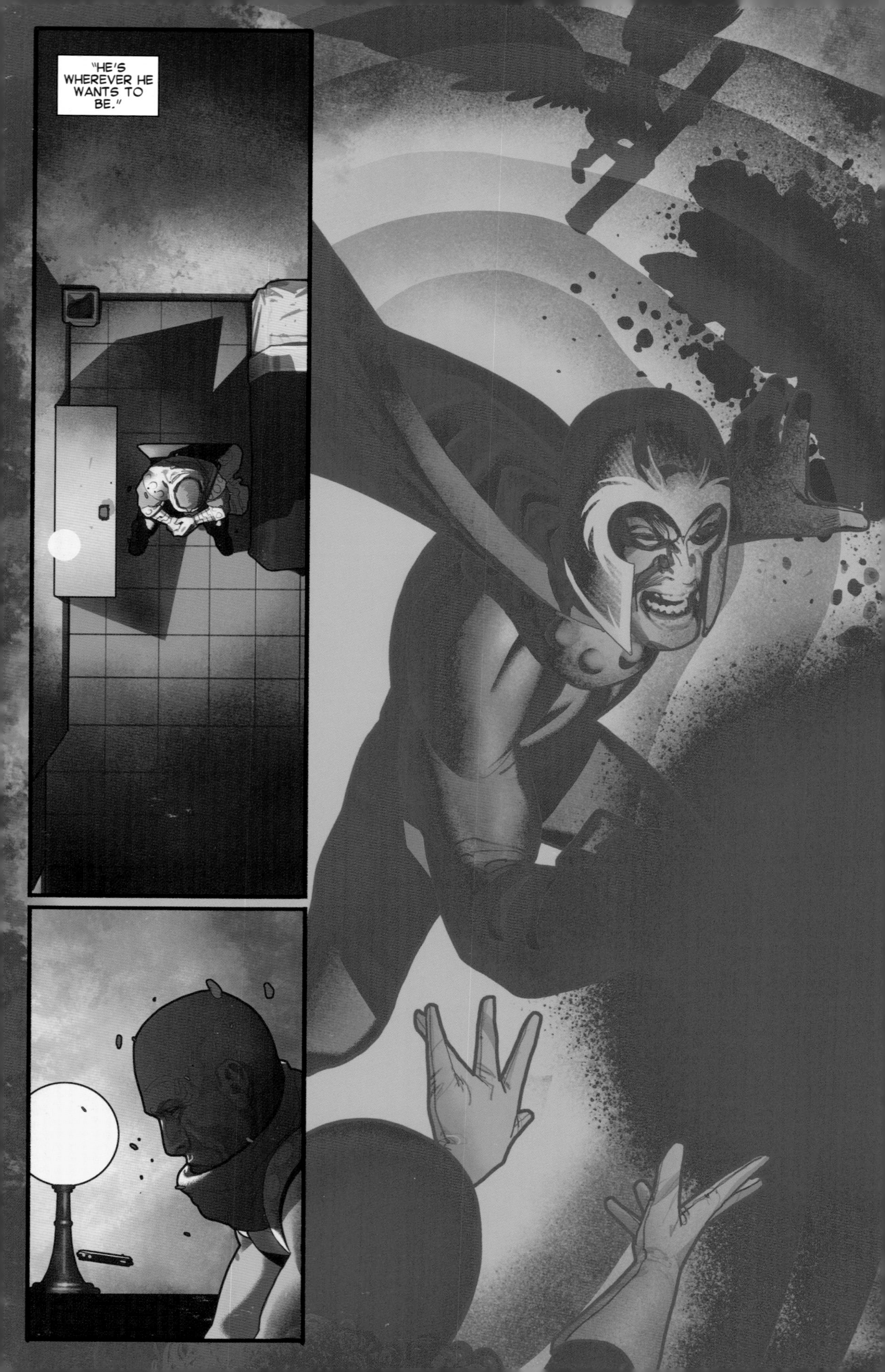
"HE'S WHEREVER HE WANTS TO BE."

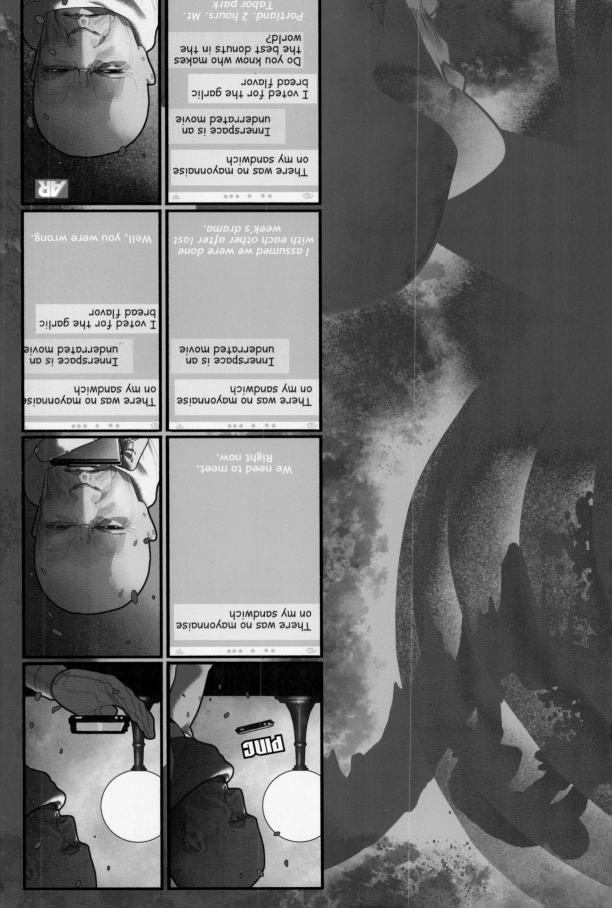

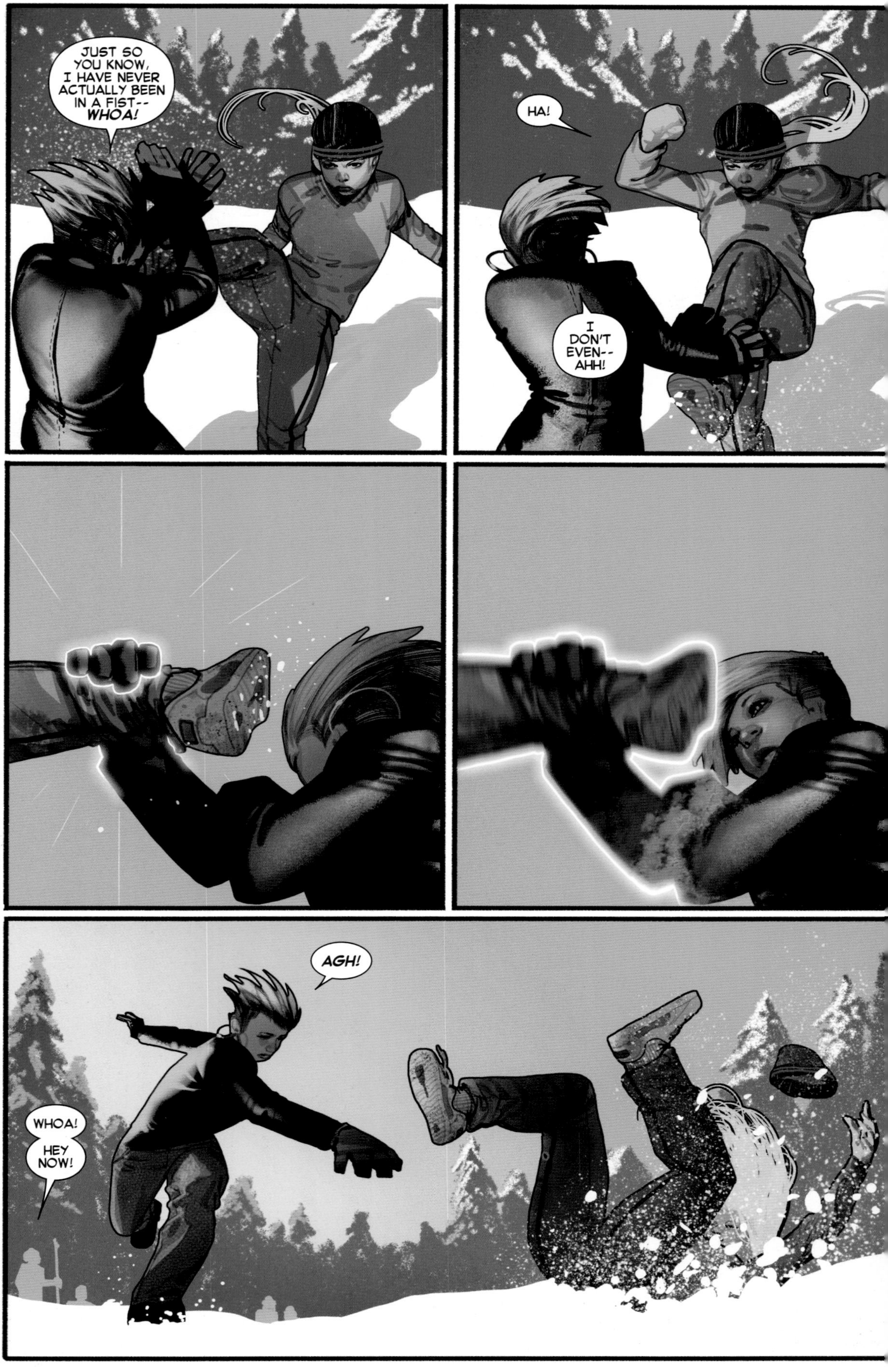
JUST SO YOU KNOW, I HAVE NEVER ACTUALLY BEEN IN A FIST-- *WHOA!*
HA!
I DON'T EVEN-- AHH!
AGH!
WHOA!
HEY NOW!

HOW DO YOU KNOW, CELESTE?

SHE'S NOT.

SHE'S JUST FREAKED OUT.

EVA!

BUT WHAT IF SHE'S RUNNING AWAY?

GIVE HER A MINUTE, CHRISTOPHER.

EVA?!

WE KNEW YOU COULD STOP PEOPLE IN TIME...WE DIDN'T KNOW YOU CAN MOVE THEM IN TIME.

IT'S JUST A LITTLE TIME DISPLACEMENT.

NOTHING HAPPENED?

NOTHING HAPPENED.

EVA, CALM DOWN.

HOW LONG WAS I GONE?

A MINUTE.

DID WE KNOW SHE COULD DO THAT?

NO, WE DID NOT.

I THINK YOU MAY HAVE TRAVELED IN TIME.

WAIT, WHAT--DID SOMETHING JUST HAPPEN?

THAT WAS FAIRLY INSANE.

MAGIK, ARE YOU OKAY?

OH MY GOD!

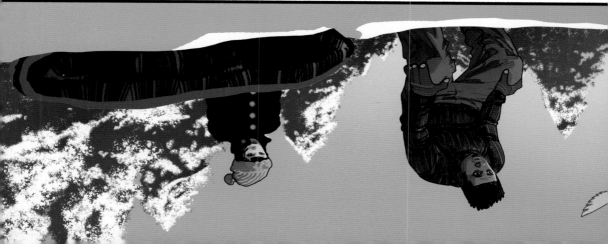

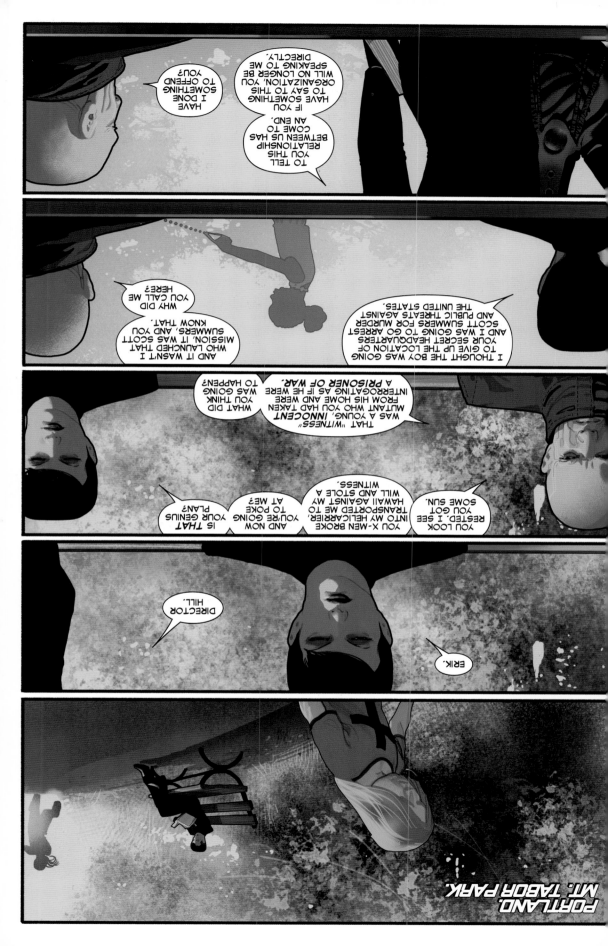

PORTLAND, MT: TABOR PARK.

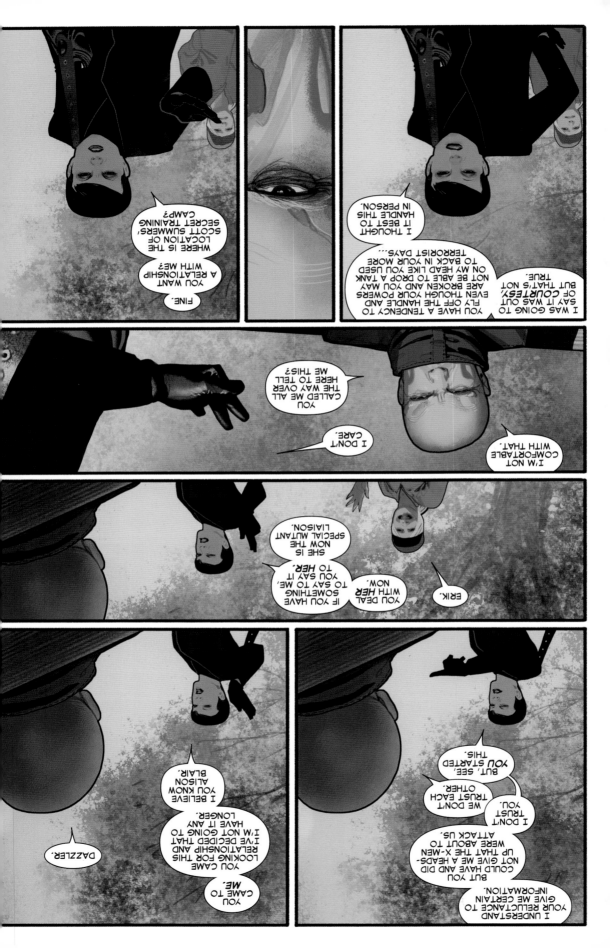

"HOLD ON...."

BRING ME SCOTT SUMMERS. HAVE FUN, KIDS.

YOU CAME TO ME, ERIK. IF YOU HAVE SOMETHING TO SAY, YOU SAY IT TO AGENT BLAIR.

WHO IS BEHIND THE SENTINEL ATTACKS ON MY PEOPLE? AND HOW DO THEY KNOW WHERE WE ARE GOING TO BE BEFORE WE DO?

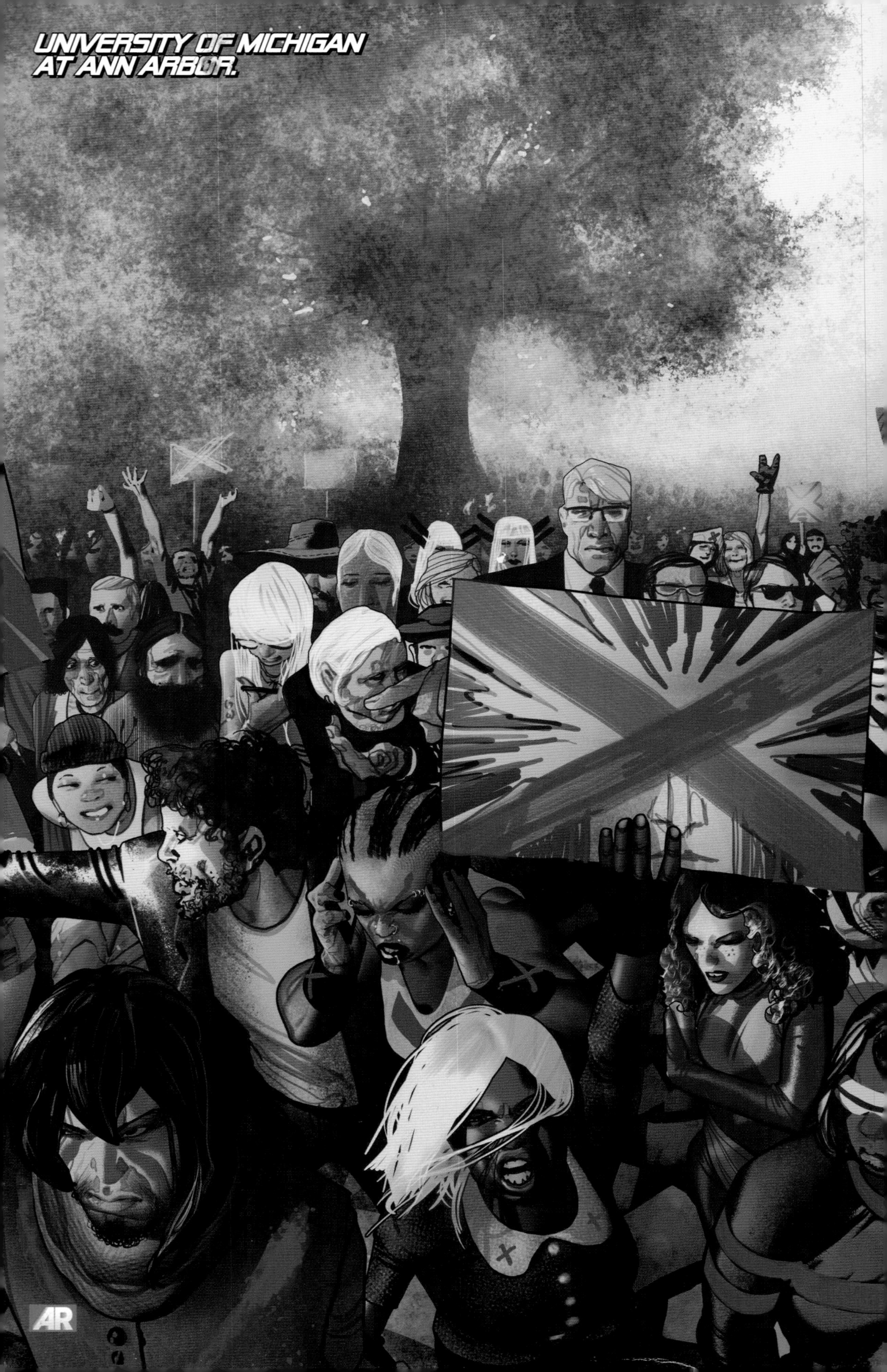
UNIVERSITY OF MICHIGAN
AT ANN ARBOR.
AR

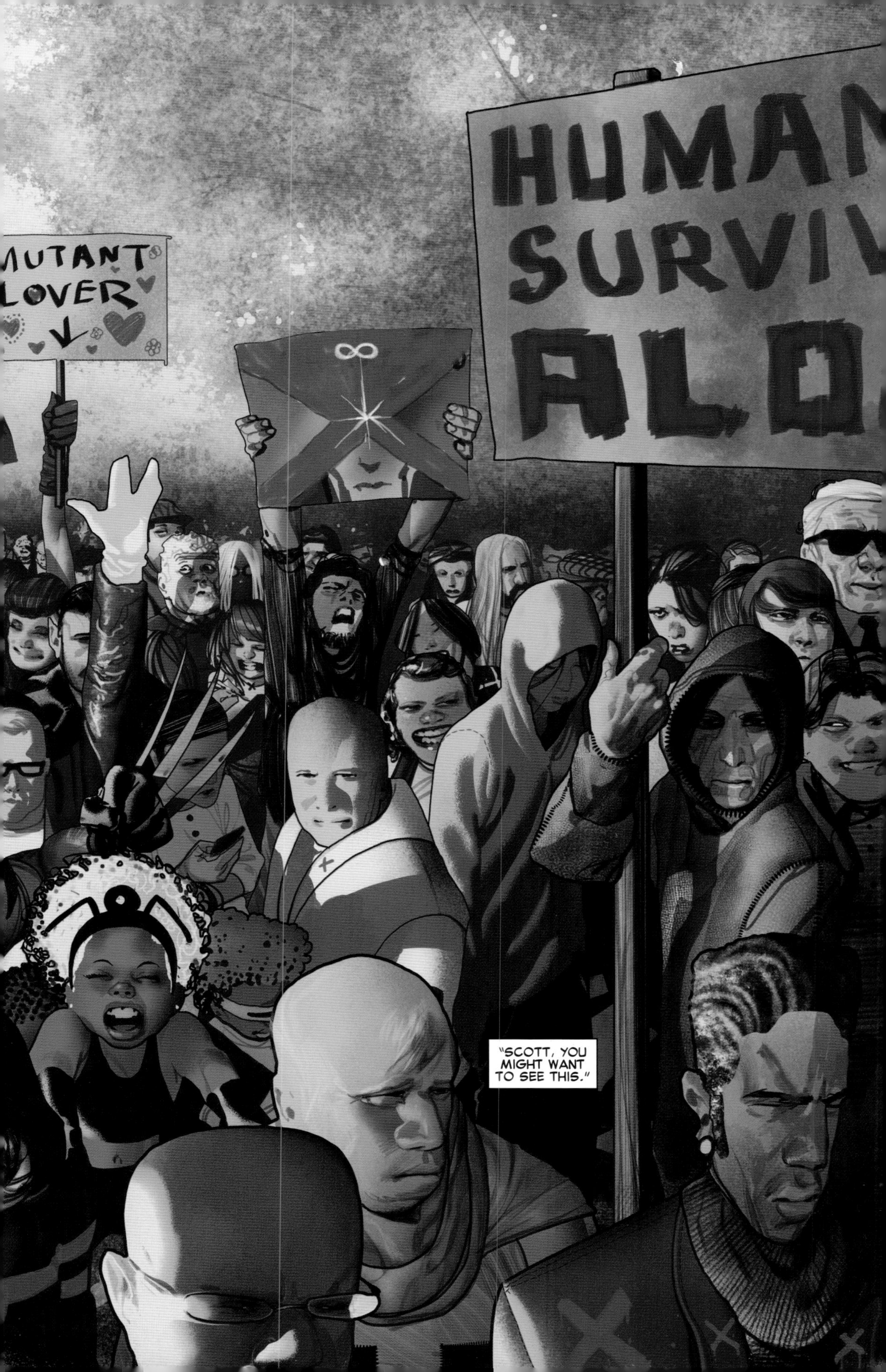

MUTANT LOVER
HUMAN SURVI ALO
"SCOTT, YOU MIGHT WANT TO SEE THIS."

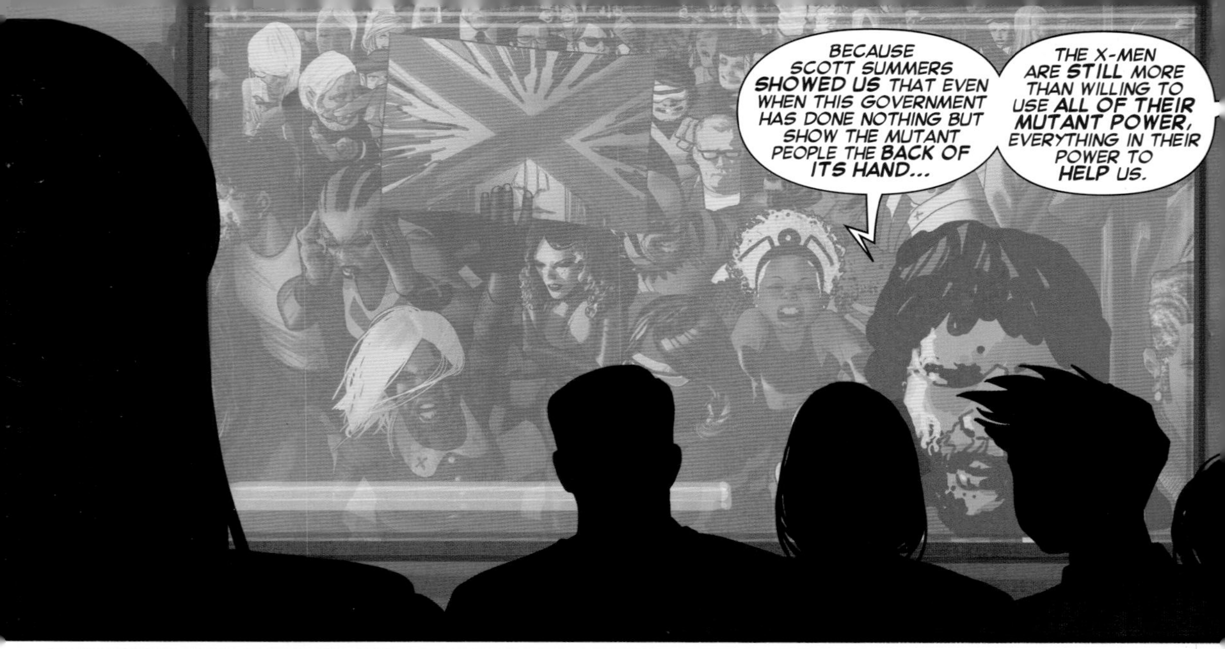
BECAUSE SCOTT SUMMERS SHOWED US THAT EVEN WHEN THIS GOVERNMENT HAS DONE NOTHING BUT SHOW THE MUTANT PEOPLE THE BACK OF ITS HAND...
THE X-MEN ARE STILL MORE THAN WILLING TO USE ALL OF THEIR MUTANT POWER, EVERYTHING IN THEIR POWER TO HELP US.

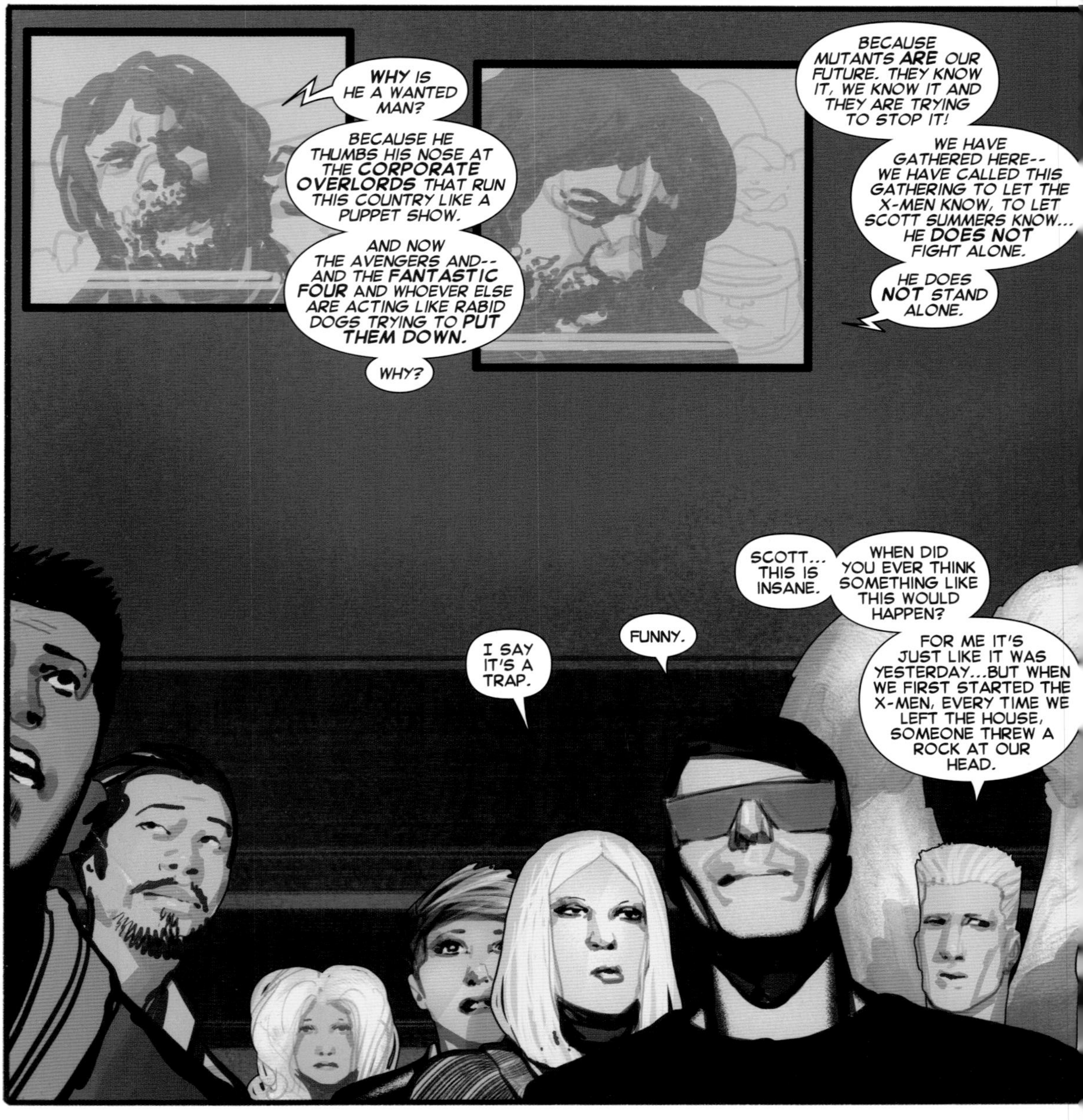
WHY IS HE A WANTED MAN?
BECAUSE HE THUMBS HIS NOSE AT THE CORPORATE OVERLORDS THAT RUN THIS COUNTRY LIKE A PUPPET SHOW.
AND NOW THE AVENGERS AND-- AND THE FANTASTIC FOUR AND WHOEVER ELSE ARE ACTING LIKE RABID DOGS TRYING TO PUT THEM DOWN.
WHY?
BECAUSE MUTANTS ARE OUR FUTURE. THEY KNOW IT, WE KNOW IT AND THEY ARE TRYING TO STOP IT!
WE HAVE GATHERED HERE-- WE HAVE CALLED THIS GATHERING TO LET THE X-MEN KNOW, TO LET SCOTT SUMMERS KNOW... HE DOES NOT FIGHT ALONE.
HE DOES NOT STAND ALONE.
SCOTT... THIS IS INSANE.
WHEN DID YOU EVER THINK SOMETHING LIKE THIS WOULD HAPPEN?
FOR ME IT'S JUST LIKE IT WAS YESTERDAY...BUT WHEN WE FIRST STARTED THE X-MEN, EVERY TIME WE LEFT THE HOUSE, SOMEONE THREW A ROCK AT OUR HEAD.
FUNNY.
I SAY IT'S A TRAP.

"CAN YOU FEEL THAT?"

ALL RIGHT... THE FOLLOWING IS STRICTLY VOLUNTARY.

WHAT ARE YOU GOING TO DO?

LIKE A FRUIT BASKET?

WE SHOULD SEND A MESSAGE BACK.

THIS IS BORDERLINE HISTORIC.

WARREN IS RIGHT.

DID ANYBODY NOTICE THAT THE MINUTE SCOTT SUMMERS AND HIS X-MEN HAD ENOUGH POWER TO CHANGE THE WORLD FOR THE BETTER THEY IMMEDIATELY WENT ABOUT TRYING TO CHANGE THE WORLD FOR THE BETTER?

WHY DID THE AVENGERS TRY TO STOP THEM?

ALL WE KNOW IS THAT SCOTT SUMMERS TRIED TO SAVE THE WORLD AND THEN ALL OF A SUDDEN HE'S A WANTED MAN.

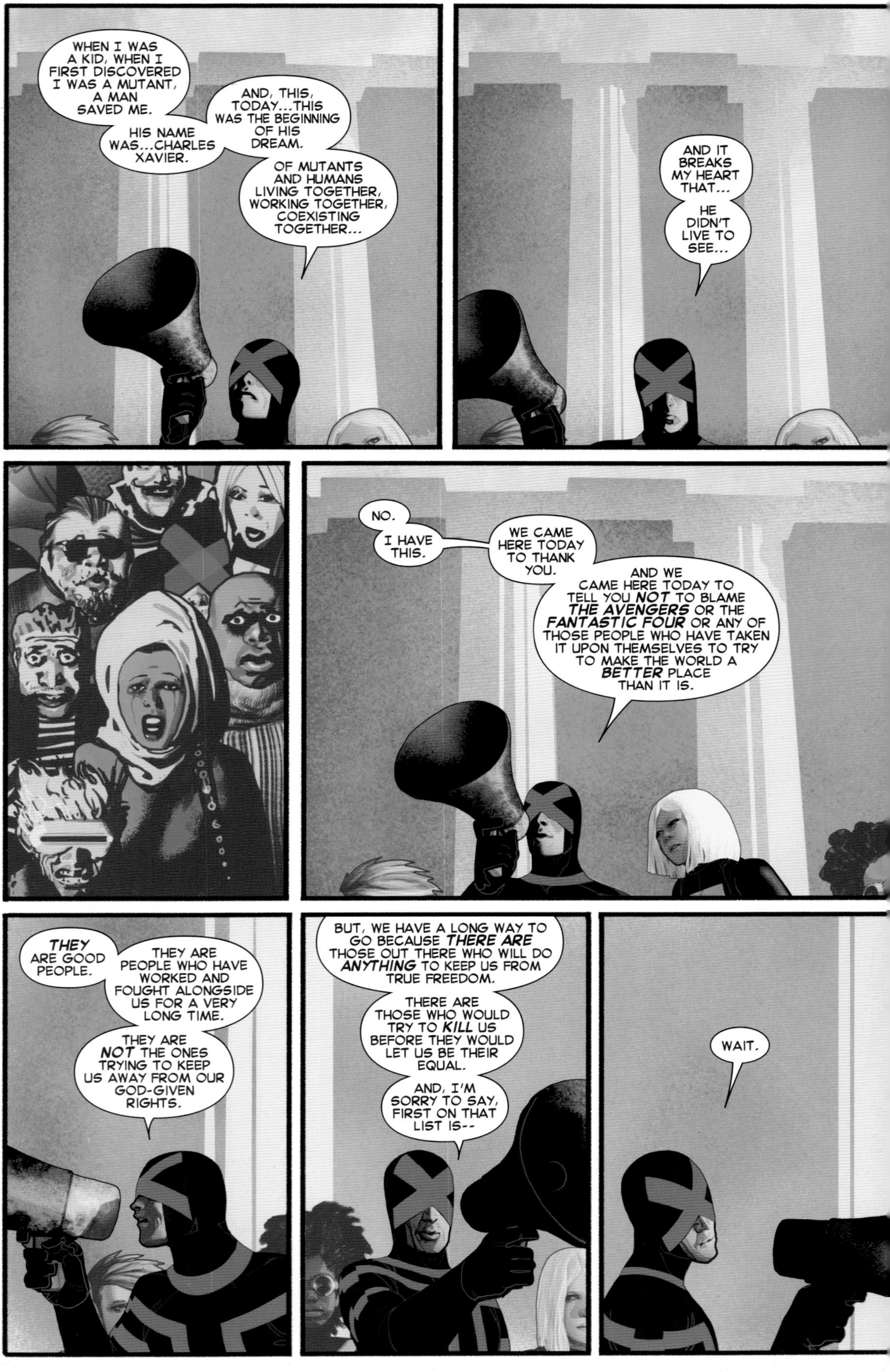
WHEN I WAS A KID, WHEN I FIRST DISCOVERED I WAS A MUTANT, A MAN SAVED ME.
HIS NAME WAS...CHARLES XAVIER.
AND, THIS, TODAY...THIS WAS THE BEGINNING OF HIS DREAM.
OF MUTANTS AND HUMANS LIVING TOGETHER, WORKING TOGETHER, COEXISTING TOGETHER...
AND IT BREAKS MY HEART THAT...
HE DIDN'T LIVE TO SEE...
NO.
I HAVE THIS.
WE CAME HERE TODAY TO THANK YOU.
AND WE CAME HERE TODAY TO TELL YOU NOT TO BLAME THE AVENGERS OR THE FANTASTIC FOUR OR ANY OF THOSE PEOPLE WHO HAVE TAKEN IT UPON THEMSELVES TO TRY TO MAKE THE WORLD A BETTER PLACE THAN IT IS.
THEY ARE GOOD PEOPLE.
THEY ARE PEOPLE WHO HAVE WORKED AND FOUGHT ALONGSIDE US FOR A VERY LONG TIME.
THEY ARE NOT THE ONES TRYING TO KEEP US AWAY FROM OUR GOD-GIVEN RIGHTS.
BUT, WE HAVE A LONG WAY TO GO BECAUSE THERE ARE THOSE OUT THERE WHO WILL DO ANYTHING TO KEEP US FROM TRUE FREEDOM.
THERE ARE THOSE WHO WOULD TRY TO KILL US BEFORE THEY WOULD LET US BE THEIR EQUAL.
AND, I'M SORRY TO SAY, FIRST ON THAT LIST IS--
WAIT.

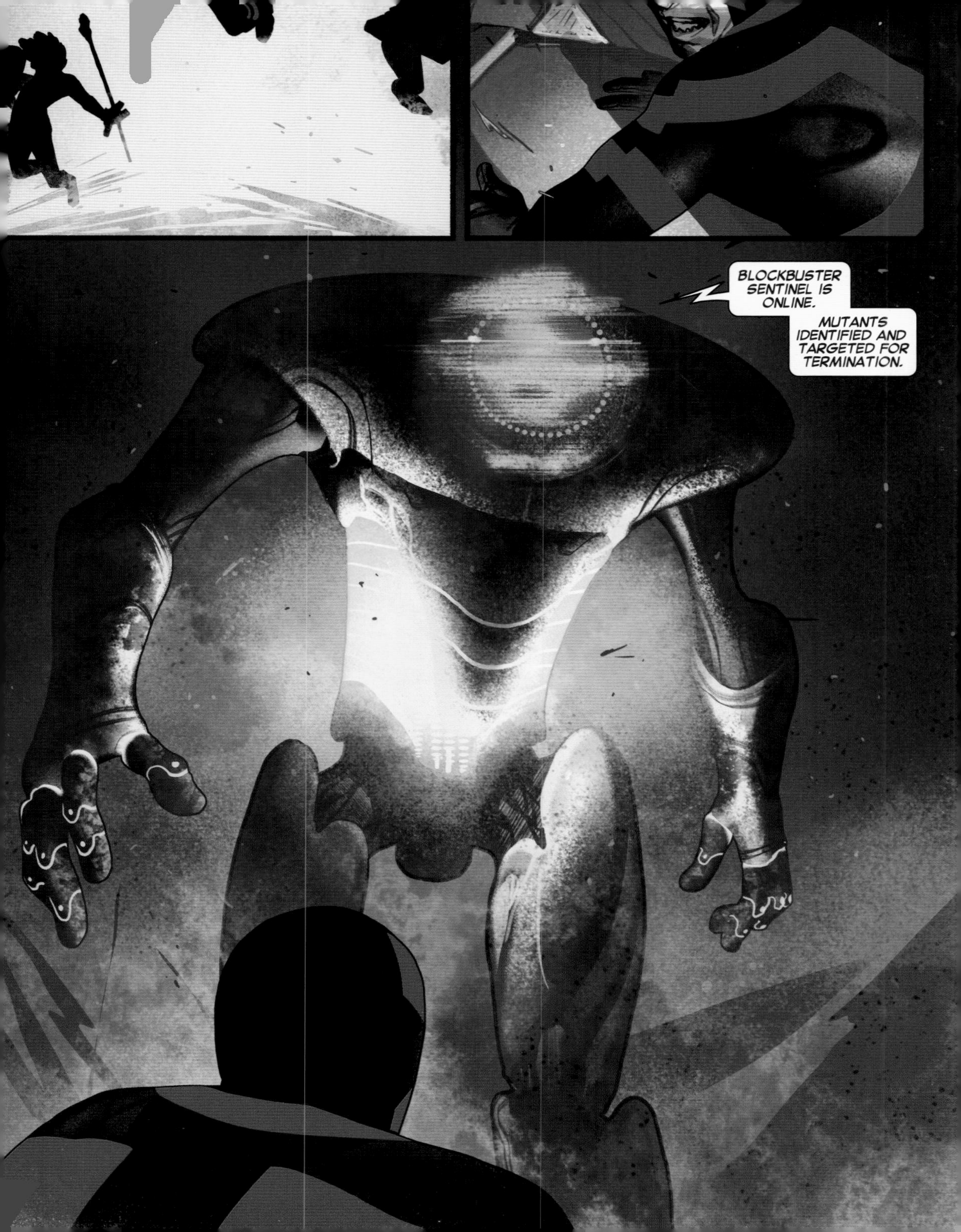
BLOCKBUSTER SENTINEL IS ONLINE.
MUTANTS IDENTIFIED AND TARGETED FOR TERMINATION.

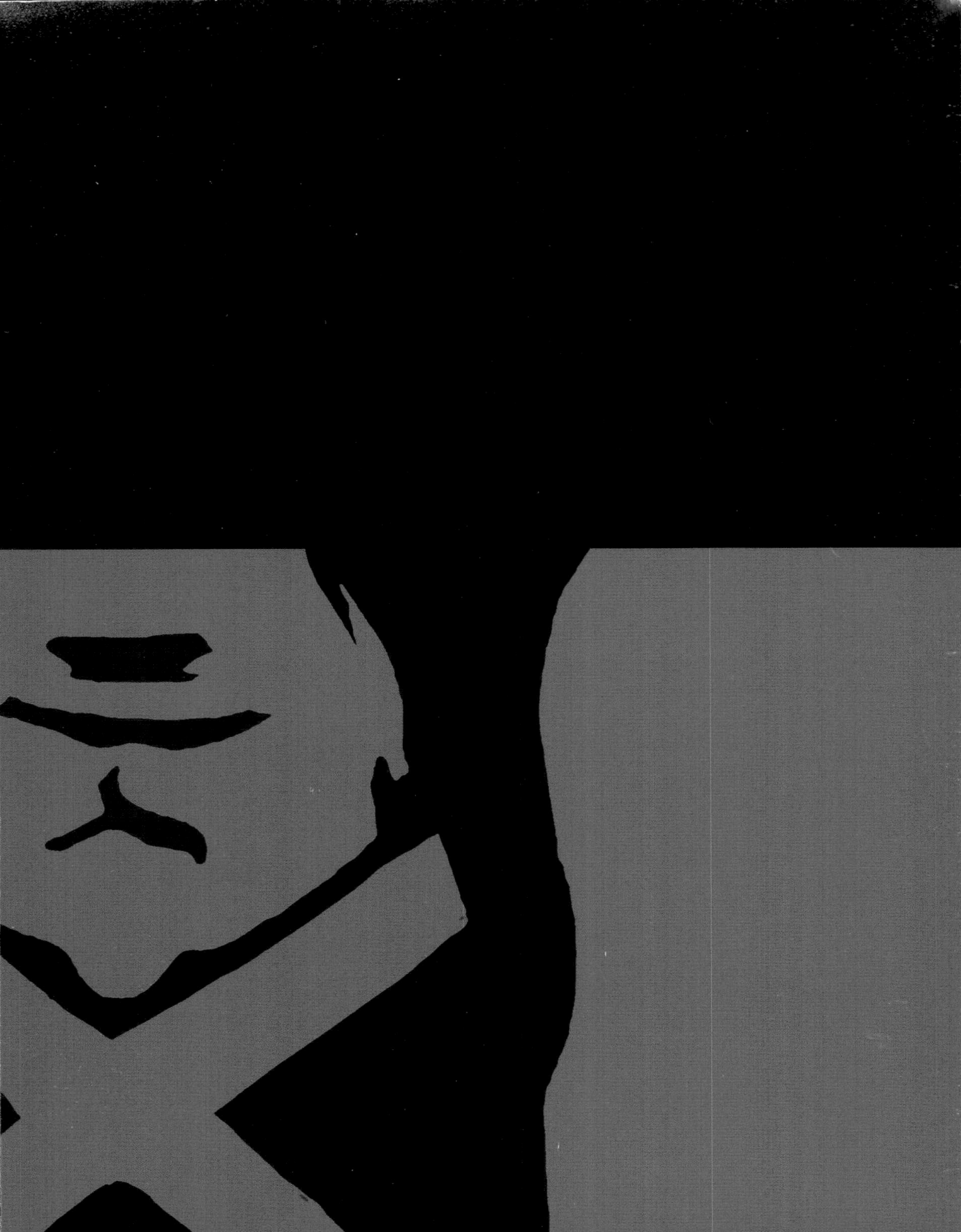

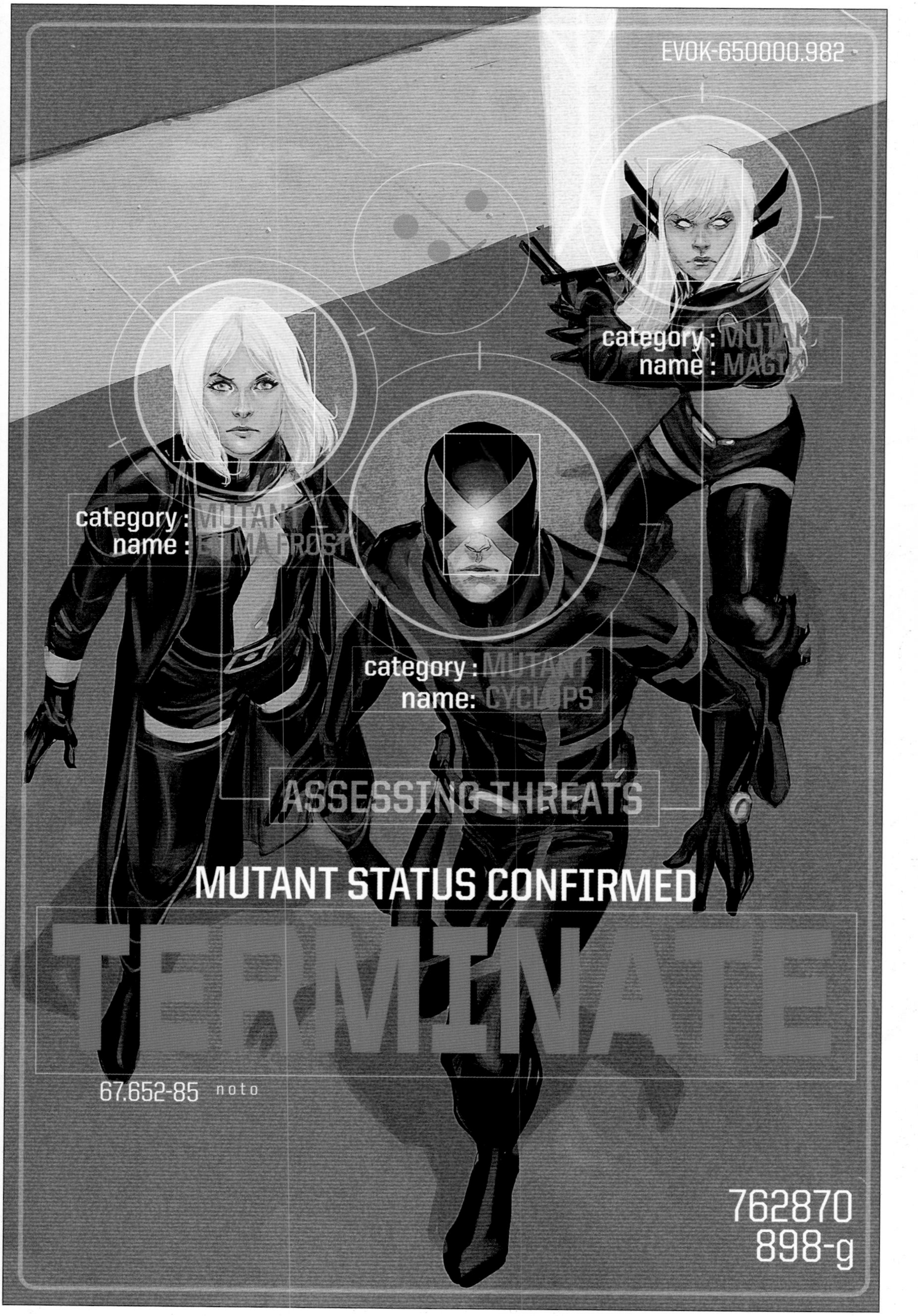

898-9
762870

67652-85 noto

TERMINATE

MUTANT STATUS CONFIRMED

ASSESSING THREATS

name: CYCLOPS
category: MUTANT

name: EMMA FROST
category: MUTANT

name: MAGIK
category: MUTANT

EVOK-650000.982

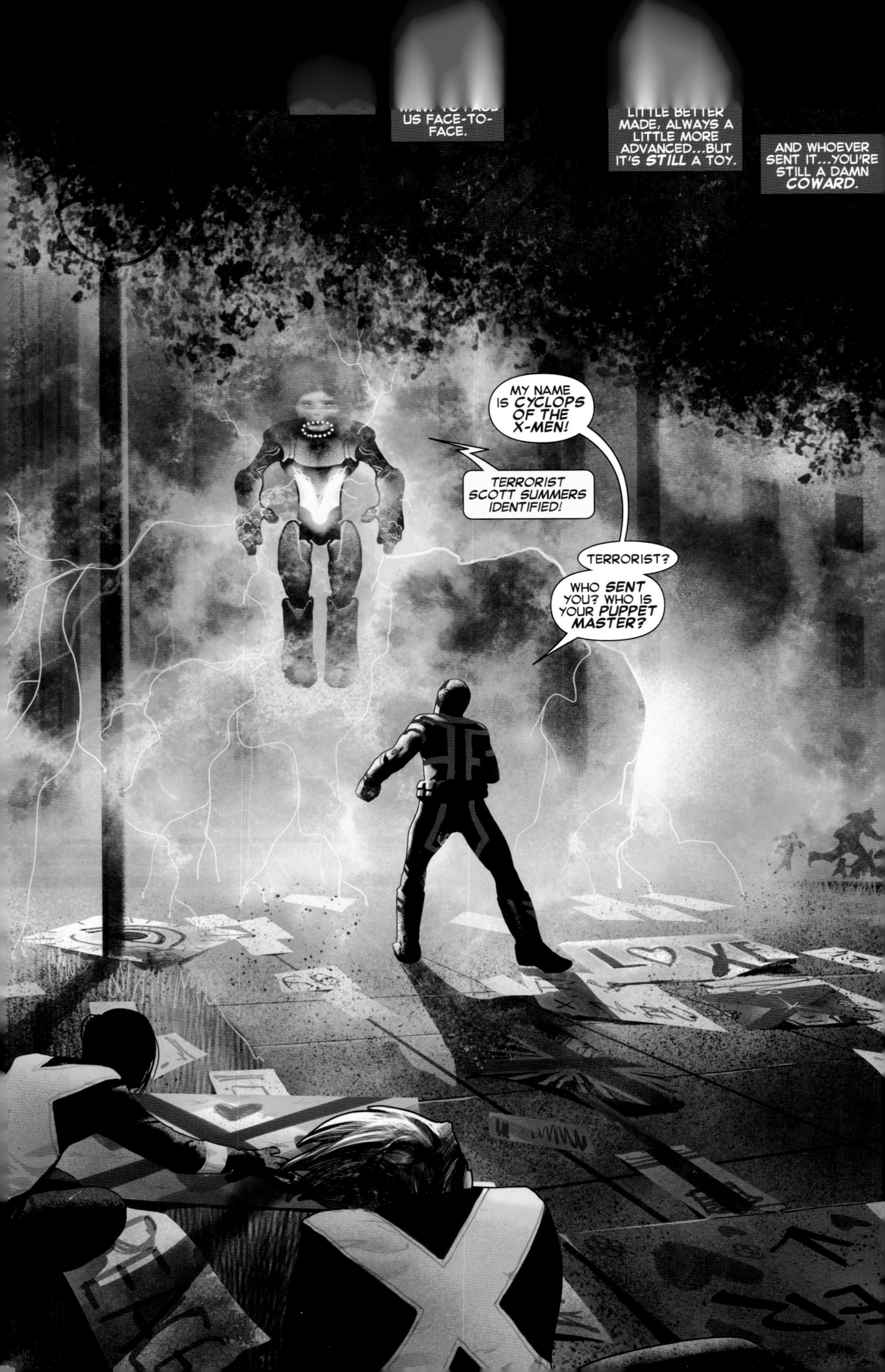
US FACE-TO-FACE.
MADE, ALWAYS A LITTLE MORE ADVANCED...BUT IT'S STILL A TOY.
AND WHOEVER SENT IT...YOU'RE STILL A DAMN COWARD.
MY NAME IS CYCLOPS OF THE X-MEN!
TERRORIST SCOTT SUMMERS IDENTIFIED!
TERRORIST?
WHO SENT YOU? WHO IS YOUR PUPPET MASTER?
LOVE

THE WHITE QUEEN.

I HOPE THIS HURTS LIKE HELL!

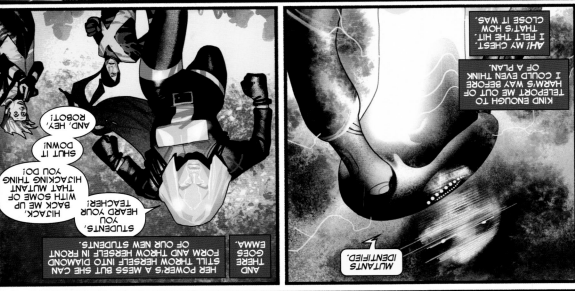

MUTANTS IDENTIFIED.

AH! MY CHEST. I FELT THE HIT. THAT'S HOW CLOSE IT WAS.

KIND ENOUGH TO TELEPORT ME OUT OF HARM'S WAY BEFORE I COULD EVEN THINK OF A PLAN.

HER POWER'S A MESS BUT SHE CAN STILL THROW HERSELF INTO DIAMOND FORM AND THROW HERSELF IN FRONT OF OUR NEW STUDENTS.

AND THERE GOES EMMA.

STUDENTS, YOU HEARD YOUR TEACHER!

HIJACK, BACK ME UP WITH SOME OF THAT MUTANT HIJACKING THING YOU DO!

SHUT IT DOWN!

AND, HEY, ROBOT!

ILLYANA RASPUTIN!

SAVED MY LIFE WITHOUT ME EVEN HAVING TO ASK.

GET THE CIVILIANS OUT OF HERE!

SECURE A PERIMETER AND LET'S TAKE THIS THING TO ROBOT HELL!

THAT WAS A HELL OF A NICE SAVE, ILLYANA.

DOESN'T GET ANY CLOSER.

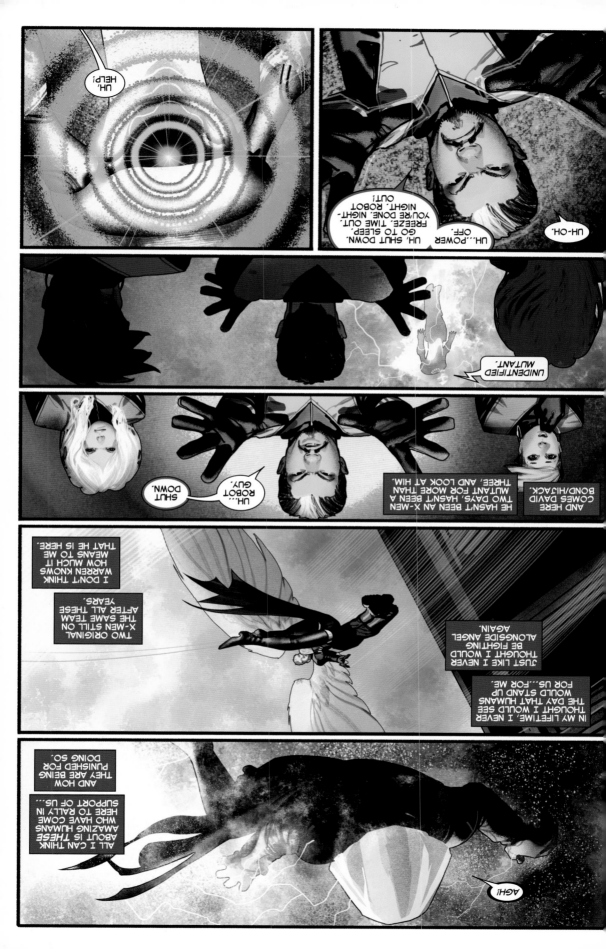

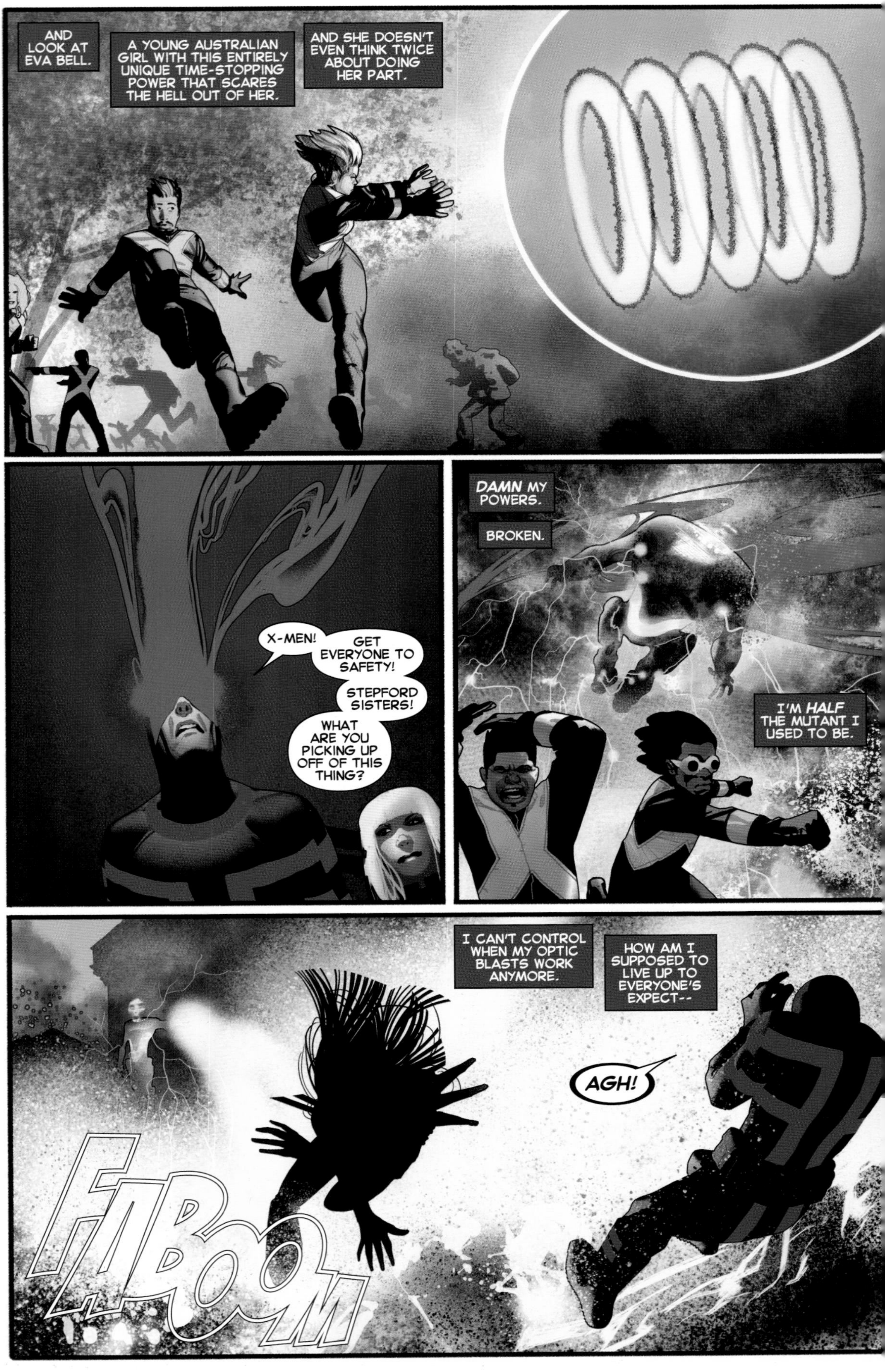
AND LOOK AT EVA BELL.
A YOUNG AUSTRALIAN GIRL WITH THIS ENTIRELY UNIQUE TIME-STOPPING POWER THAT SCARES THE HELL OUT OF HER.
AND SHE DOESN'T EVEN THINK TWICE ABOUT DOING HER PART.
X-MEN!
GET EVERYONE TO SAFETY!
STEPFORD SISTERS!
WHAT ARE YOU PICKING UP OFF OF THIS THING?
DAMN MY POWERS.
BROKEN.
I'M HALF THE MUTANT I USED TO BE.
I CAN'T CONTROL WHEN MY OPTIC BLASTS WORK ANYMORE.
HOW AM I SUPPOSED TO LIVE UP TO EVERYONE'S EXPECT--
AGH!
FTROOM

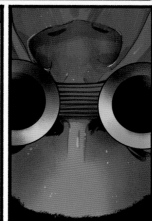

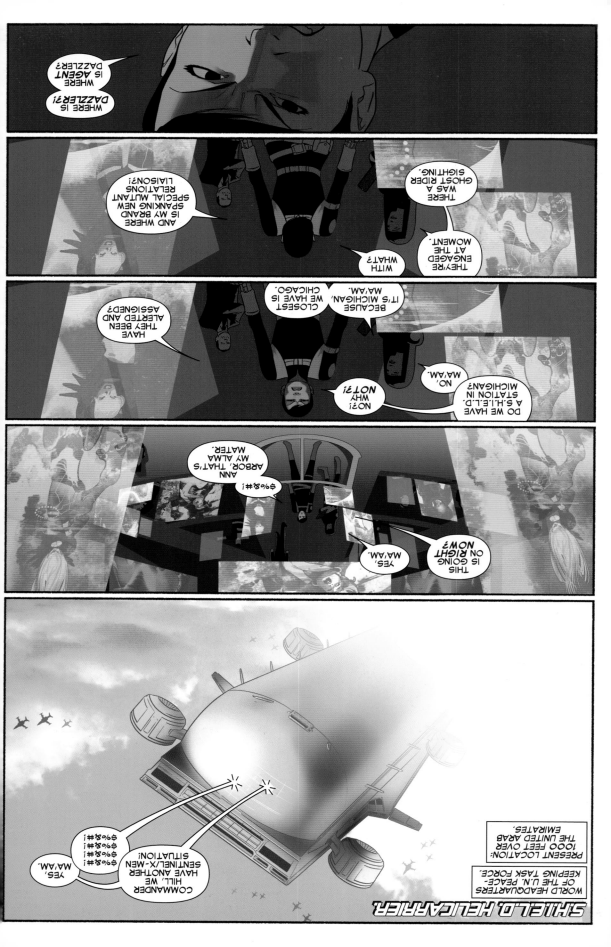

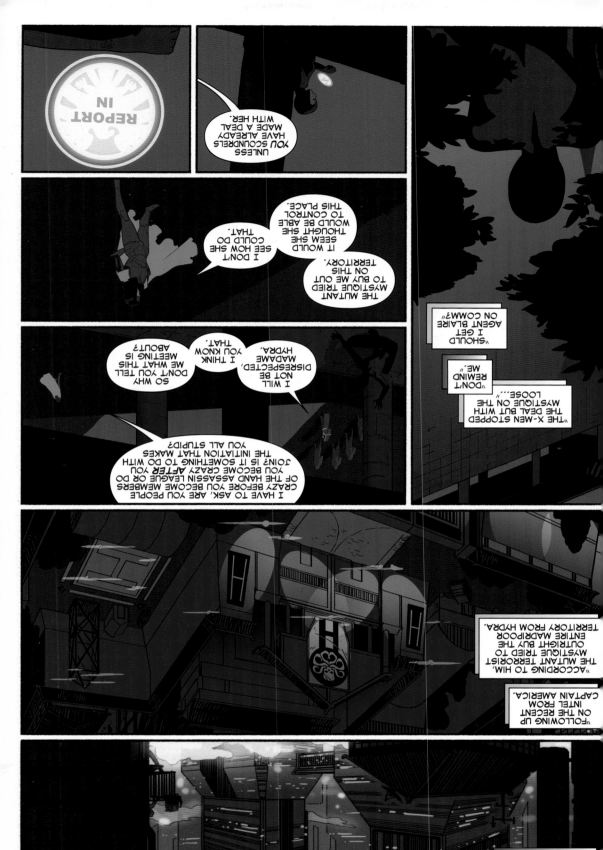

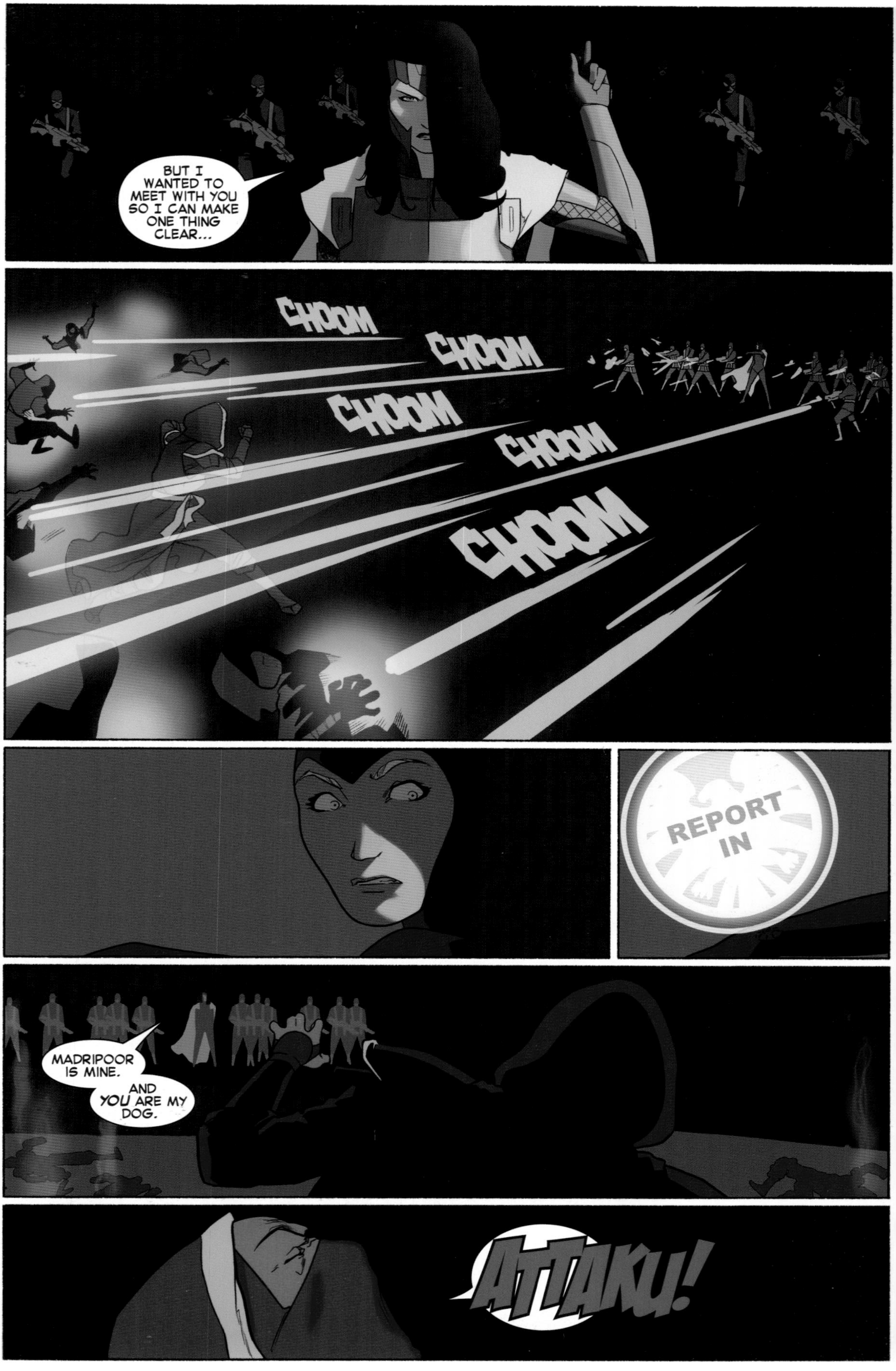
BUT I WANTED TO MEET WITH YOU SO I CAN MAKE ONE THING CLEAR...
CHOOM
CHOOM
CHOOM
CHOOM
CHOOM
REPORT IN
MADRIPOOR IS MINE.
AND *YOU* ARE MY DOG.
ATTAKU!

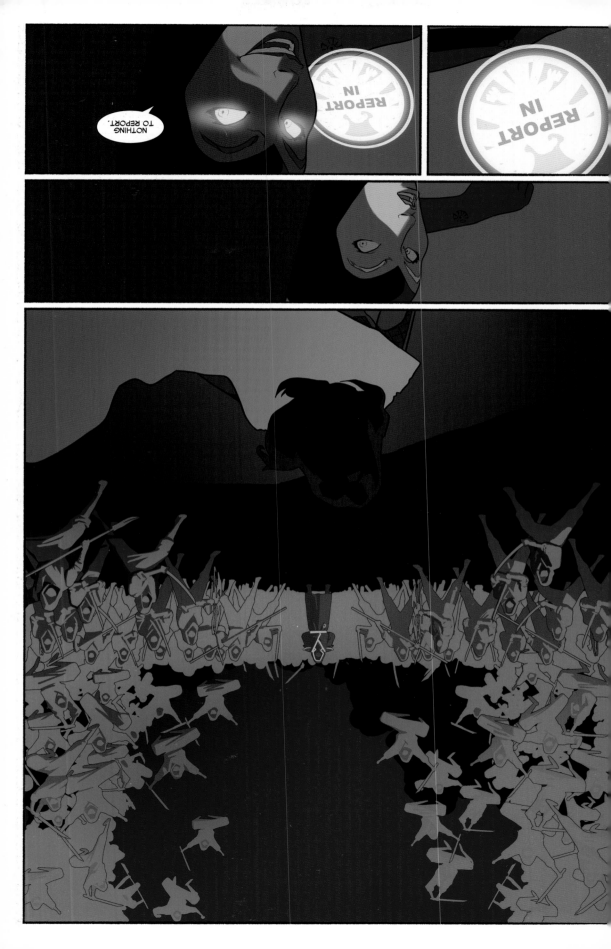

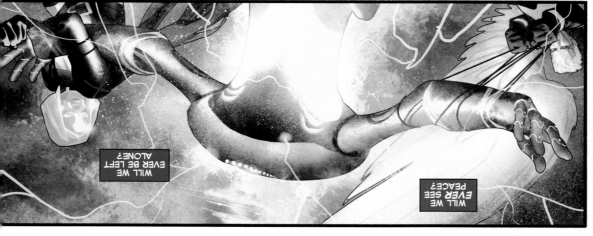

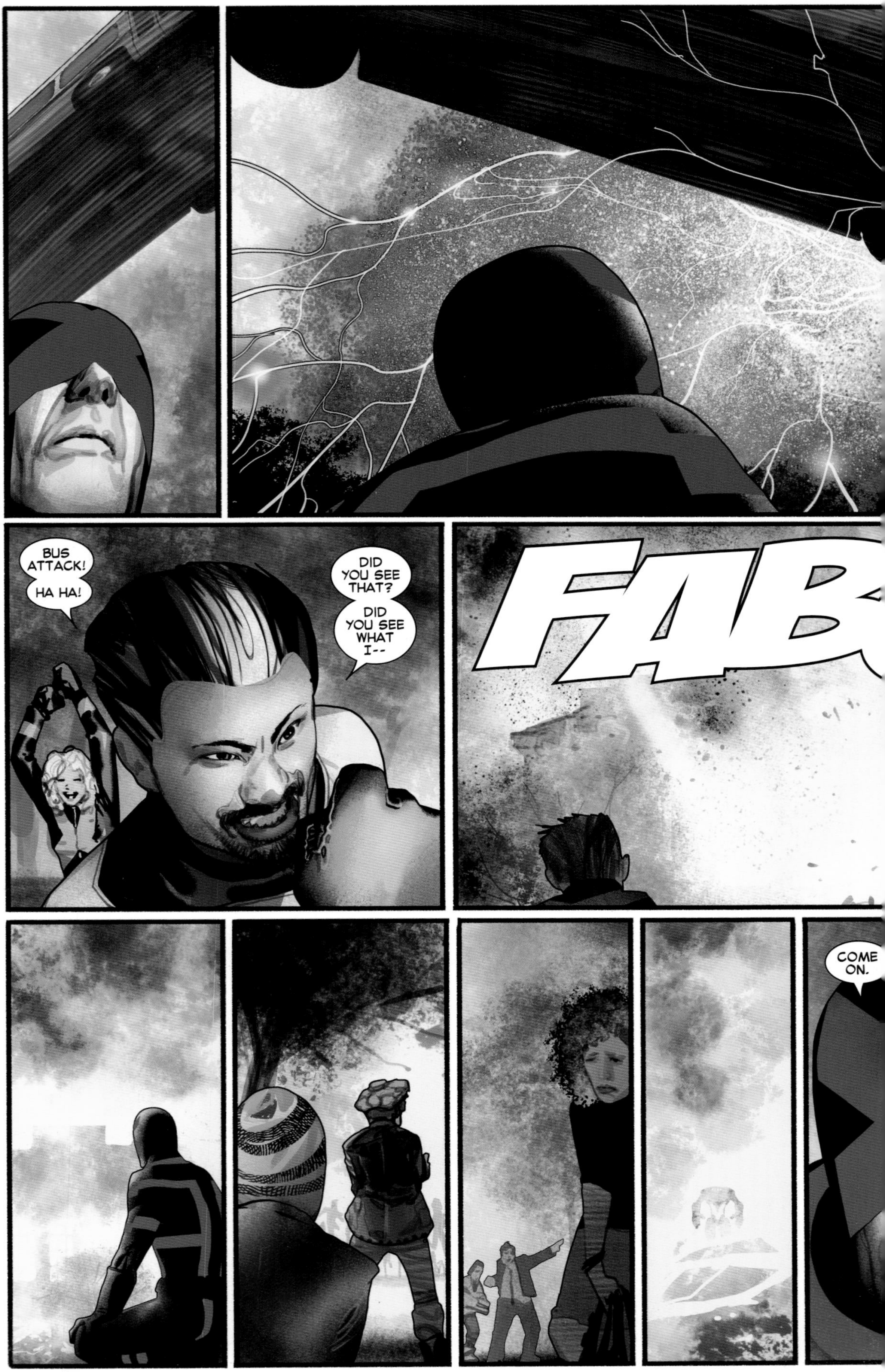
BUS ATTACK!
HA HA!
DID YOU SEE THAT?
DID YOU SEE WHAT I--
FAB
COME ON.

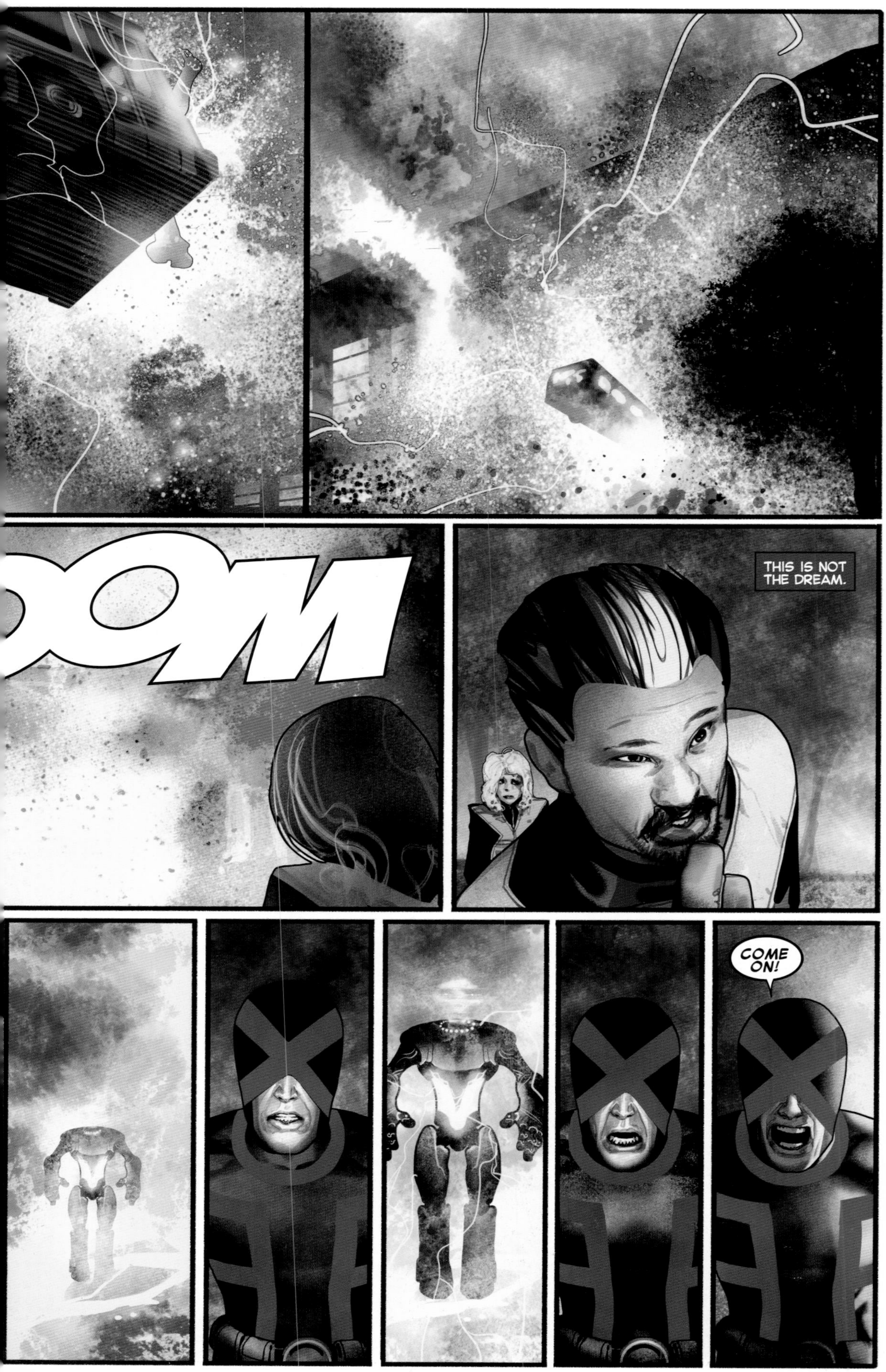
OOM
THIS IS NOT THE DREAM.
COME ON!

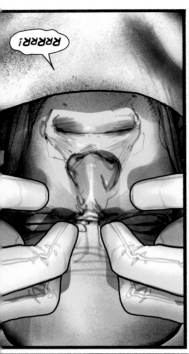

RRRR!

CHUCK CHUCK CHUCK

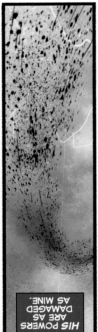

HIS POWERS ARE AS DAMAGED AS MINE.

MAGNETO!

WHERE THE HELL HAVE YOU BEEN?!

YOU ARE RIGHT, ILLYANA. THIS CREATURE IS NOT MADE OF A METAL I CAN CONTROL.

THIS WAS MADE TO KILL US.

SO WE'RE SCREWED?

HARDLY.

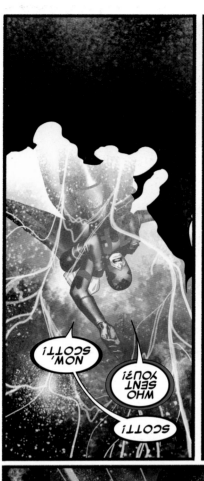

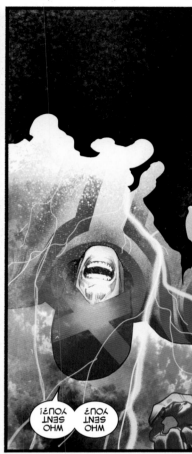

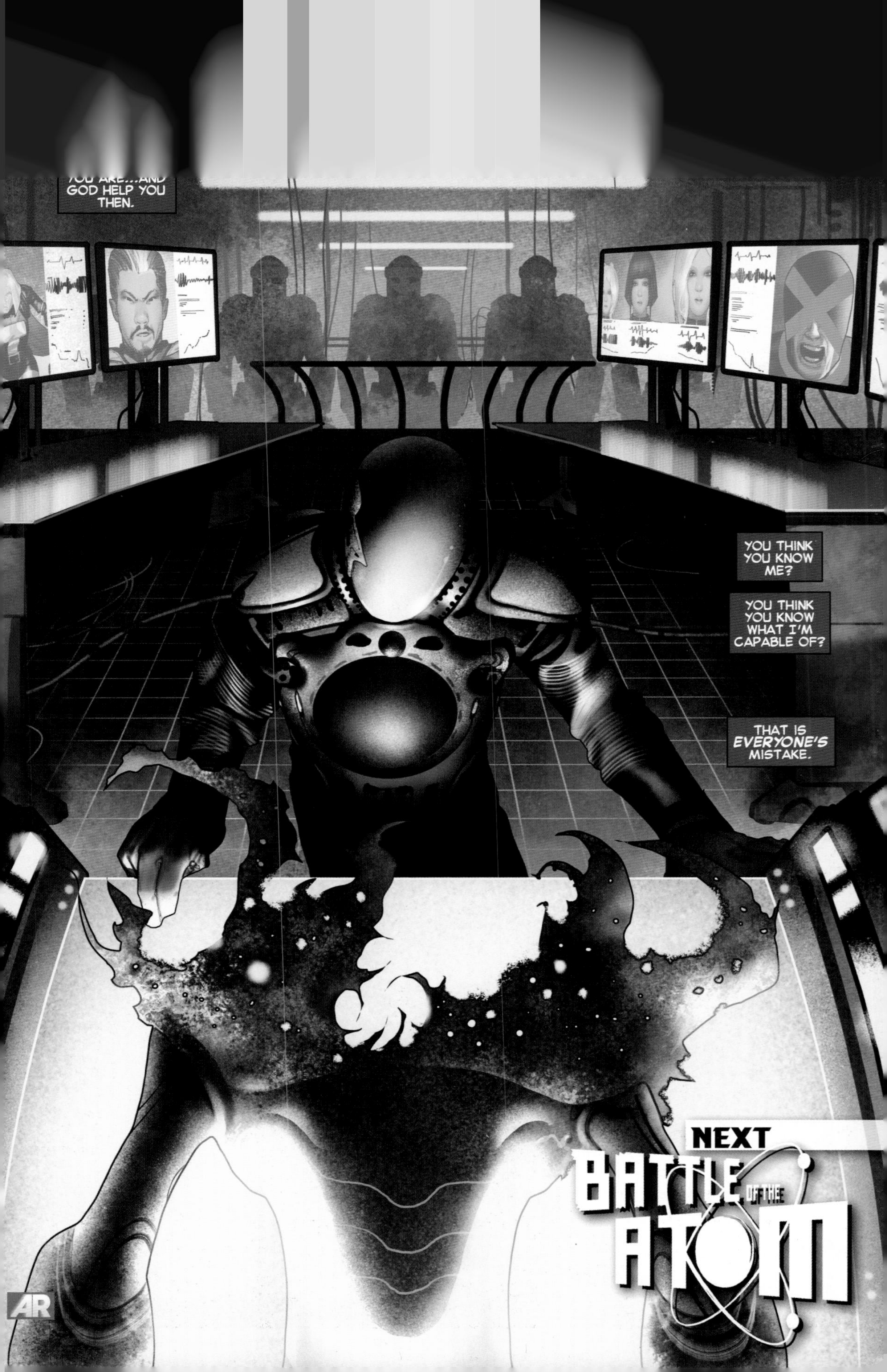
YOU ARE...AND GOD HELP YOU THEN.
YOU THINK YOU KNOW ME?
YOU THINK YOU KNOW WHAT I'M CAPABLE OF?
THAT IS EVERYONE'S MISTAKE.
NEXT
BATTLE OF THE ATOM
AR

UNCANNY X-MEN VARIANT COVERS

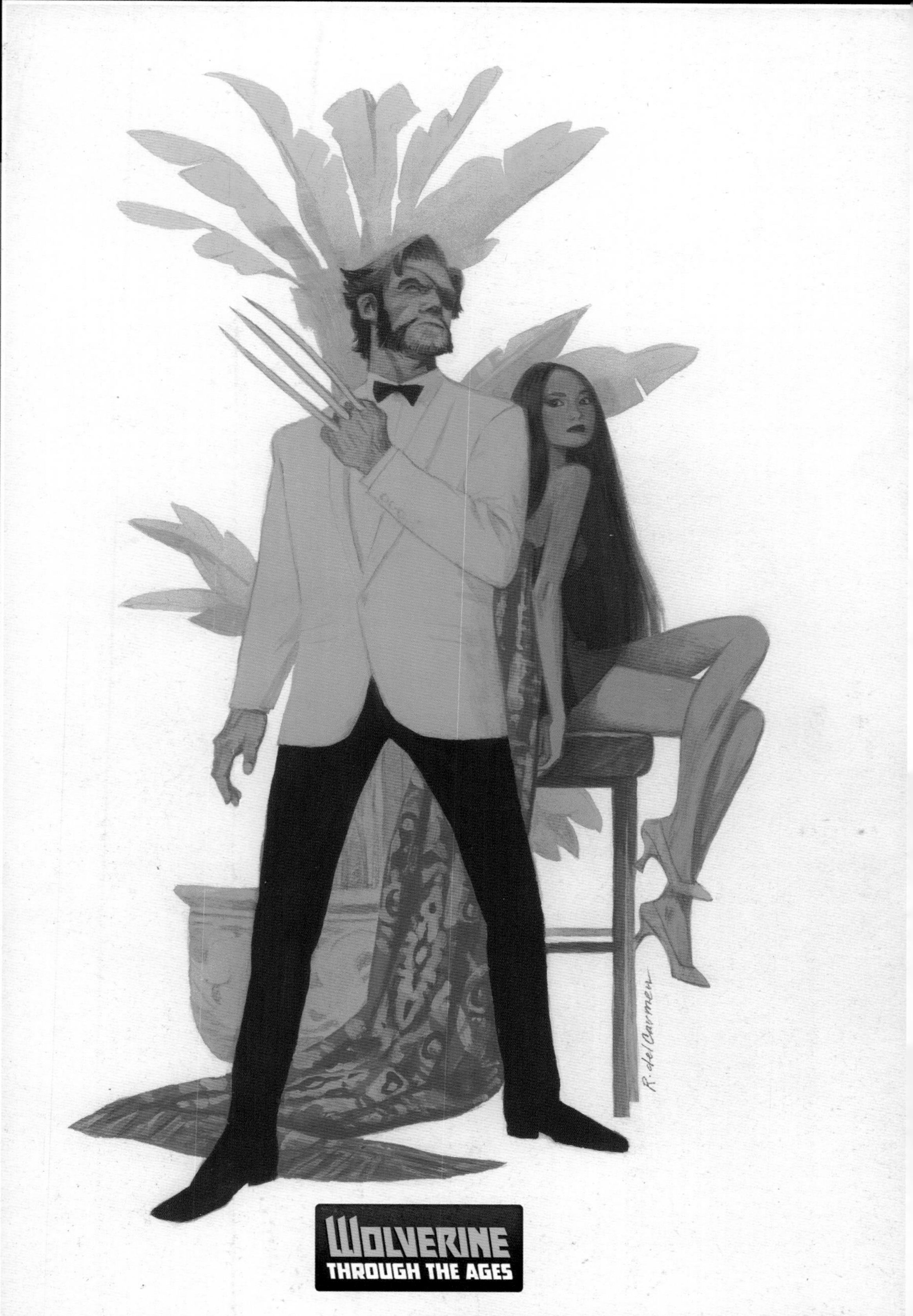
R. del Carmen
WOLVERINE
THROUGH THE AGES